Visual QuickStart Guide

PageMaker 5
for Macintosh

Suzanne Bennie, Carrie Webster & Paul Webster

Webster & Associates

Peachpit Press

PageMaker 5 for Macintosh: Visual QuickStart Guide
Webster & Associates

Peachpit Press, Inc.
2414 Sixth Street
Berkeley, CA 94710
(510) 548-4393 (phone)
(510) 548-5991 (fax)

Notice of Liability:

The information in this book is distributed on an "As is" basis, without warranty. While every precaution has been taken in the preparation of this book, neither the author nor Peachpit Press shall have any liability to any person or entity with respect to any liability, loss, or damage caused or alleged to be caused directly or indirectly by the instructions contained in this book or by the computer software and hardware products described therein.

Trademarks:

Throughout this book, trademarked names are used. Rather than put a trademark symbol with every occurrence of a trademarked name, we are using the names only in an editorial fashion and to the benefit of the trademark owner, with no intention of infringement of the trademark. Where those designations appear in this book, the designations have been printed in initial caps.

Published 1993

0 9 8 7 6 5 4 3 2

ISBN: 1 56609 035 0
Printed and bound in the United States

Printed on recycled paper

Why a Visual QuickStart Guide?

Virtually no one actually reads computer books; rather, people typically refer to them. This series of **Visual QuickStart Guides** has made that reference easier thanks to a new approach to learning computer applications.

Although conventional computer books lean towards providing extensive textual explanations, a **Visual QuickStart Guide** takes a far more visual approach—pictures literally show you what to do, and text is limited to clear, concise commentary. Learning becomes easier, because a **Visual QuickStart Guide** familiarizes you with the look and feel of your software. Learning also becomes faster, since there are no long-winded passages through which to comb.

It's a new approach to computer learning, but it's also solidly based on experience: Webster & Associates have logged thousands of hours of classroom computer training, and have authored many books on computer applications.

All the chapters graphically overview the major PageMaker features; these chapters are easy to read and, with the extensive use of screen shots, allow you to grasp the essential concepts quickly.

Chapters 1 and **2** provide an overview of how to install PageMaker 5 and how it operates, as well as how to start using PageMaker.

Chapters 3 through **5** show you what you need to know about managing and linking files.

Chapters 6 and **7** cover everything you need to know about graphics in PageMaker.

Chapters 8 through **13** illustrate the major features you will need when working in PageMaker, including the Aldus Additions.

Chapters 14 through **17** cover advanced features of PageMaker.

Acknowledgments

The authors wish to acknowledge the effort and dedication of the following people:

- Stephanie Berglin
- Jenny Hamilton
- Sean Kelly
- Tony Webster

Special thanks to the following people from Aldus Australia:

- Graham Freeman
- Carrie Platt
- Fergus Hammond

Thanks also to Peachpit Press for editorial assistance.

Contents

Chapter 6: Creating Graphics

Chapter 7: Imported Graphics

Chapter 8: Working with Templates

Chapter 9: Aldus Additions

Chapter 15: Creating a Table of Contents

Chapter 16: Creating an Index

Chapter 17: Dictionary Editor

INTRODUCTION 1

INSTALLATION SUMMARY

Installing PageMaker 5 is a relatively simple operation. The following instructions summarize what you need to do.

Figure 1. Insert disk number 1. Double-click on the *Aldus Installer/Utility* icon in the *Utilities* folder.

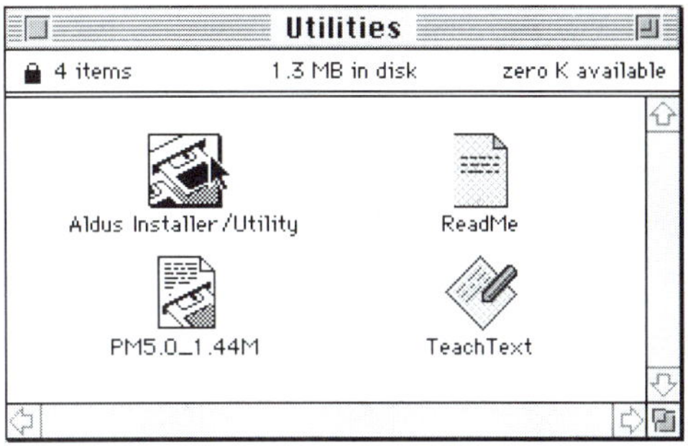

Figure 2. This opens the *Aldus Installer Main Window* dialog box where you can choose your installation options. For a simple installation, ensure that *Install everything* is selected and then click on *Install.*

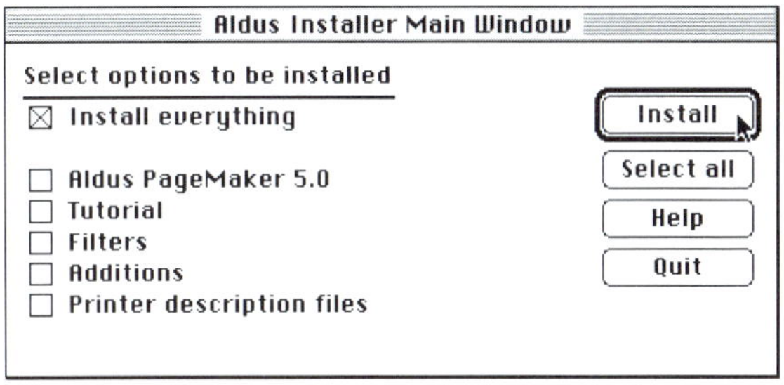

Figure 3. The next dialog box that appears is the *Aldus dictionaries.* There is only one dictionary available, so click on the *OK* button.

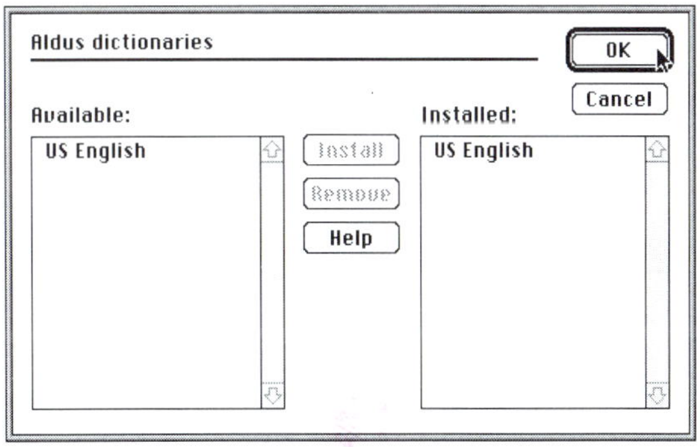

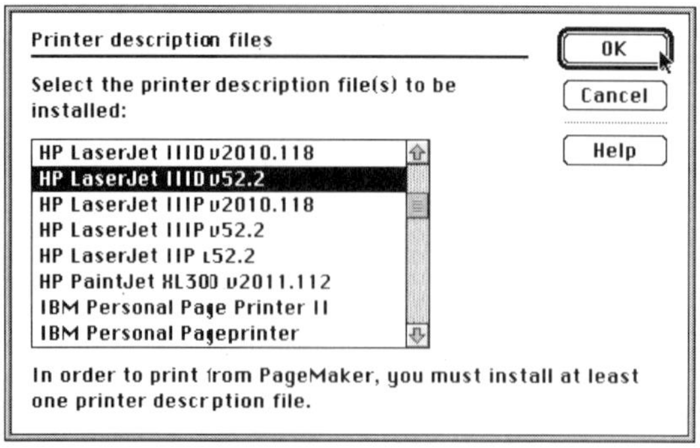

Figure 4. In the *Printer description files* dialog box that appears, select a printer description and then click on the *OK* button.

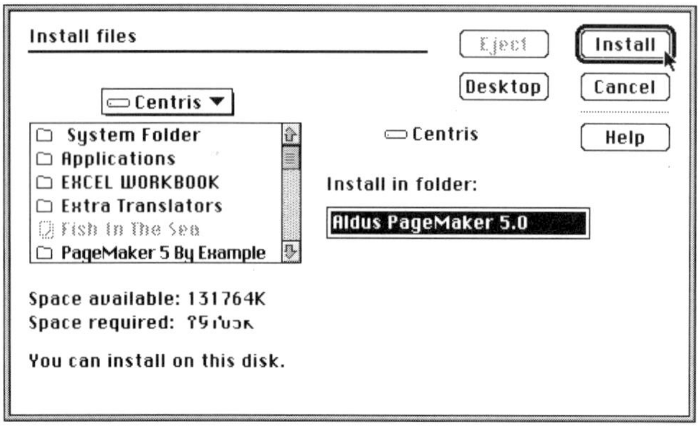

Figure 5. The *Install files* dialog box appears next. Choose where you want the PageMaker folder and then click on the *Install* button.

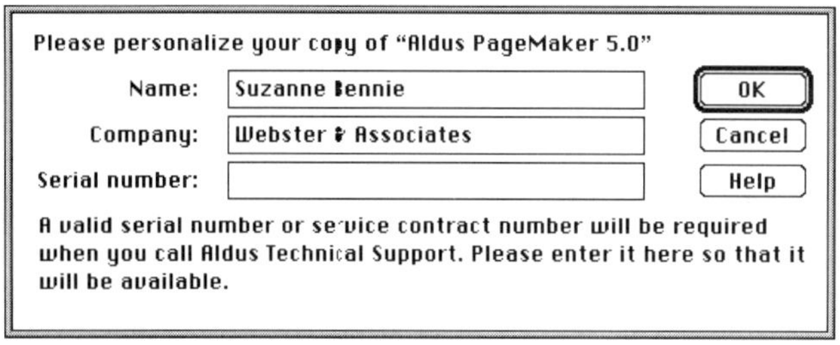

Figure 6. The next dialog box to appear is the *Personalize your program* dialog box. Type in your name, company and serial number and click on *OK*.

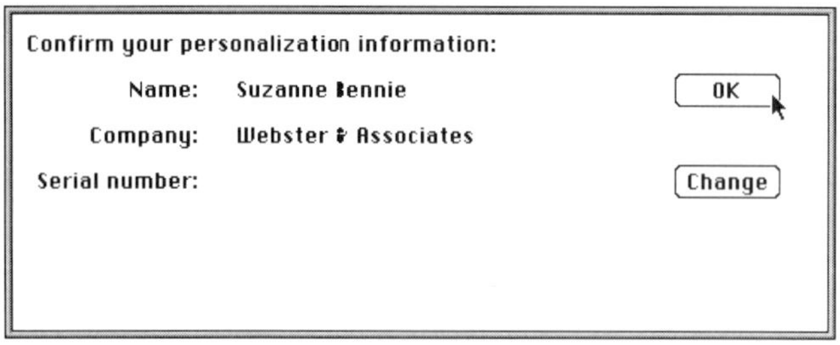

Figure 7. Click on *OK* to confirm the information you have entered, or click on *Change* if you need to make an alteration.

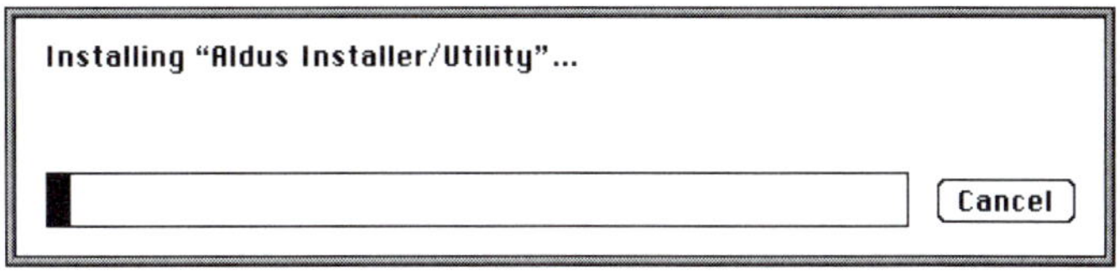

Figure 8. After you click on *OK,* PageMaker begins installation.

Figure 9. After a few moments, the dialog box asking you to swap disks appears. Insert Disk 2 in the drive. Soon you will be asked to insert the remaining disks. Follow the same steps as for Disk 2.

Figure 10. Once you have inserted the last disk this screen prompt appears confirming that you have installed the program. Click on *Quit.*

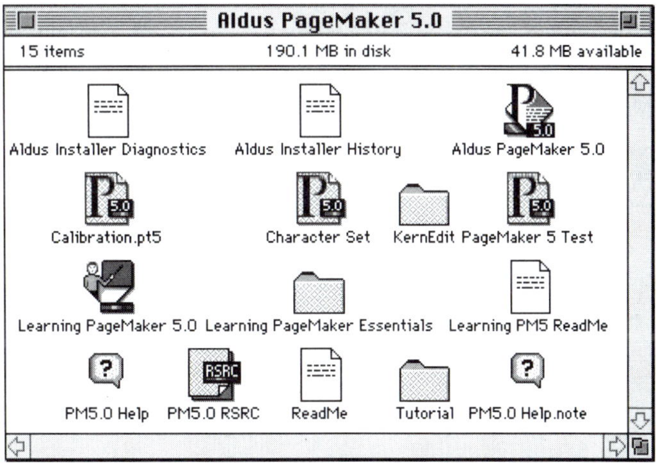

Figure 11. PageMaker is now in the *Aldus PageMaker 5.0* folder on your hard disk.

STARTING PAGEMAKER

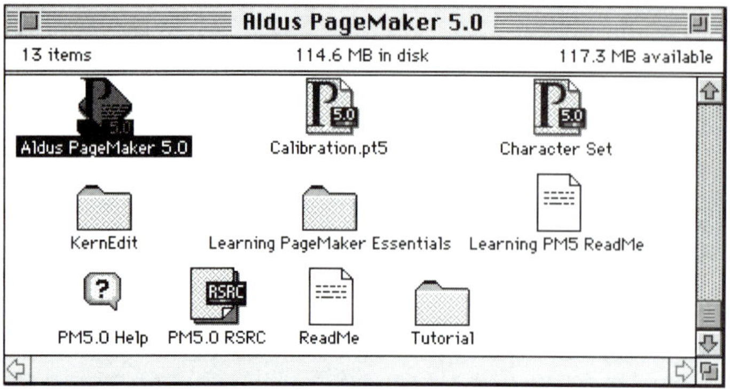

Figure 12. Opening PageMaker 5 is a matter of finding its icon on the desktop and double-clicking on it.

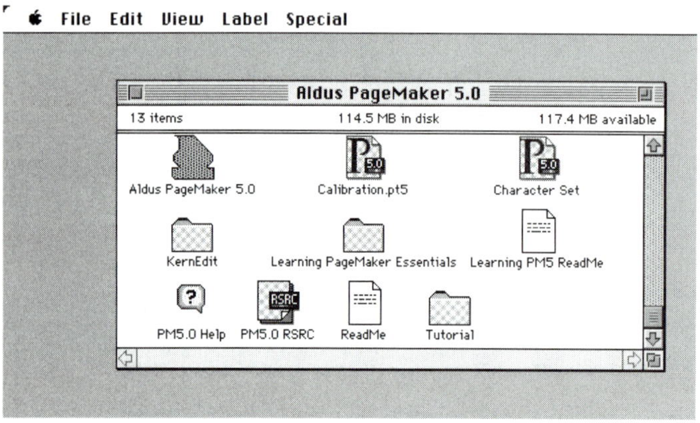

Figure 13. Once you have opened PageMaker, your screen will be similar to the one shown here. At this point you have the choice of creating a new publication, or opening a previously saved one. You can find these commands in the **File** menu.

Figure 14. To create a new publication select *New* from the **File** menu. Similarly, to open a previously saved publication, select the *Open* command.

PAGE SETUP

Figure 15. The *New* command opens the *Page setup* dialog box. This lets you define attributes for your publication.

In Chapter 2, we change dialog box options. For now, click the mouse on the *OK* button.

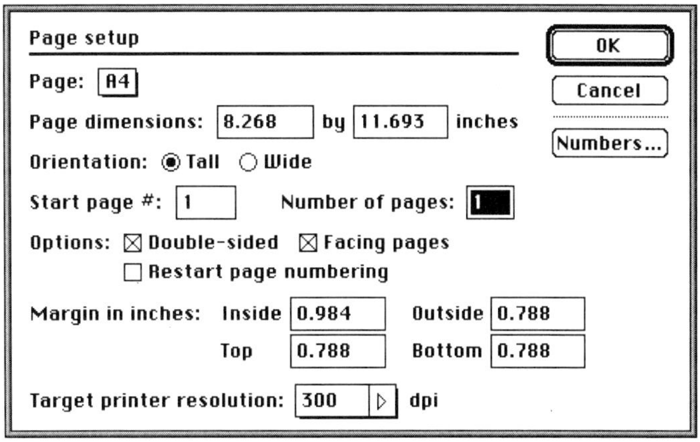

Figure 16. After selecting *OK* in the *Page setup* dialog box, this is how a new publication looks.

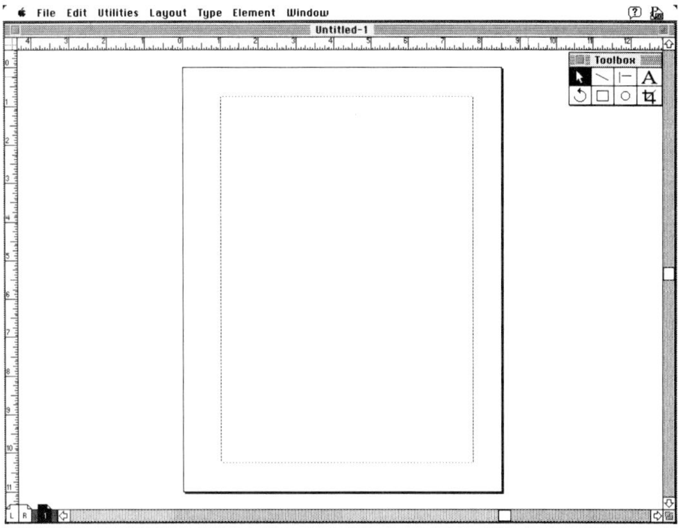

THE PAGEMAKER SCREEN

Figure 17. This is the PageMaker screen. Your screen may not contain all these components when you first open PageMaker.

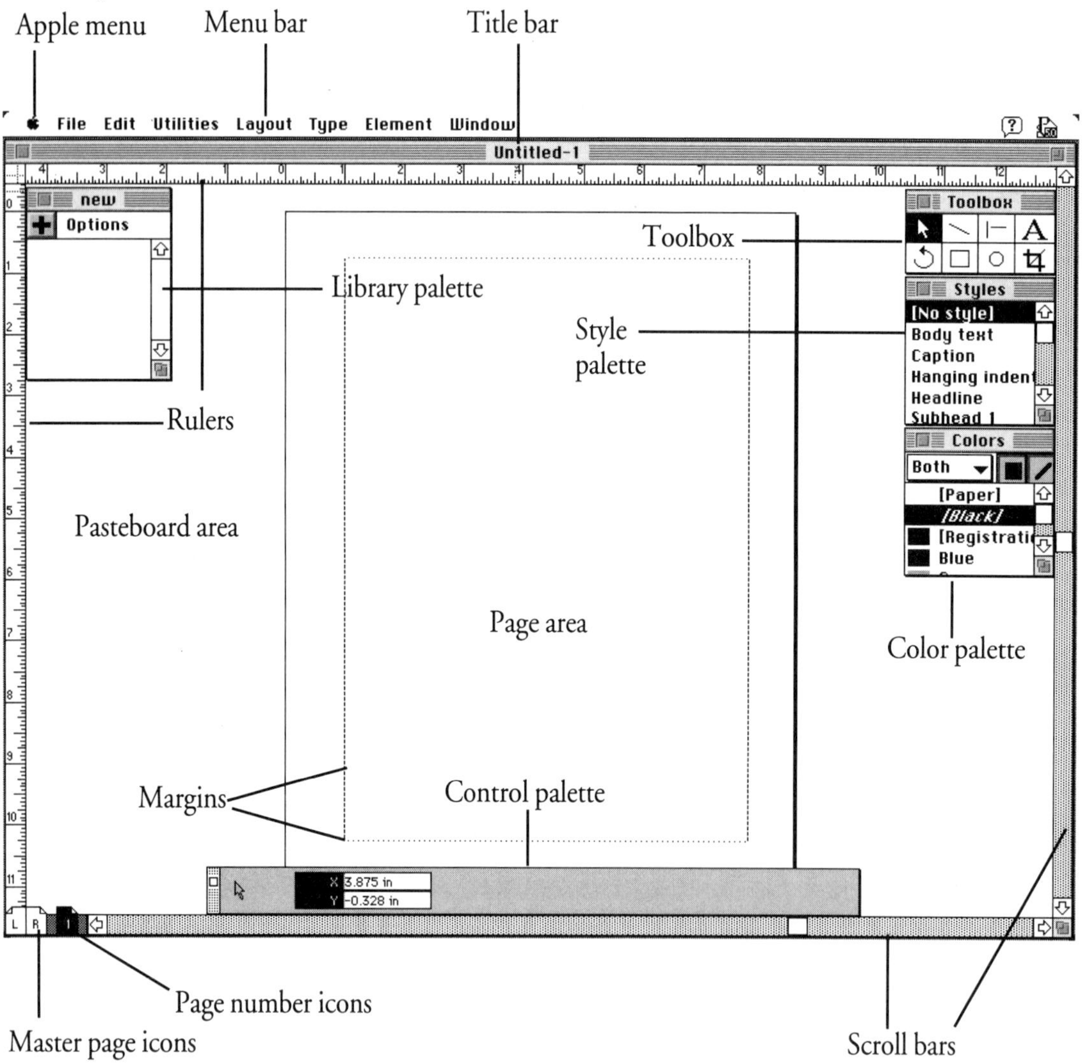

SCREEN COMPONENTS

THE MENU BAR

Figure 18. Clicking on any name in the menu bar produces the pull-down menu commands you use to operate PageMaker.

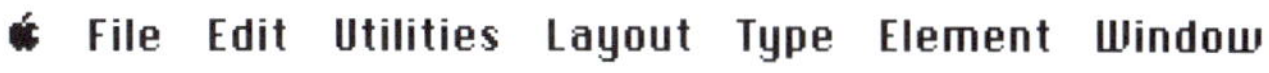

THE TITLE BAR

Figure 19. The current publication title bar contains the name of the PageMaker publication. If you haven't named it, it reads **Untitled-1**.

THE ZOOM BOX

Figure 20. The zoom box is on the title bar. You use it to increase or decrease the size of the current window.

PAGE NUMBER ICONS

Figure 21. Page number icons indicate how many pages are in your publication, and which page or pages you are currently viewing.

MASTER PAGE ICONS

Figure 22. Clicking on the master page icons takes you to the master pages in your publication. You can have left and right master pages, or just a right master page for a single-sided document.

SCROLL BARS

Figure 23. Use the scroll bars to move around the screen so you can see different parts of your page.

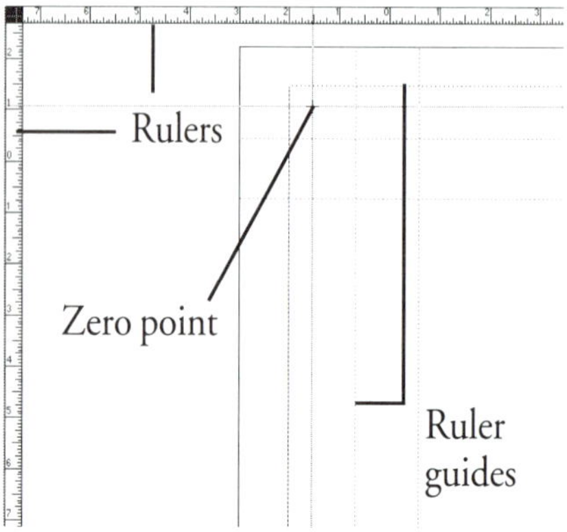

RULERS AND RULER GUIDES

Figure 24. Use the rulers to measure distance on the screen. You can change the measurement units and move the zero point to any area on the screen.

Ruler guides are non-printing guides that you drag with the mouse onto the page from either of the rulers. You can move them with the mouse once they are on the page.

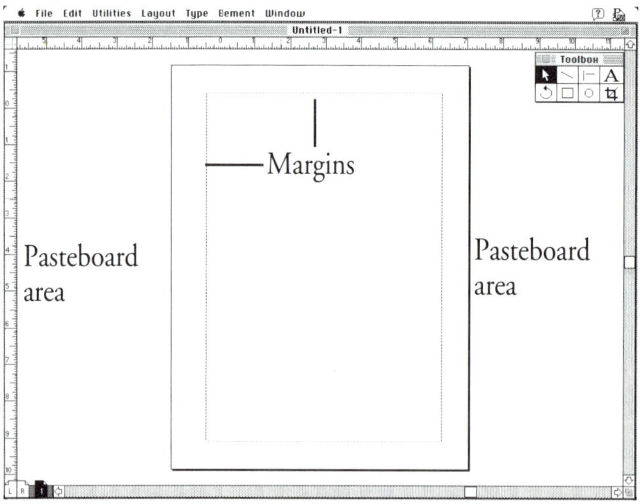

MARGINS AND PASTEBOARD AREA

Figure 25. Margins are non-printing guides that show the defined print area.

The pasteboard area is like a desk around your page where you can put text or graphics. PageMaker saves any object on the pasteboard with the publication.

PAGE AREA

Figure 26. The page area represents your page and its boundaries.

STYLE PALETTE

Figure 27. You use the style palette in conjunction with the text tool to apply styles to paragraphs of text.

COLOR PALETTE

Figure 28. You use the color palette to apply color to selected text and graphic areas.

LIBRARY PALETTE

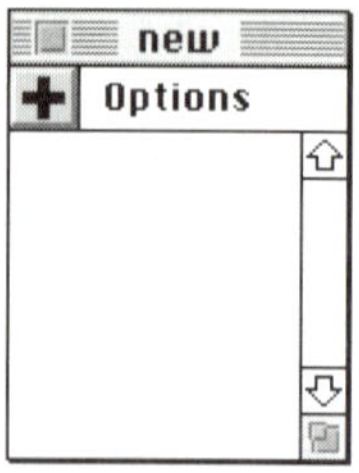

Figure 29. You use the Library palette to store and retrieve images and text files that you frequently need in publications.

CONTROL PALETTE

Figure 30. Use the Control palette to place, rotate, skew and resize objects precisely on the page.

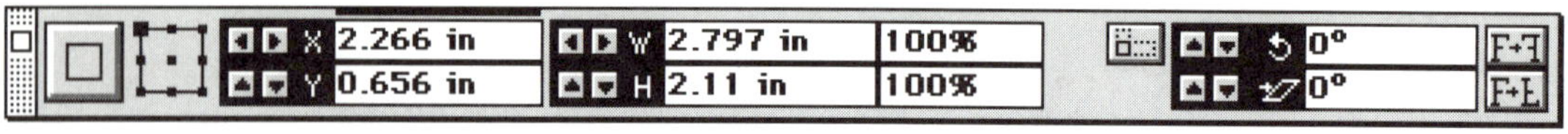

Figure 31. If you are using the text tool, you can also use the Control palette to apply fonts, point sizes, leading, kerning, styles, indents, and more, to text on the page.

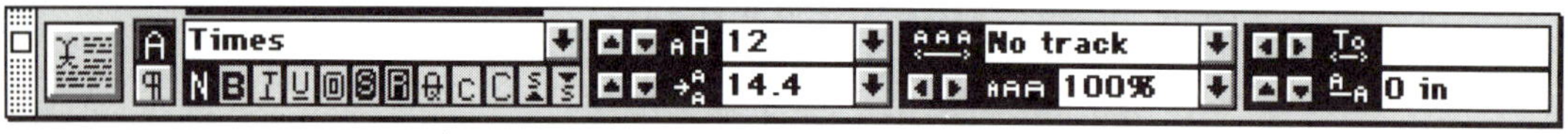

MOUSE CURSOR

Figure 32. The mouse cursor is the icon that you move around the screen by moving the mouse. The shape of the cursor changes depending upon what tool you have selected and what you are doing with PageMaker.

TOOLBOX

Figure 33. The toolbox contains a number of tools that you use to manipulate, create, resize and move text and graphics on the screen.

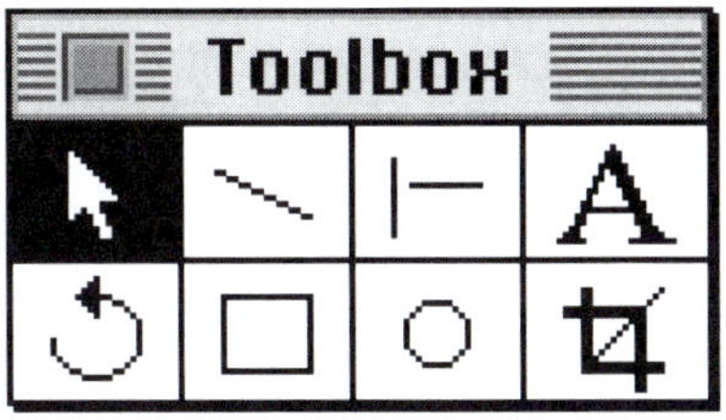

Use the pointer tool to select, move and resize text blocks and graphics on the page.

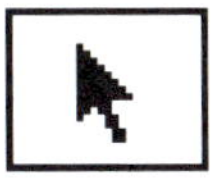

Use the line tool to draw straight lines at any angle.

Use the constrained line tool to draw lines at 45 degree orientations.

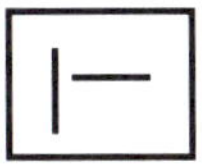

Use the text tool to edit and apply attributes to text, as well as to create text files.

Use the rotation tool to rotate objects on the page.

Use the rectangle tool to draw squares and rectangles.

Use the ellipse tool to draw circles and ellipses.

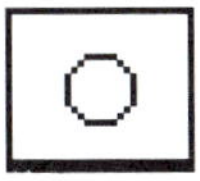

Use the cropping tool to crop imported graphics files.

CHANGING VIEWS

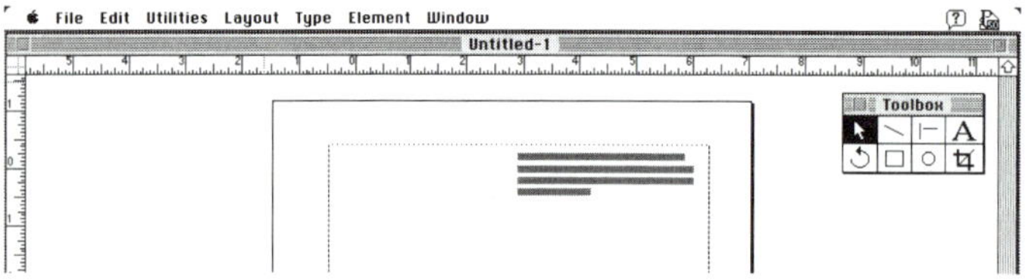

Figure 34. You often need to change views in PageMaker so that you can edit and format text, and select, move and align objects on the page precisely. The default view in PageMaker is in *Fit in window* view.

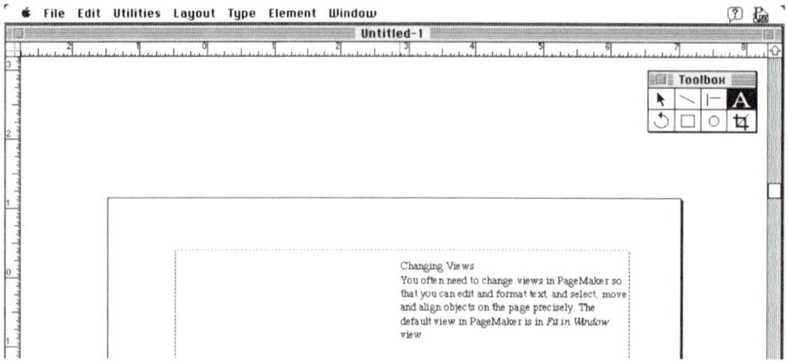

Figure 35. The quickest way to change to *Actual size* is to select something in the area you would like to enlarge and then press Command+1.Press Command+W to return to *Fit in window* view. You can also hold Command+ Option and click where you want, this takes you from any view to *Actual size* view. Command +Option+Shift and click takes you from any view to 200% view.

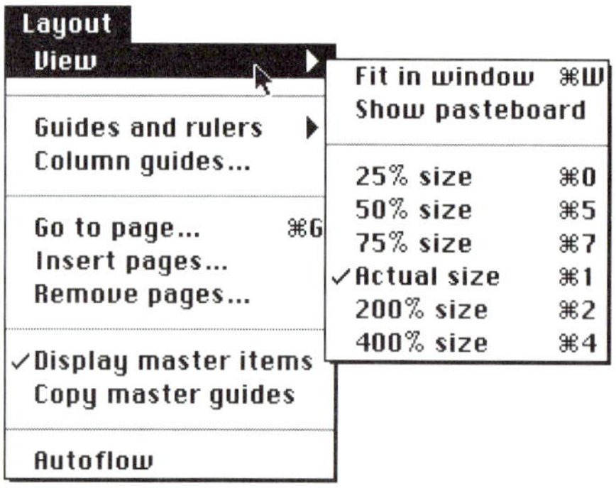

Figure 36. An alternative to using the keyboard is to select a view size from the *View* submenu in the Layout menu. You have more of a range here, as well as more keyboard shortcuts, displayed to the right of the commands.

Figure 37. Hold Command+Spacebar to activate a magnifying tool. Click the mouse button to enlarge an area on the page (Command+ Option+T to reduce) or drag over the area you want to enlarge.

SETTING UP A PUBLICATION

2

NEW OR EXISTING PUBLICATIONS

After opening PageMaker, you have the choice of creating a new publication or opening an existing one.

NEW PUBLICATION

Figure 1. To create a new publication, select *New* from the **File** menu. This opens the *Page setup* dialog box. In this dialog box you can set up various options for your publication: the page size, orientation, and number of pages, whether it is double- or single-sided, the margins, and the starting page number.

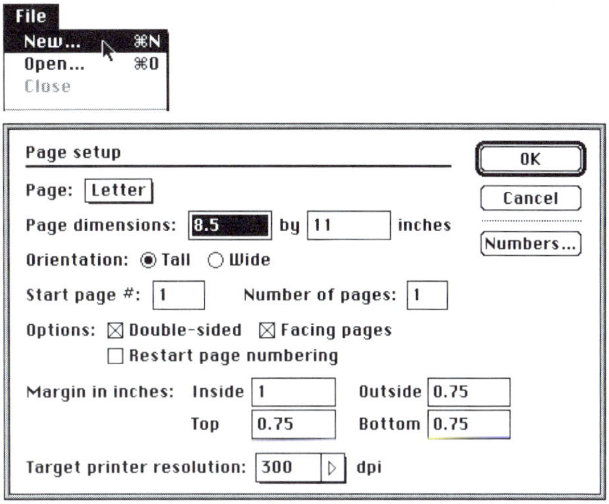

OPENING AN EXISTING PUBLICATION

Figure 2. To open an existing publication, select *Open* from the **File** menu. The *Open publication* dialog box appears. In this dialog box you have access to all folders on your Mac, including floppy drives. Make your selection and click on *OK.*

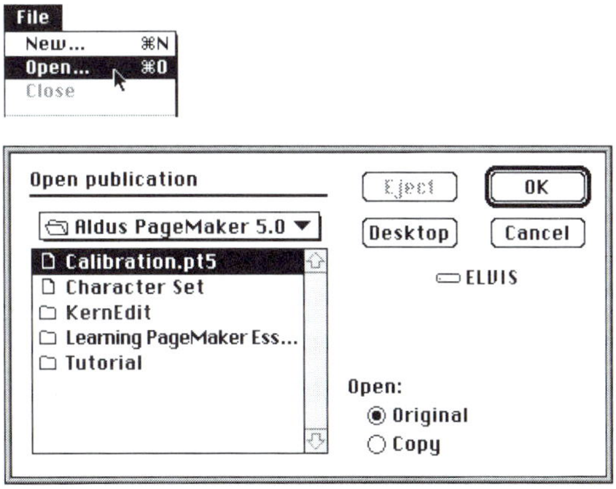

OPENING MULTIPLE PUBLICATIONS

Figure 3. If you already have a publication open and you want to open another, select *Open* from the **File** menu. (Select *New* if you want to create a new publication.)

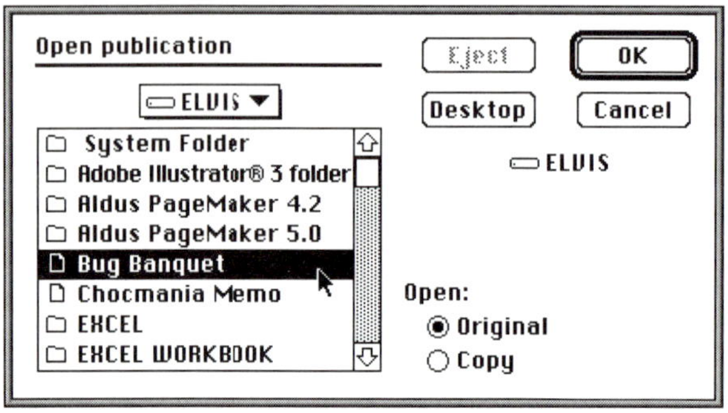

Figure 4. In the *Open publication* dialog box, find and select the file you want to open and click on *OK*.

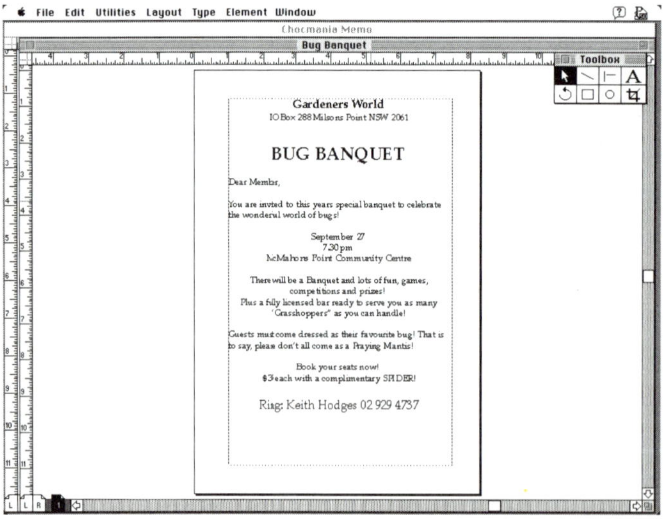

Figure 5. When the screen returns, you see two windows. The window in front is the file you just opened and the window behind it is the file you previously opened.

You can open as many files as your computer's memory allows, one on top of the other.

USING MULTIPLE FILE WINDOWS

Figure 6. You can bring any file to the front in two ways, using the mouse and using the menu.

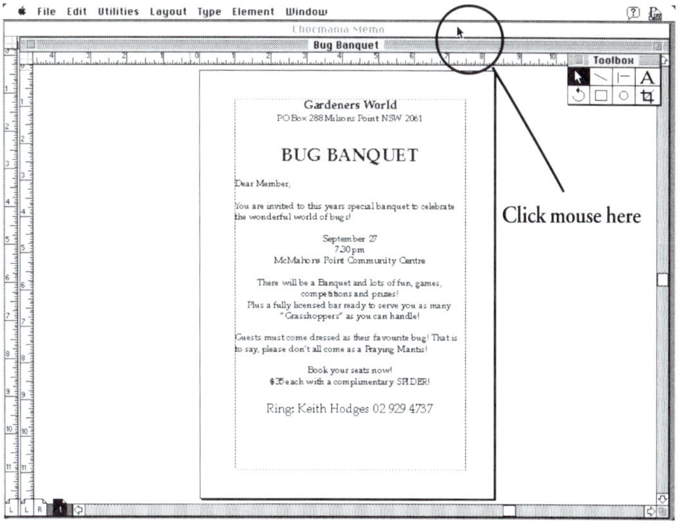

Figure 7. You can click on the exposed part of the file you want active. The window you click on moves to the front of the other windows. Note that you can no longer see the file that was originally at the front.

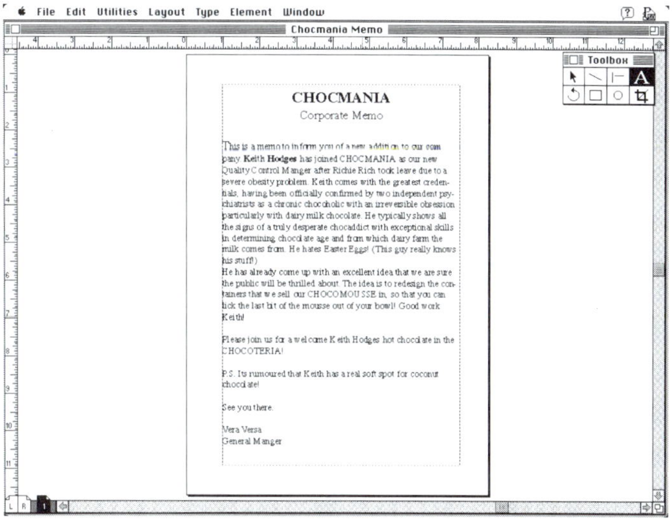

Figure 8. The second method is to move the files to the front using the Window menu. When you select this menu, all PageMaker files you have open are listed at the bottom. Select the file that you want to work on.

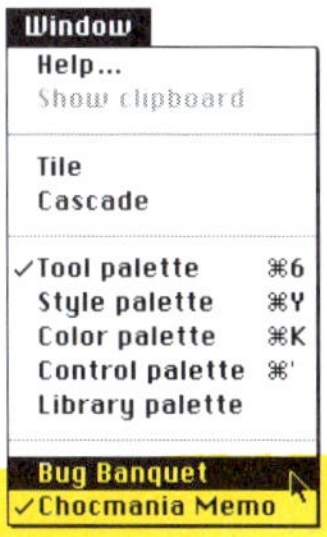

ARRANGING WINDOWS

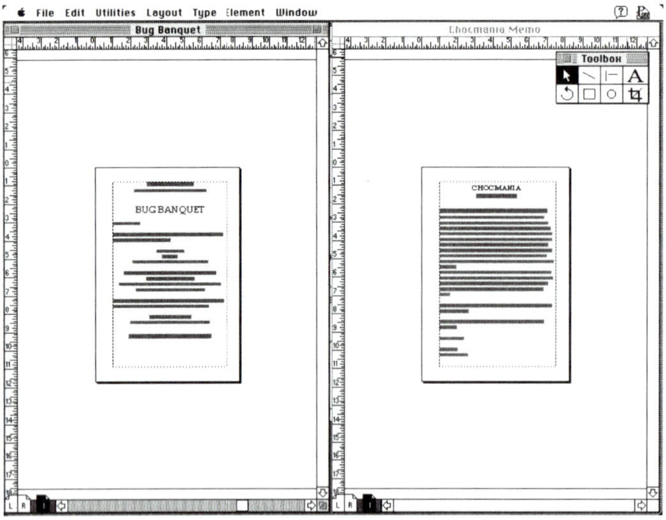

Figure 9. Use the *Tile* command in the Window menu to arrange all the open publications on the screen.

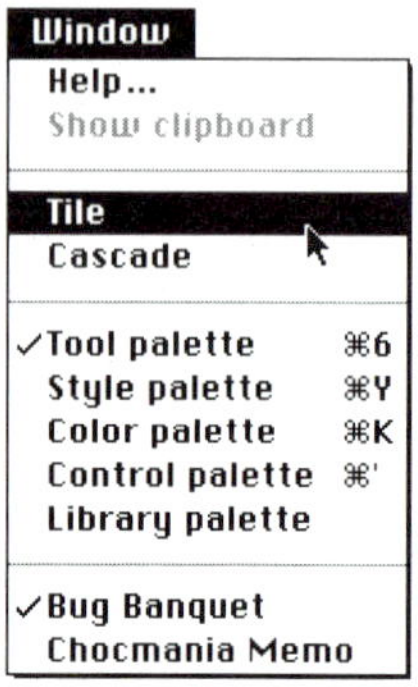

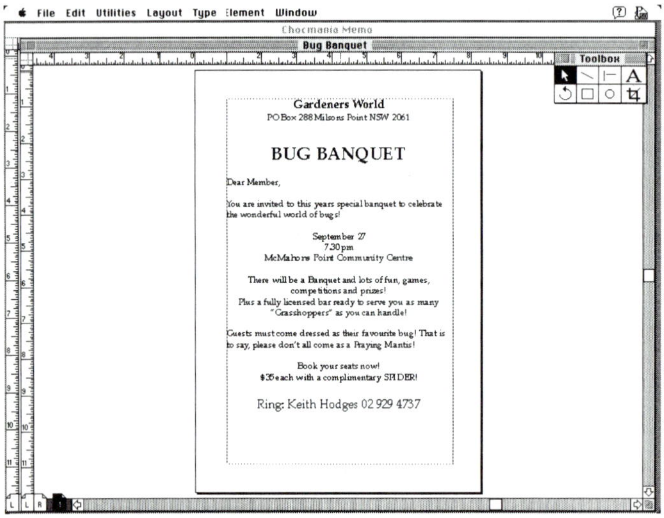

Figure 10. Use the *Cascade* command to overlay all the open publications, with just the title bars of the inactive publications showing.

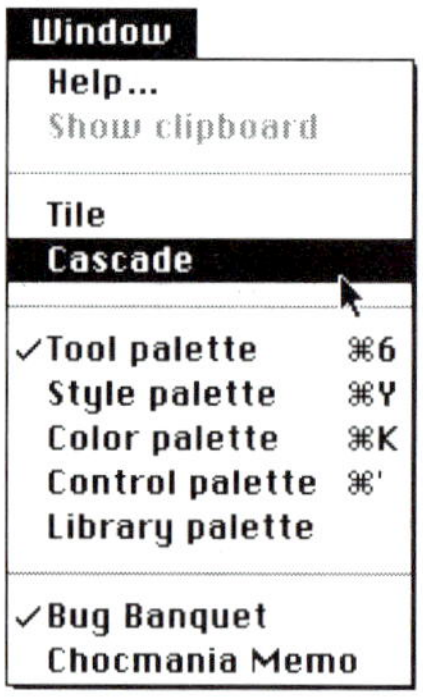

RESIZING PUBLICATION WINDOWS

Figure 11. You can resize publication windows using the zoom box or the size box. The zoom box enlarges a window to fill almost the entire screen. If you click on the zoom box while the window is enlarged, the window resizes to the size it was before you zoomed it.

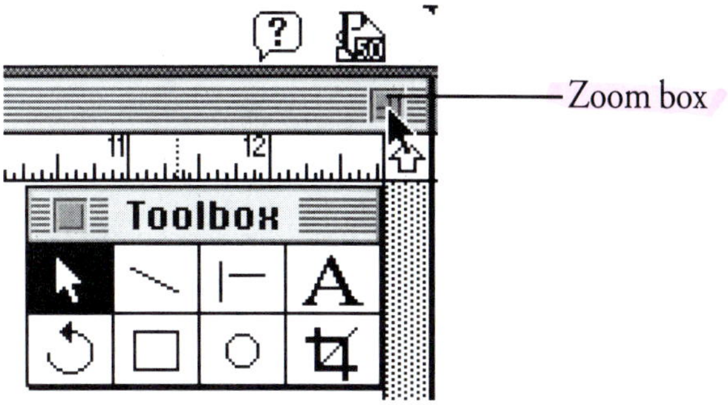

Figure 12. The size box in the bottom right-hand corner of the window lets you enlarge or reduce the publication window by clicking and dragging the size box.

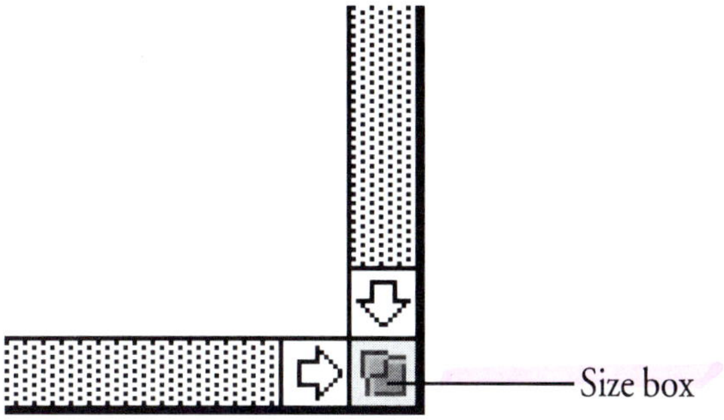

PLACING FILES

Figure 13. Use the *Place* command from the **File** menu to load all text and graphics files into new and existing PageMaker publications. Selecting *Place* opens the *Place document* dialog box.

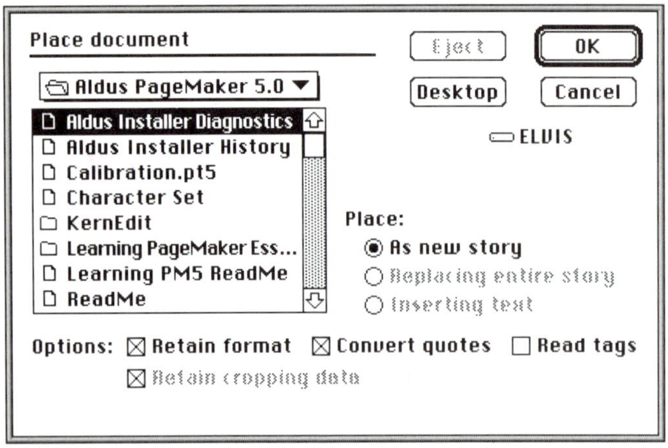

Figure 14. In the *Place document* dialog box you can move around your hard disk to find the necessary file.

PLACING TEXT FILES

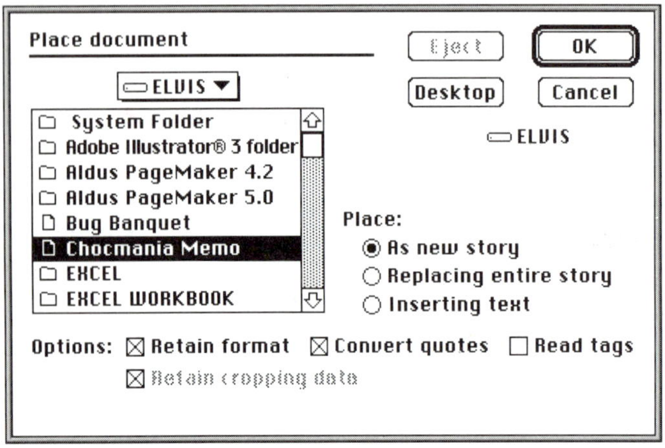

Figure 15. The *Place document* dialog box shows the options PageMaker gives you for placing text.

The options at the top-right are *As new story* (default setting for a new story), *Replacing entire story* (lets you replace the selected story with the new text file) and *Inserting text* (lets you insert a new text file at the insertion point).

The options at the bottom-right include *Retain format* (from your word processor), *Convert quotes* (turning straight quotes into typesetting quotes) and *Read tags* (discussed in Chapter 11). The *Retain cropping data* option is used for imported graphics, and is explained in Chapter 6.

AUTO AND MANUAL TEXT FLOW

Figure 16. After clicking on a text file name and choosing *OK* in the *Place document* dialog box, you get a mouse cursor on screen in one of two modes:

(a) Manual (b) Autoflow

(a) Manual text flow (default setting), or
(b) Autoflow.

Manual text flow lets you load text into one column and then stop. Autoflow lets you load all text into as many columns or pages as you need, creating the pages as it goes.

Figure 17. Once the mouse cursor changes to a loaded text cursor as shown here, you can flow the text onto the page. Put the cursor where you want the text to start and click the mouse button.

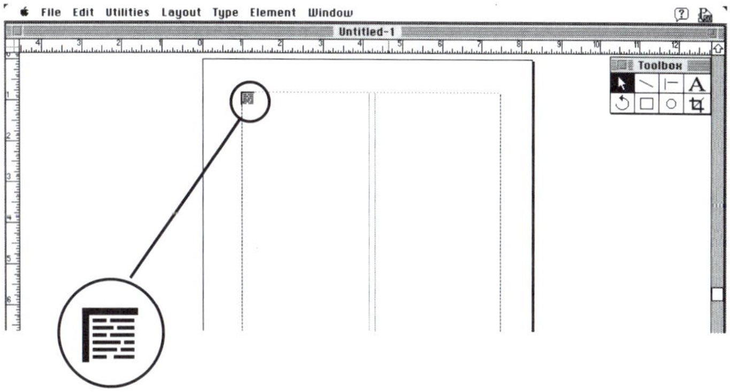

MANUAL TEXT FLOW

Figure 18. Manual text flow places the text in one column and then stops. If you have no text left to flow, the windowshade handle at the bottom is empty. In this figure it has a down-arrow in it, which means you have more text available.

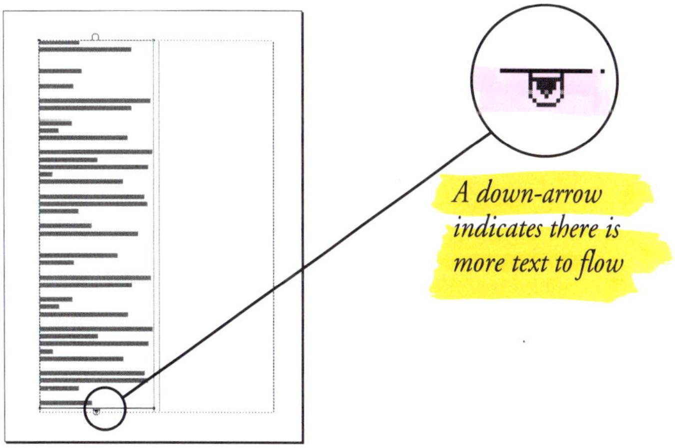

Figure 19. To continue flowing the text, click the mouse on the down-arrow symbol to re-activate the loaded text cursor.

Figure 20. Position the loaded text cursor at the top of the next column (or wherever you wish to place the text), and click again. The text flows down this column and stops at the bottom (even if you have more text available).

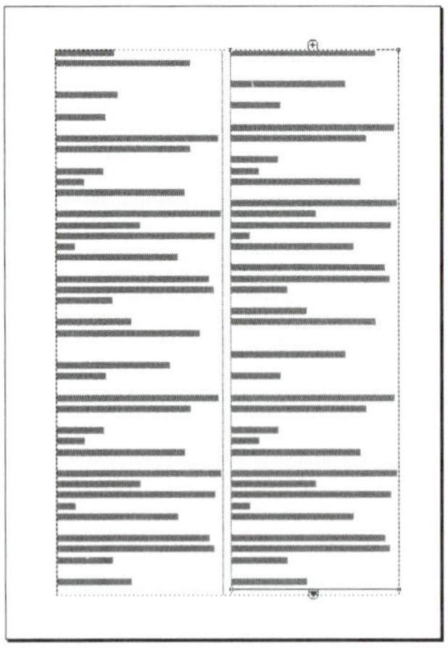

Figure 21. Repeat the process outlined in the two figures above until text runs out. Click on the page number icons to "turn" the pages as needed or create new pages using *Insert pages* from the **Layout** menu. You can click on the page number icons with the loaded mouse cursor without losing the rest of the text.

You have finished placing the text file when the bottom windowshade handle is empty.

AUTOFLOW

Figure 22. Autoflow lets you flow text across as many columns and pages as necessary to import the text file completely. Activate this mode by choosing *Autoflow* from the **Layout** menu. A tick alongside the *Autoflow* command indicates that you have turned automatic text flow on.

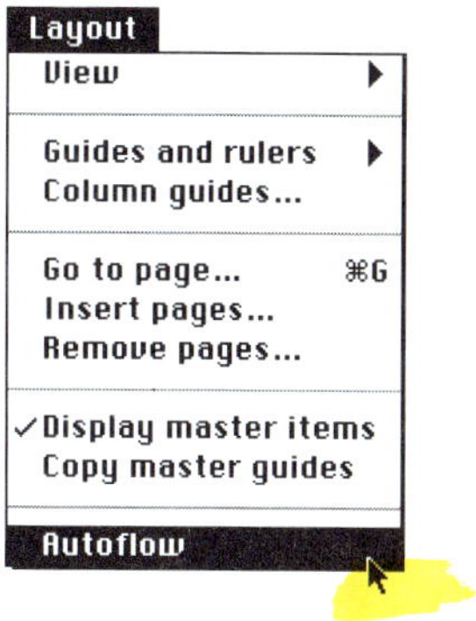

Figure 23. If you place a file in Autoflow mode, the cursor changes to the automatic text flow icon after you select a text file from the *Place document* dialog box (Figure 15) and click on *OK.* Clicking once in this mode causes the text to flow continuously until finished. PageMaker generates extra pages, if required.

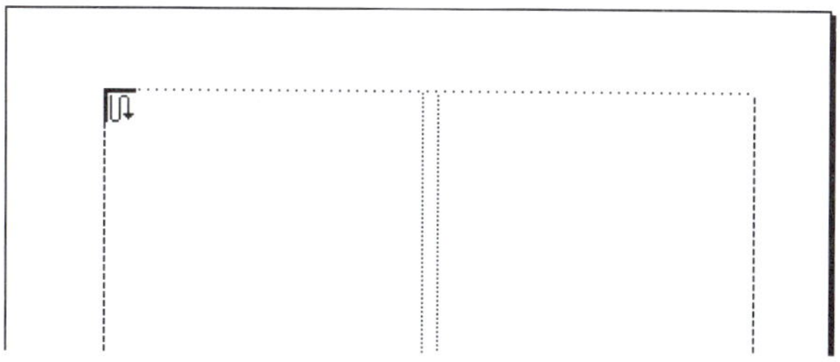

Figure 24. Note that we have placed the text file using *Autoflow*, and PageMaker has automatically selected both text blocks.

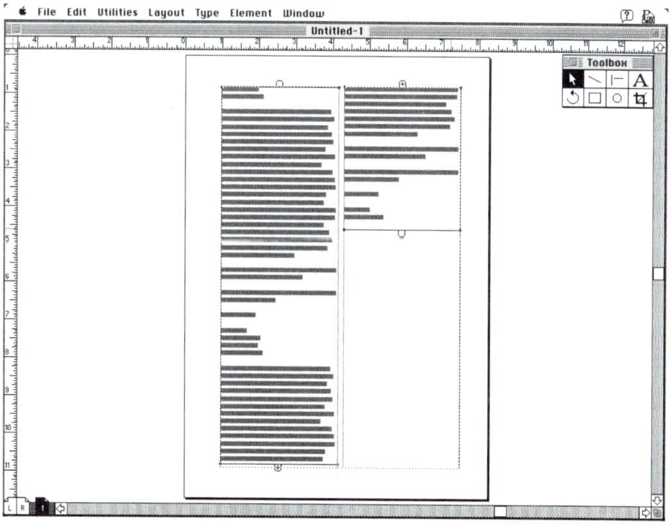

To get semi-automatic text flow, hold down the Shift key before clicking the mouse cursor to place text in manual or automatic modes.

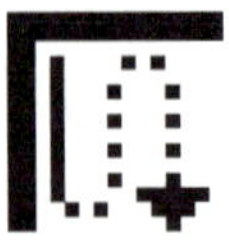

Figure 25. The cursor changes to the semi-automatic text flow icon as shown here. Text flows down the column and PageMaker automatically reloads the cursor to flow again, without you having to click on the bottom windowshade handle first (as discussed in Figure 20).

PLACING GRAPHICS

(a) Bitmap graphic

(b) Draw graphic (EPS, PICT)

(c) TIFF graphic

(d) Encapsulated PostScript file (EPSF)

Figure 26. PageMaker can place a variety of graphic file types including: (a) *paint*, (b) *draw*, (c) *TIFF*, (d) *Encapsulated PostScript*. The different icons PageMaker displays for these different graphic types are shown here.

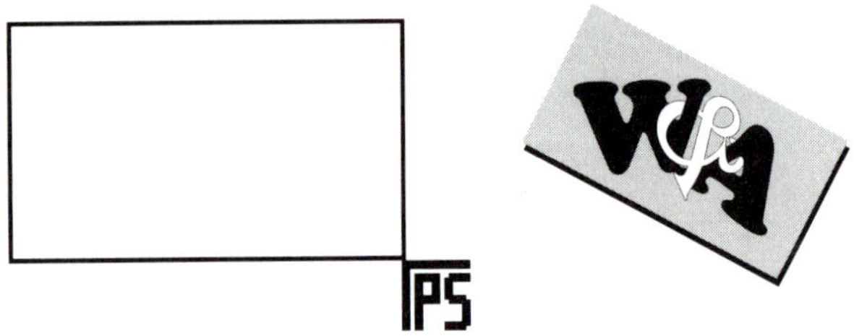

Figure 27. You can place graphics in the same way as text. Select the *Place* command, choose the graphic file, place the cursor where you want the graphic to go and click the mouse.

Unfortunately, you don't know how big the graphic will be on the page when you place files this way. It is better to do what is shown here. Drag the mouse on the page until you have a box as big as you want the graphic to be and then release the mouse. The graphic appears only in the defined area. For more details on placing and proportionally resizing external graphics, see Chapter 7.

LIBRARY PALETTE

Use the Library palette to store, organize, search for and retrieve graphic and text files that you use often.

You can create several different object libraries and you can arrange each library by subject. For example you may want to create a library containing only EPS files and then assign it a subject name—such as "animals." The library palette can display "thumbnail" images of the objects, and you can search the library based on keywords and other attributes you assigned to the objects.

CREATING AND OPENING A LIBRARY

Figure 28. Open the Library palette through the *Library palette* command in the **Window** menu.

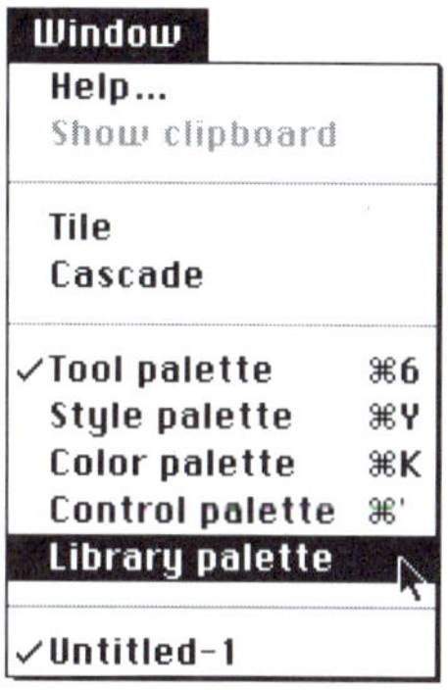

Figure 29. If you have not opened a Library palette with the current publication, or it is a new publication, an *Open library* dialog box appears.

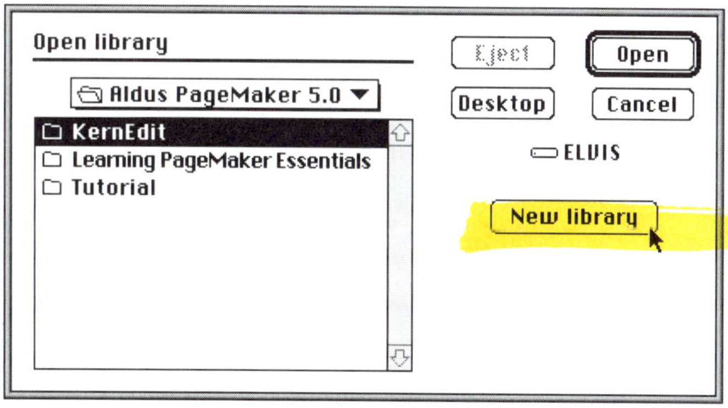

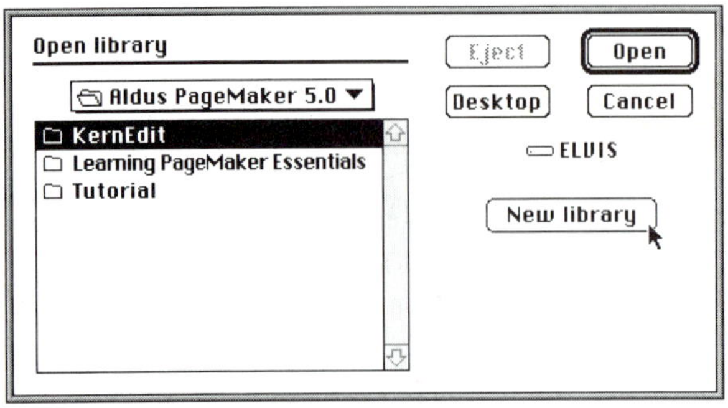

Figure 30. In the *Open Library* dialog box, choose an already library or click on the *New Library* button. Here, we are creating a new library.

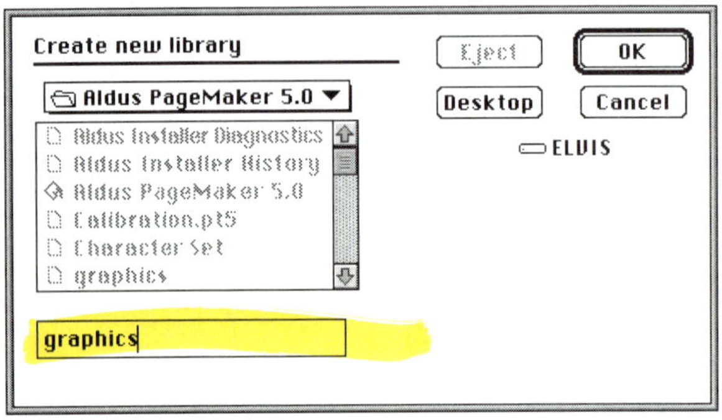

Figure 31. In the *Create new library* dialog box, type a name for the library. In this example, we are creating a library called "graphics."

ADDING FILES TO A LIBRARY

Figure 32. To add files to the currently opened library, select any text or graphic objects on the page, then click on the + button on the Library palette.

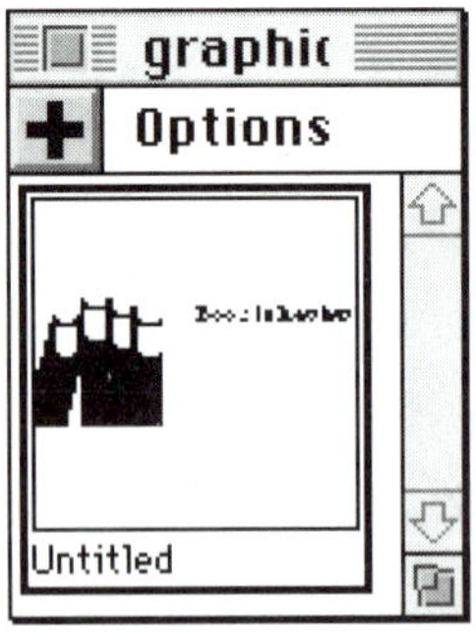

Figure 33. The objects you have added to the library are now visible in the Library palette. If you have added a number of items, you may need to scroll down the list.

ADDING AND EDITING ITEM INFORMATION

Figure 34. If you wish to add or edit any information on an object already in the Library palette, double-click on this item in the Library palette window to open the *Item information* dialog box. You can then make any changes.

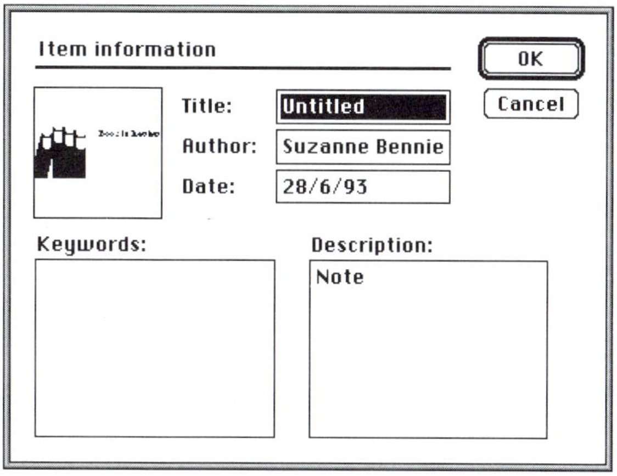

PLACING A LIBRARY PALETTE OBJECT ON THE PAGE

Figure 35. Select the object from the Library palette window with the mouse and drag the object onto the page. The mouse cursor changes shape. PageMaker places a copy of the object when you release the mouse at that location.

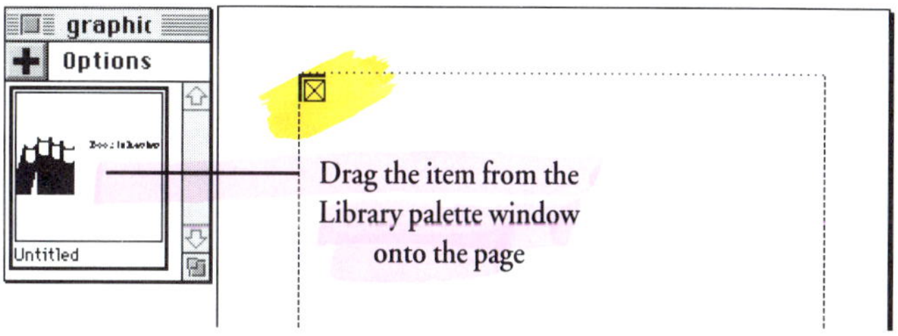

REMOVING ITEMS FROM A LIBRARY

Figure 36. To remove an item from a library, click on the item in the Library palette and then select *Remove item* from the **Options** menu.

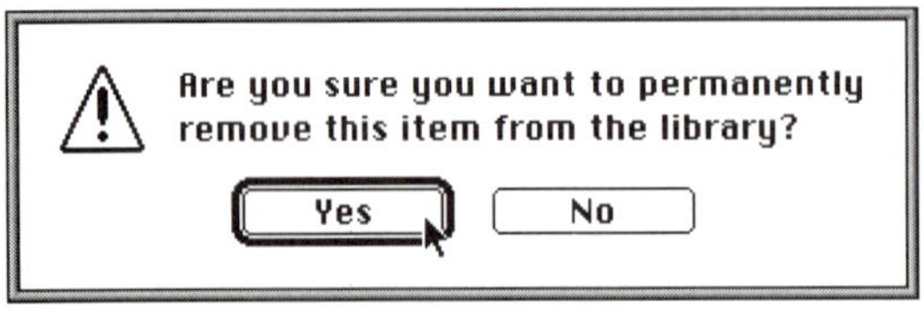

Figure 37. An alert box appears asking you to confirm that you want to remove the library item.

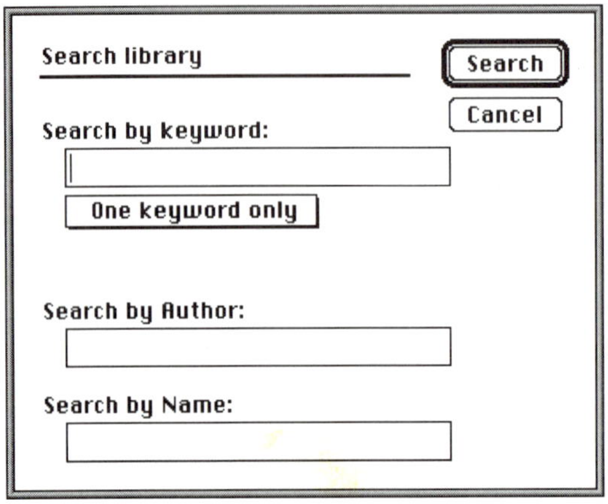

SEARCHING FOR ITEMS

Figure 38. To search for a specific item that you have added to a library, select *Search library* from the **Options** menu. You can search by keyword, author or name. Leave any unwanted search option blank. Click on the *Search* button to start the search.

THE OPTIONS MENU

Figure 39. The *New library*, *Open library*, *Search library* and *Remove item* commands have all been described earlier in this section.

Select the *Show all items* command to list all the items in the Library palette after you have conducted a search for specific items.

Import Fetch items command lets you import cataloged image files created with Aldus Fetch. The *Preferences* command lets you open the *Library Preferences* dialog box, where you can choose to *Make Color Thumbnails* or *Edit items after adding.*

The last three commands, *Display images, Display names* and *Display both,* let you choose which way you display objects in the Library palette. These commands are self-explanatory.

CLOSING THE LIBRARY PALETTE

Either select *Library palette* in the **Window** menu or click on the Library palette close box in the top left corner to close the Library palette.

COLUMN AND MARGIN GUIDES

Figure 40. You can adjust the number of columns using the *Column guides* command in the **Layout** menu. This opens the *Column guides* dialog box. In the example dialog box, we have changed the number of columns to 3. The maximum number of columns you can have is 40.

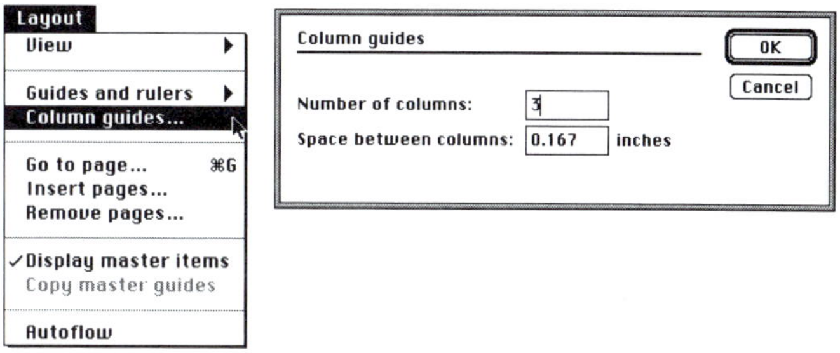

Figure 41. If you have already placed text on a page, changing the number of columns does not alter its layout. You must manually resize this text with the mouse, or delete and re-flow it onto the page. (See the **Resizing Text Blocks** section in Chapter 4 for more information.)

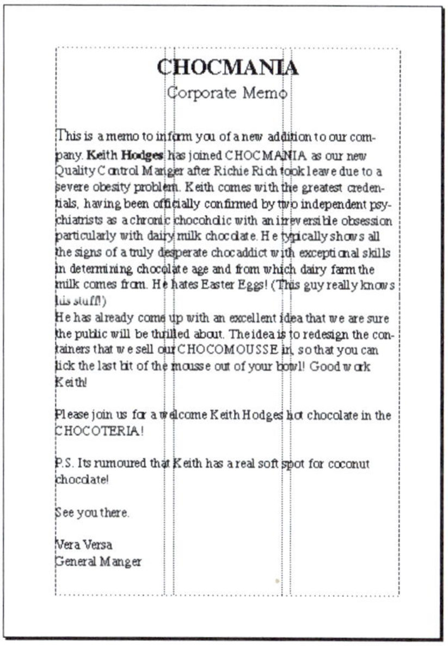

Note: You set up the margins in the Page setup dialog box as discussed earlier in this chapter.

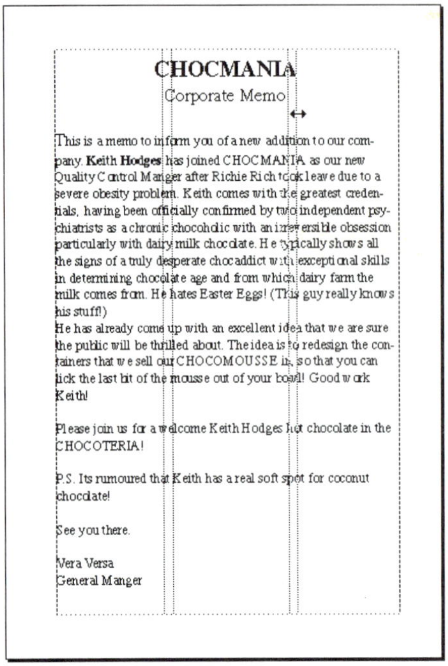

CHOCMANIA

Corporate Memo

This is a memo to inform you of a new addition to our company. **Keith Hodges** has joined CHOCMANIA as our new Quality Control Manger after Richie Rich took leave due to a severe obesity problem. Keith comes with the greatest credentials, having been officially confirmed by two independent psychiatrists as a chronic chocoholic with an irreversible obsession particularly with dairy milk chocolate. He typically shows all the signs of a truly desperate chocaddict with exceptional skills in determining chocolate age and from which dairy farm the milk comes from. He hates Easter Eggs! (This guy really knows his stuff!)
He has already come up with an excellent idea that we are sure the public will be thrilled about. The idea is to redesign the containers that we sell our CHOCOMOUSSE in, so that you can lick the last bit of the mousse out of your bowl! Good work Keith!

Please join us for a welcome Keith Hodges hot chocolate in the CHOCOTERIA!

P.S. Its rumoured that Keith has a real soft spot for coconut chocolate!

See you there.

Vera Versa
General Manger

Figure 42. You can change margin and column guides on the screen. Put the mouse over the column guide or margin, so that the mouse changes to a double-headed arrow. Hold the mouse down and reposition the margin or column guide, then release the mouse.

SAVING PUBLICATIONS

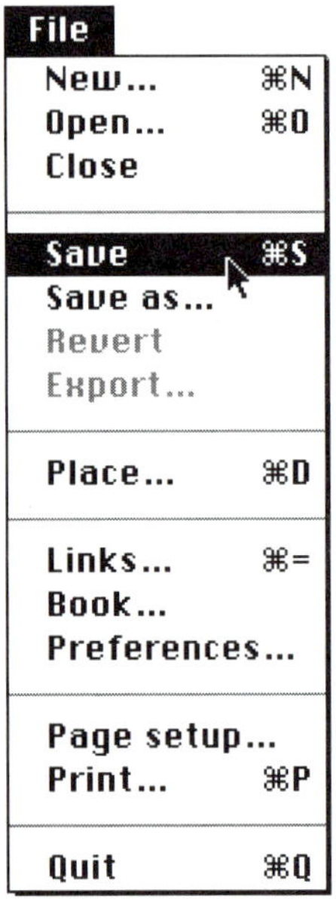

Figure 43. You can save a PageMaker publication even before loading any text or graphics. You save the publication with the *Save* command in the **File** menu. The first time you *Save,* the *Save publication as* dialog box appears, which lets you name your document. Once you have named your document, the *Save* command simply saves to disk any new changes you have made to your publication.

Figure 44. The *Save publication as* dialog box lets you type a name for the publication in the filename text box. In this dialog box choose the folder and disk where you want to save the file.

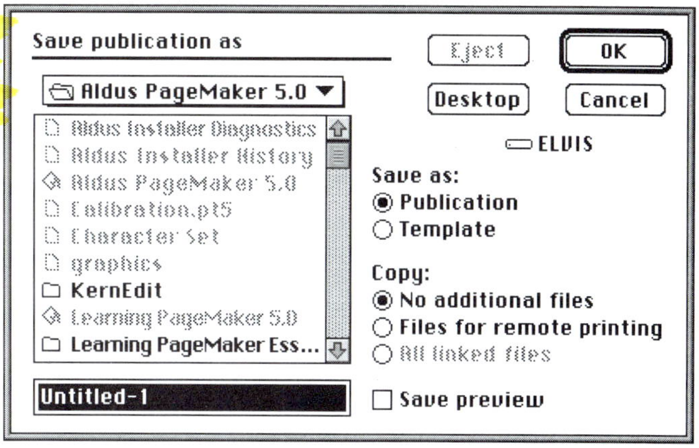

THE SAVE AS COMMAND

Figure 45. If you are working on a large PageMaker publication, using the *Save* command periodically to save your changes also saves unnecessary elements, such as spelling corrections and deleted paragraphs. To compress the size of a publication, use the *Save as* command and give your file the same name just before you close the document.

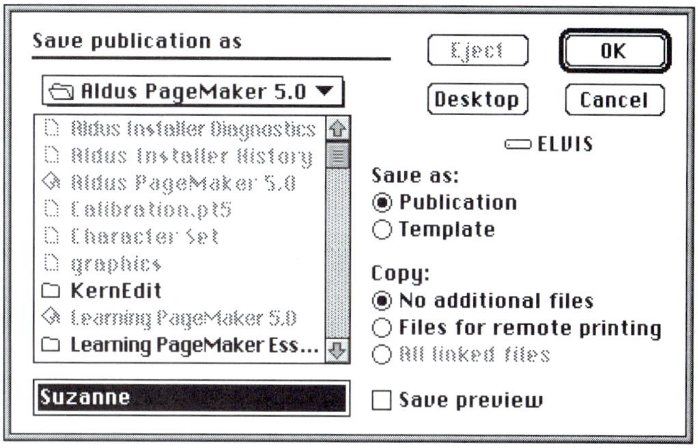

Figure 46. Type in the current name of the publication and select *OK*, and this alert box appears. Select *Replace* to overwrite the file.

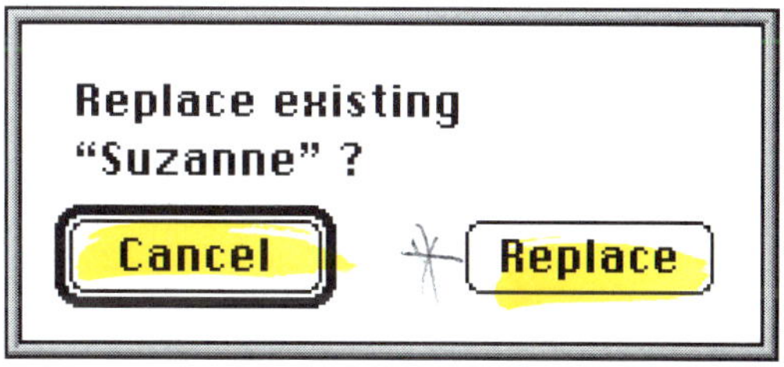

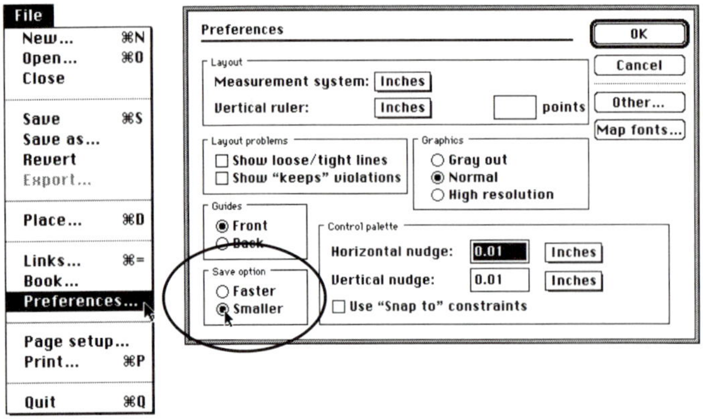

Figure 47. If you want PageMaker to compress a file to its smallest size every time you save it, select the *Smaller* option in the *Preferences* dialog box. Keep in mind that this considerably slows down the time it takes to save.

You can also use the *Save as* command to create a copy of your publication. Just type a new name into the File name text box of Figure 44 and select *OK*.

Linking Files 3

Link Options

PageMaker lets you link files you have placed so you can update imported text and graphics quickly and easily when you change the original file. PageMaker's linking, publishing and subscribing, and OLE (object linking and embedding) allows you to create different types of links from within PageMaker. If the program you are linking from is compatible with PageMaker, a type of link called a hotlink is established where you can open the program you created the original document in from within PageMaker, edit the object and update your publication. You can use publishing and subscribing and OLE to import objects created in programs that don't directly support PageMaker-compatible formats.

Figure 1. This table describes the different types of links that are available in PageMaker, and why you use them.

Link Type	Description	Function
Linking	Using the Place command automatically imports files and links them. All files are linked to their original file. This is the easiest and the best form of linking.	For placing files that originate from programs that are PageMaker compatible. You can edit the original files in their original program, and then update these files in PageMaker. You can do this manually or have PageMaker do it automatically.
OLE	You can use OLE (Object Linking and Embedding) to link files that are not PageMaker compatible. You do this by copying the object onto the clipboard and selecting paste.	OLE linking is used to link graphics that you use more than once in a publication. OLE embedding is useful for graphic files used once in a publication. Not many packages support OLE.
Publishing and Subscribing	Publishing and Subscribing is only available under System 7 and lets you publish text or graphics from an application as an edition in and then subscribe to the edition from PageMaker.	Publishing and subscribing is useful when you want to use an object in multiple publications, because you can update the subscriptions automatically.

LINKING FILES

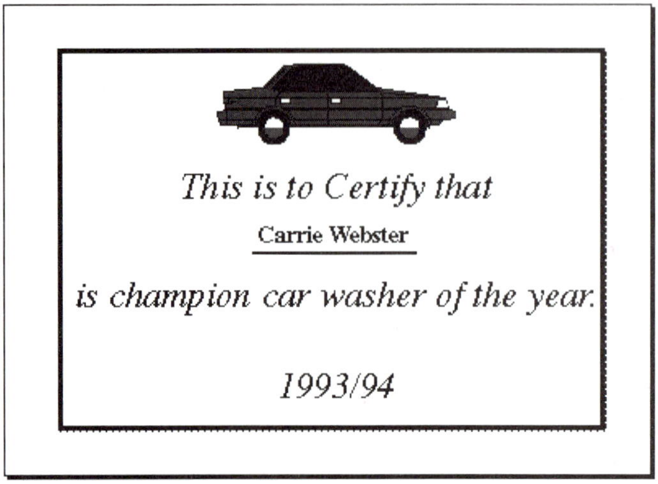

Figure 2. By default, PageMaker automatically links imported text and graphics to their original external files. This lets you update these publications if you modify the external files.

Figure 3. The *Links* command from the **File** menu gives you access to the *Links* dialog box (Figure 4).

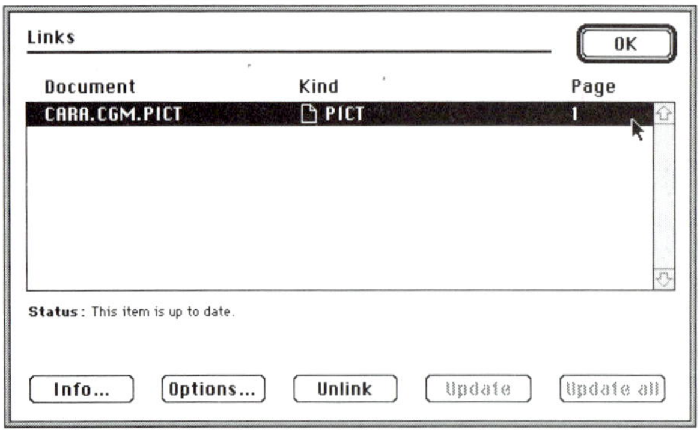

Figure 4. Selecting a file from the *Links* dialog box gives the current file status. The *Update* and *Update all* buttons update single linked elements or all publication files, respectively. The right-most column displays page number and other additional information.

The *Unlink* button allows you to sever the link between the selected file and its original. See Figures 5 through 9 for descriptions of the *Link info* and *Link options* buttons.

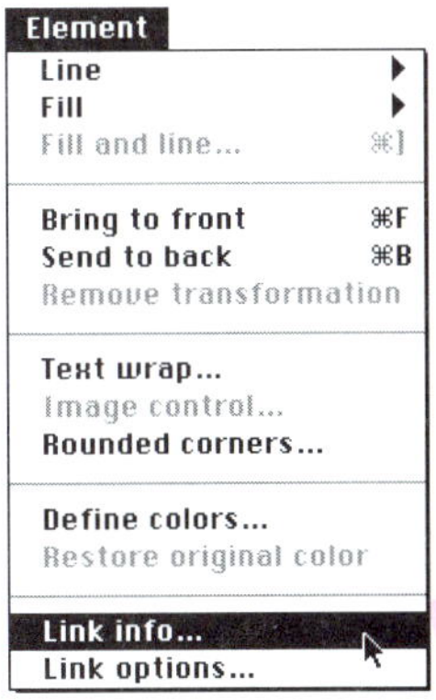

Figure 5. You can open the *Link info* dialog box with the *Link info* button shown in Figure 4 or by selecting a graphic or text block and choosing *Link info* from the **Element** menu.

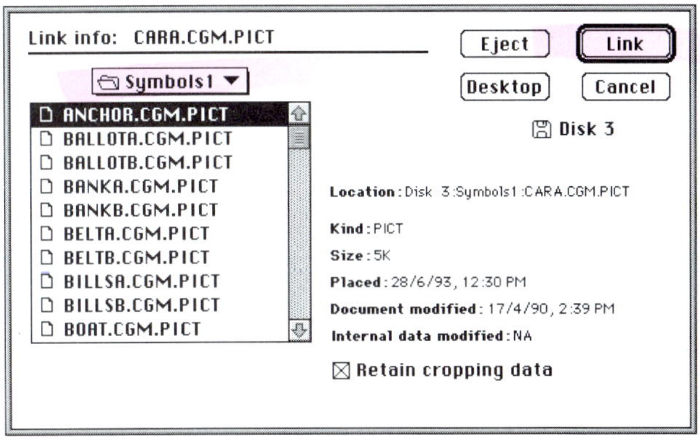

Figure 6. The *Link info* dialog box lets you update or re-establish a link between text or graphic elements and external files. You have to re-establish a link if you move or rename the external file. All you need to do is select the new or moved file and click on the *Link* button.

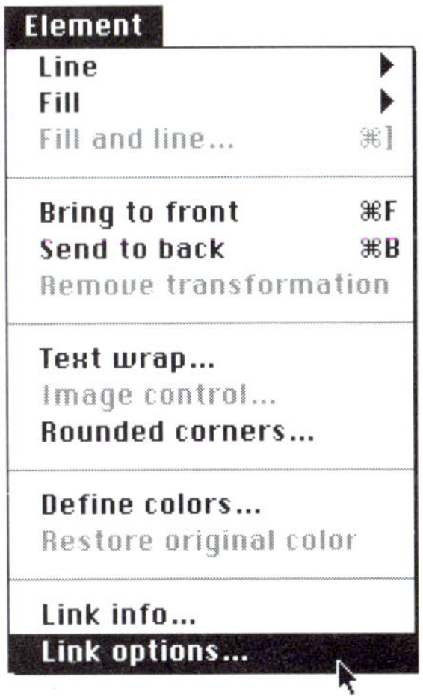

Figure 7. You get to the *Link options* dialog box through the *Link options* button shown in Figure 4, or by selecting *Link options* from the **Element** menu (if you selected a linked element).

Figure 8. The *Link options* dialog box contains three options that give you control over how linked files are updated. (These options are self-explanatory.)

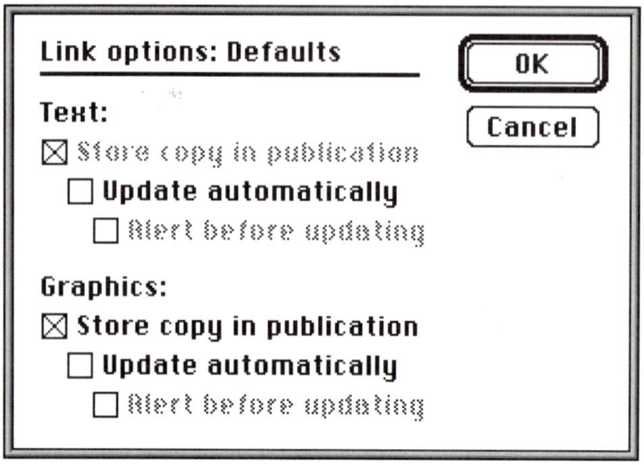

Figure 9. The *Link options* command in the **Element** menu activates the *Link options: Defaults* dialog box when you have nothing selected or you have no publications open. Use this dialog box to set default values.

OTHER LINK COMMANDS

PASTE LINK COMMAND

Figure 10. Use the *Paste link* command to paste a graphic as an OLE-linked object. You can also do this with the *Paste link* button in the *Paste special* dialog box (Figure 11). You must save the external program file before copying it to the clipboard or you can't select *Paste link* in PageMaker, or, if you did not create the graphic in an OLE-compatible program, you will not be able to access this command.

Object created and saved in OLE program and copied to clipboard

OLE-linked object in PageMaker

PASTE SPECIAL COMMAND

Figure 11. Use the *Paste special* command to open the *Paste special* dialog box. Often when you cut or copy an object to the clipboard, the object is stored in more than one format. When you use the *Paste* command to insert an object, PageMaker takes the format that displays the truest image.

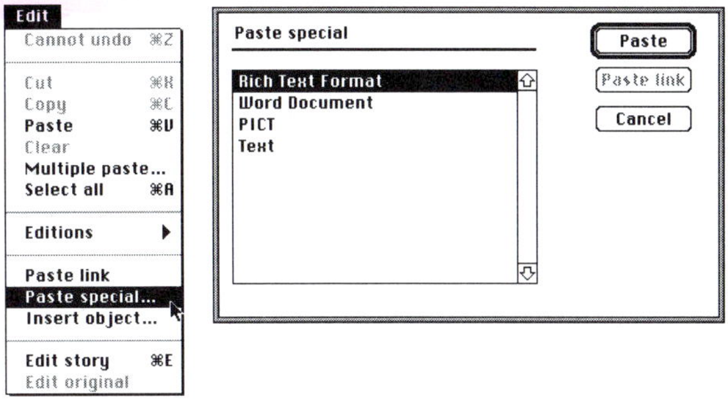

In the *Paste special* dialog box, you can select the format you want. The highest quality format is listed first. The *Paste* button in the *Paste special* dialog box pastes the selected format without linking it to the external file. The *Paste link* button sets up a link to the external file. You use it in the same way that you use the *Paste link* command (see Figure 10).

INSERT OBJECT COMMAND

Figure 12. Open the *Insert object* dialog box by selecting *Insert object* in the **Edit** menu. Double-click on the type of object you want to create and the OLE-compatible program opens.

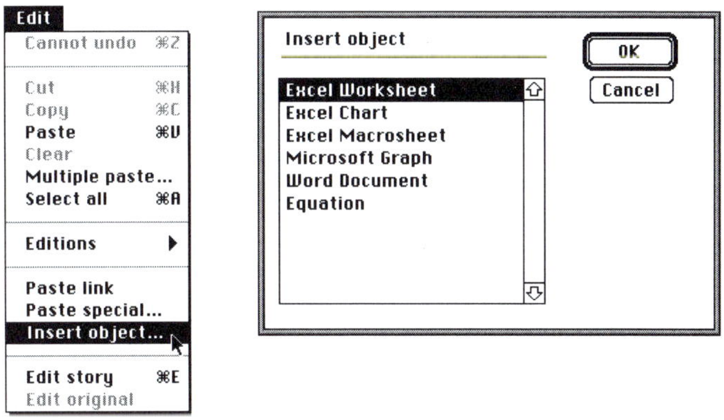

When you have finished creating the element, select *Update* or *Exit & return to PageMaker* from the **File** menu of the program that you are in. This inserts the element you have created into PageMaker as an OLE-embedded object.

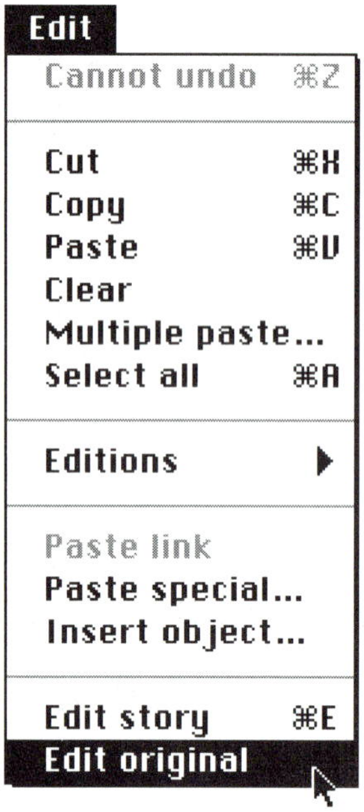

EDIT ORIGINAL COMMAND

Figure 13. Use the *Edit original* command to open the original program you used to create the selected object. You can then edit the object and save the file, which automatically updates the object in your PageMaker publication.

If you have selected an OLE-linked or -embedded object, the *Edit original* command changes to reflect the type of object you have selected.

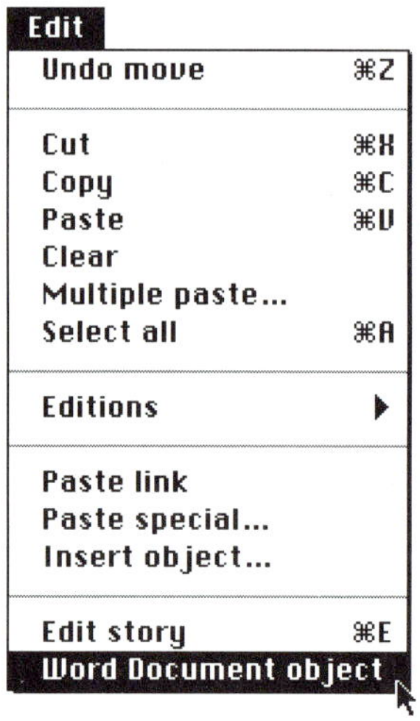

Figure 14. In the example, we have selected a Word graphic and the command *Word Document object* appears in the **Edit** menu.

Figure 15. Word opens with the selected graphic ready to update.

Alternatively, to open the original program, all you need to do is double-click on the object.

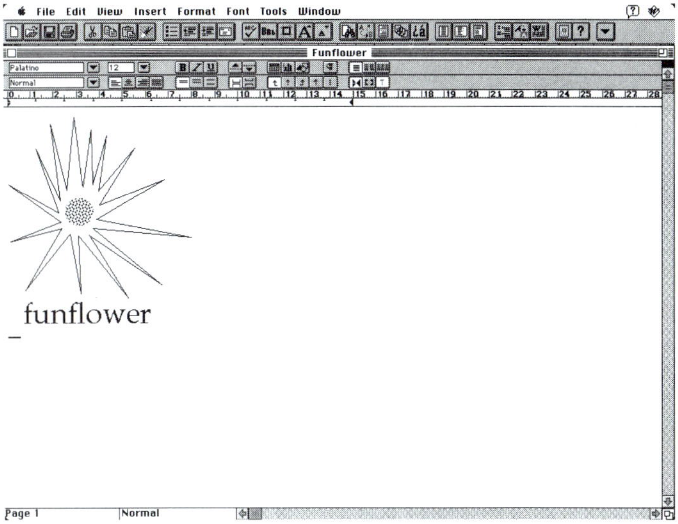

Publishing and Subscribing

Publishing and subscribing is only available with System 7. It enables you to import text or graphics created in another application by creating a publisher and subscribing to an edition. This is an especially good method to use if you want to subscribe to the same edition from multiple applications as you can update all of the subscribers simultaneously.

Subscribing

Figure 16. To create an edition, you must first publish it from within its original document. This usually involves choosing a command such as *Create Publisher* and then saving the edition. From within PageMaker you can then choose *Subscribe to* from the *Editions* submenu in the **Edit** menu.

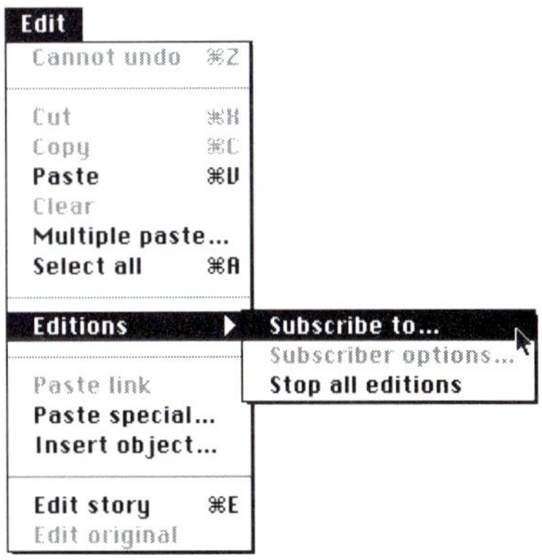

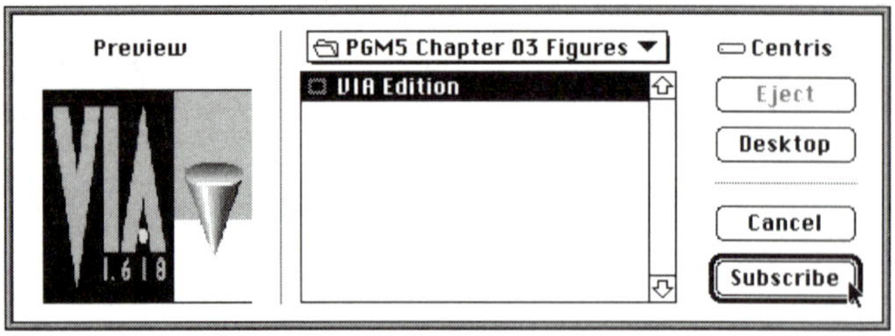

Figure 17. In the *Edition* dialog box that appears, choose the edition you want to subscribe to and then click on the *Subscribe* button.

Figure 18. Position the cursor where you want the object to be placed and either click the mouse button or click and drag the mouse to insert the object.

SUBSCRIBER OPTIONS

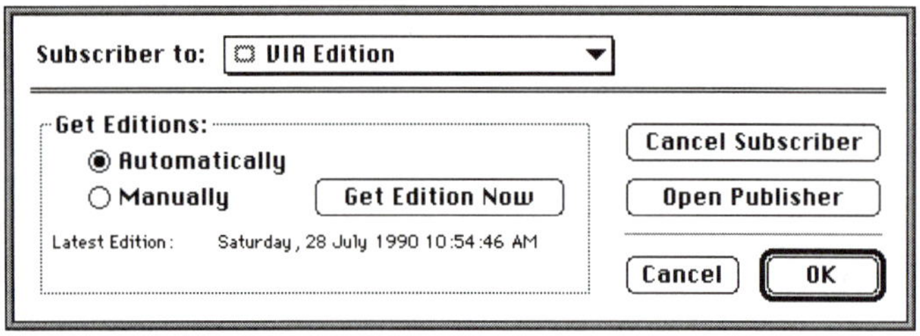

Figure 19. You can specify link options by choosing *Subscriber options* from the *Editions* submenu. This opens the *Subscriber options* dialog box. In this dialog box you choose whether you want the edition to be updated automatically or manually. Clicking on *Get edition now* updates the subscriber in your publication immediately. Clicking on *Cancel subscriber* button cancels the subscriber and the object becomes an unlinked file. Choosing *Open publisher* launches the edition file and the application it was created in.

The *Subscriber options* command appears dimmed if you have not selected a subscriber object.

Figure 20. If you select *Stop All Editions* PageMaker stops updating subscribers that have the *Automatically* option selected in the *Subscriber options* dialog. A check mark appears next to the command in the *Editions* submenu; you reselect the command to turn automatic updating on again.

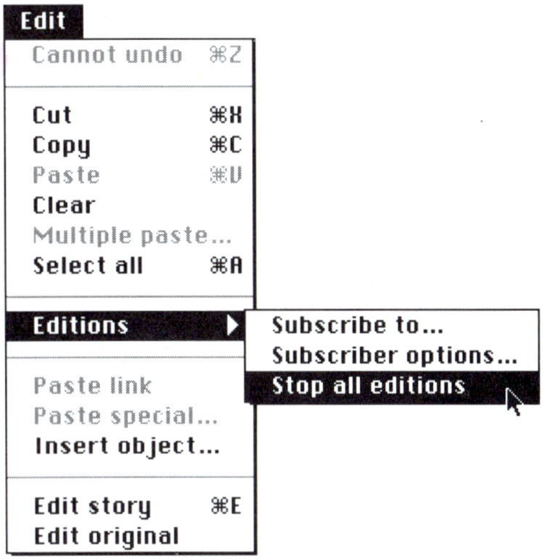

Text 4

General Editing

You can edit text in PageMaker in either layout mode, or in Story editor mode. Editing in Story editor mode is the easier of the two methods. We discuss this method later on in this chapter from Figures 75 through 87. We briefly look first at editing in layout mode, as it is still useful for small text changes and for viewing the layout.

You can delete and insert text in PageMaker just as you would in a word processor. First use the text tool to add an insertion point in the text. If you want to delete text to the left, press the Delete key. If you want to insert text, simply type in the text. You can move the text insertion point in your publication up, down, right or left by using the arrow keys on the keyboard. Alternatively, you can create a new insertion point by moving the cursor to a new location and clicking.

Figure 1. To copy or delete large blocks of text, you need to highlight the text first. You can do this in a number of ways. One way is to simply hold the mouse button down and move it over a section of text. When you release the mouse button the text appears selected, which is shown as white on a black background (reversed).

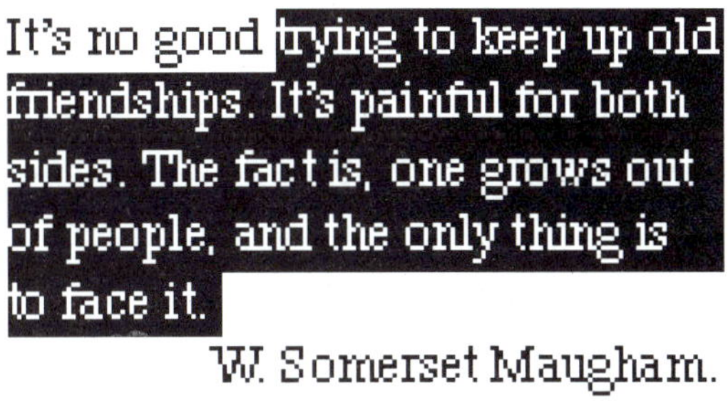

Figure 2. Double-clicking on a word automatically selects it. If you then hold the Shift key down and click the mouse button on consecutive words, you continue to highlight text a word at a time. The same procedure applies to paragraphs, but initially you need to triple-click.

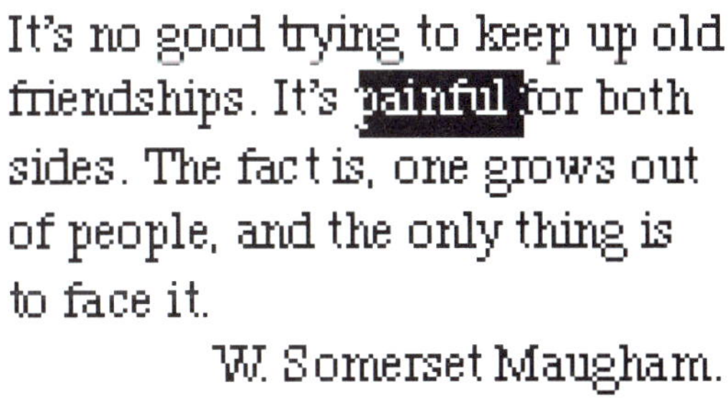

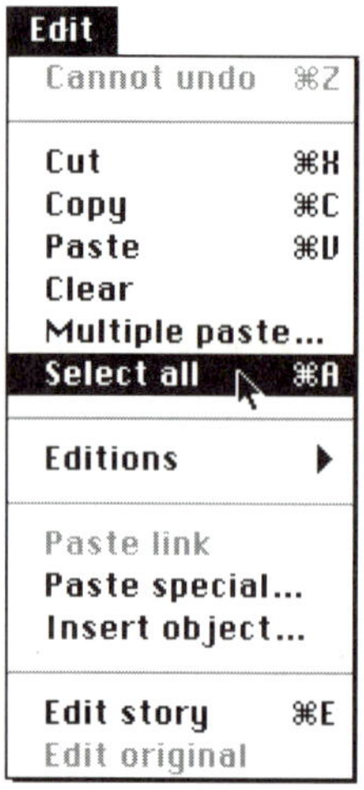

Figure 3. There are two other ways you can select the text. Click the cursor anywhere in the text and choose *Select all* from the **Edit** menu. Alternatively, click at the beginning of the text, move to the end of the text block, hold down the Shift key and click again. This selects everything in between these two points.

For the rest of the chapter, when we refer to selecting or highlighting text, you can use any of the methods we have discussed.

CUT, COPY, AND PASTE COMMANDS

Highlight the text, and then choose the Cut command.

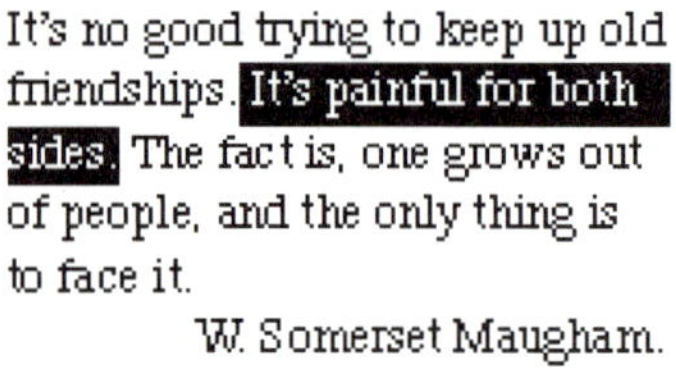

The Cut command has removed the highlighted text from the screen.

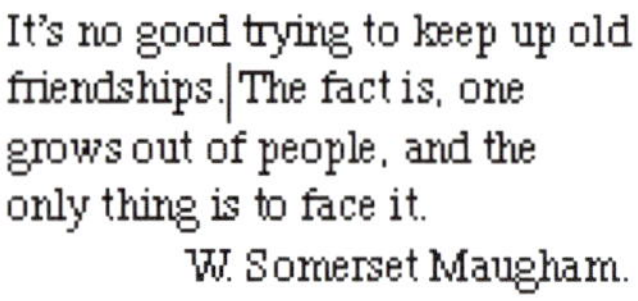

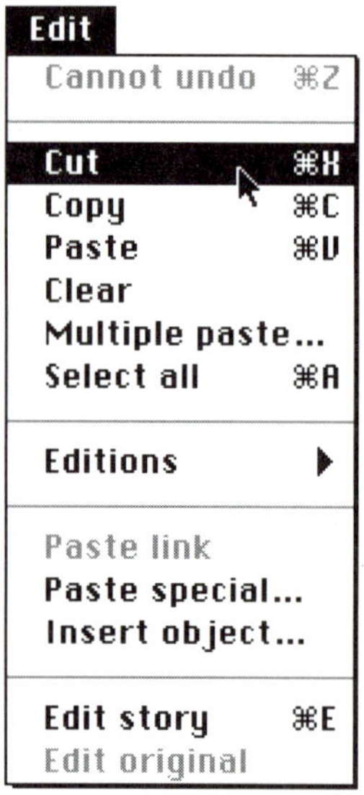

Figure 4. To remove text from a page, first highlight the text you want to delete. Select *Cut* from the **Edit** menu. This removes the text from the page and makes a copy of it to the clipboard.

Figure 5. To copy selected text to the clipboard without removing it from the page, select *Copy* from the **Edit** menu.

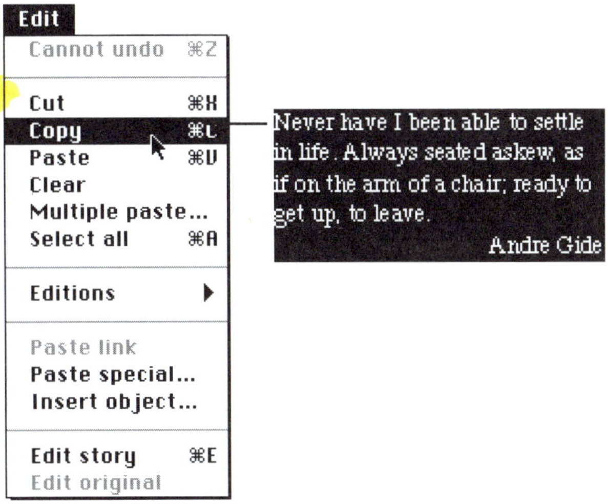

Figure 6. To paste text that you have cut or copied to the clipboard, click on the page where you want the text pasted. Select *Paste* from the **Edit** menu, and your text automatically appears on the page. In this example, the text copied in Figure 5 is pasted onto the text in Figure 6.

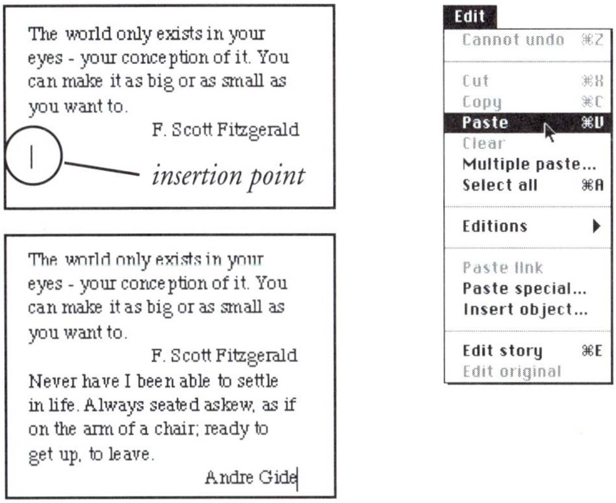

Figure 7. You can also cut and copy text by selecting a text block with the pointer tool before selecting the *Cut* or *Copy* command. To paste the text back onto the page, you can keep the pointer tool selected before selecting *Paste*, or you can click on the page to insert the text within another text block.

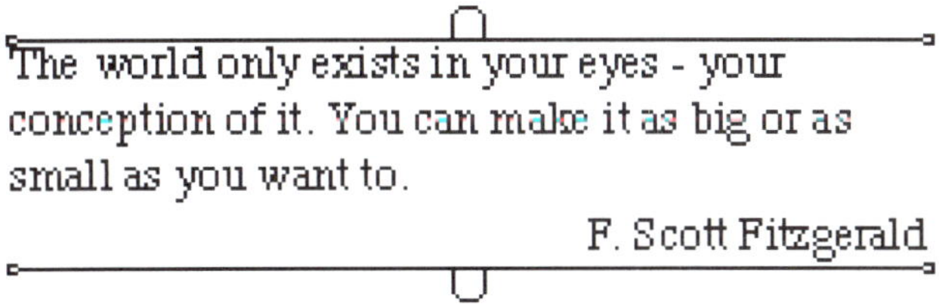

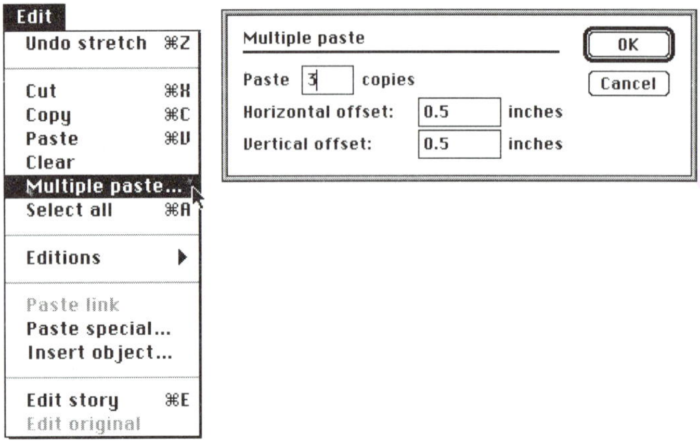

MULTIPLE PASTE COMMAND

Figure 8. Use the *Multiple paste* command to paste more than one copy at a time of your cut or copied text. If you selected the text with the text tool, the pasted text appears at the insertion point.

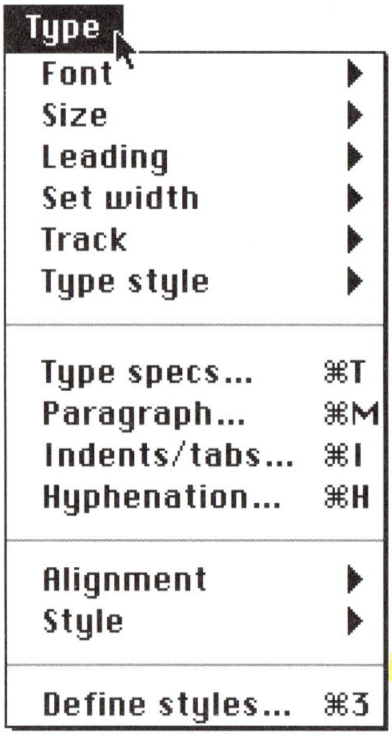

THE TYPE MENU

Figure 9. The Type menu is one of the menus within PageMaker 5 that has a series of submenus available. Each command with the ▶ symbol to the right causes a submenu to appear. When it is selected, a submenu lets you select a command quickly; you don't have to open a dialog box.

If you select any commands in the submenu without first highlighting text or with the pointer tool selected (except for *Define styles*), you set the text defaults for the publication. If you highlight the text first, then you affect only this text.

Figure 10. The *Font* command displays the fonts you can select. This includes all the PostScript printer fonts and any additional downloadable fonts you have added to your system.

Depending on how many fonts you have loaded, you might not have enough room on your menu to display all the fonts.

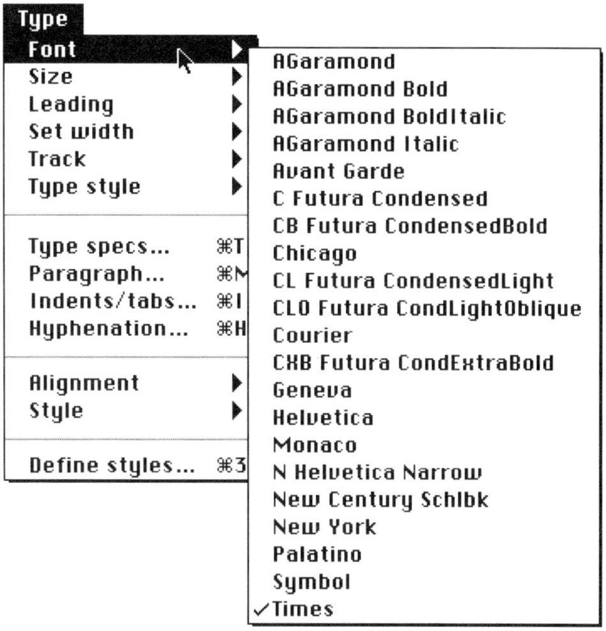

Figure 11. Selecting the *Size* command invokes a submenu as shown. Not all point sizcs are available in this submenu. Choosing *Other*, at the top, lets you key in any point size between 4 and 650 points in 0.1 point increments.

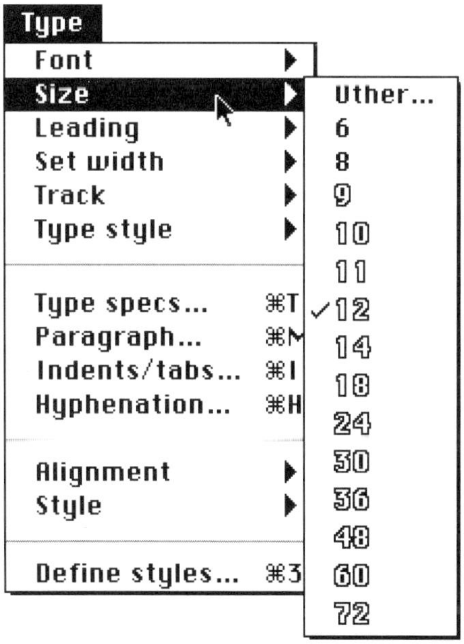

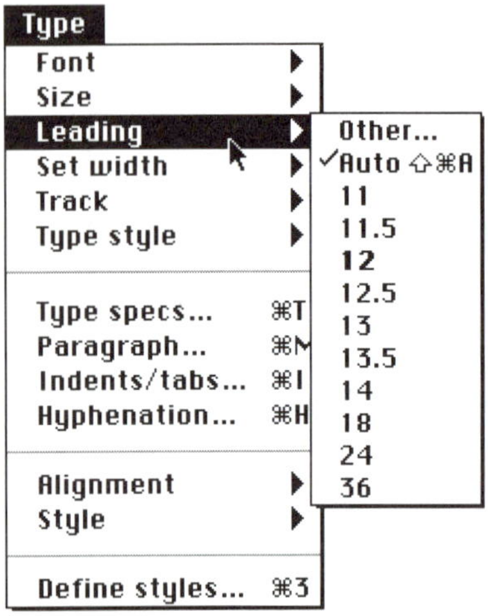

LEADING IS THE

SPACE BETWEEN

LINES OF TEXT

Figure 12. This is the submenu for *Leading*; which is the vertical spacing between text. Choose any of the values shown or select *Other* to add your own value. *Other* lets you choose a value from 0 to 1300 points in 0.1 point increments. *Auto*, by default, is set to 120% of the text point size (in the *Paragraph specifications* dialog box).

The text in this figure has had the leading increased to 24.

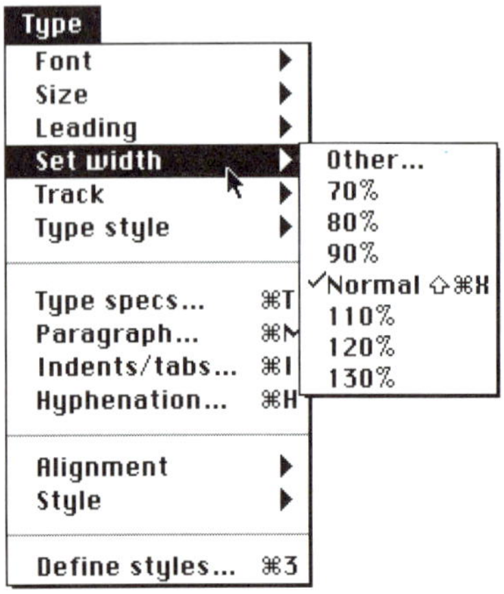

SET WIDTH

SET WIDTH

Figure 13. The *Set width* command controls the width of characters from 5% to 250% in 0.1% increments. Again, choose *Other* if you want a specific value that is not included in the submenu. This option allows you to condense or expand each character of any font.

Compare the two examples in this figure. The top text is set at *Normal* while the text below has been set to *130%*.

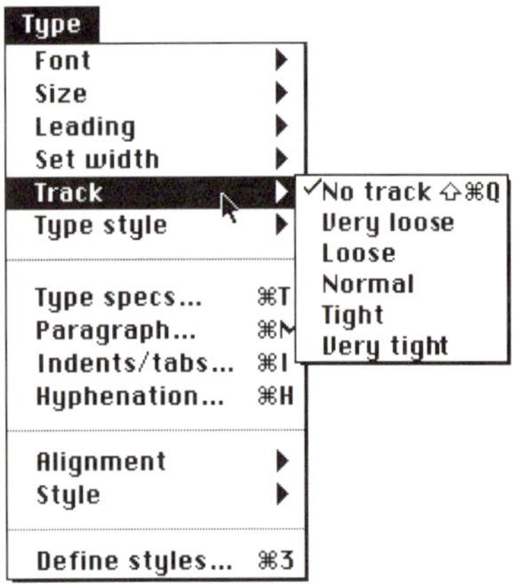

TRACK

TRACK

Figure 14. The *Track* command has its own submenu as shown. Use tracking to adjust the spacing between characters and words. As you can see in the submenu you have five levels of tracking, from very loose to very tight. Compare the two examples in this figure. The top text is *Normal* while other text is *Very tight.*

Figure 15. You can make simple style changes to the text with the *Type style* command. You can see what's available in this submenu. You can apply more than one style to selected text, but you must re-select the *Type style* submenu for each additional style.

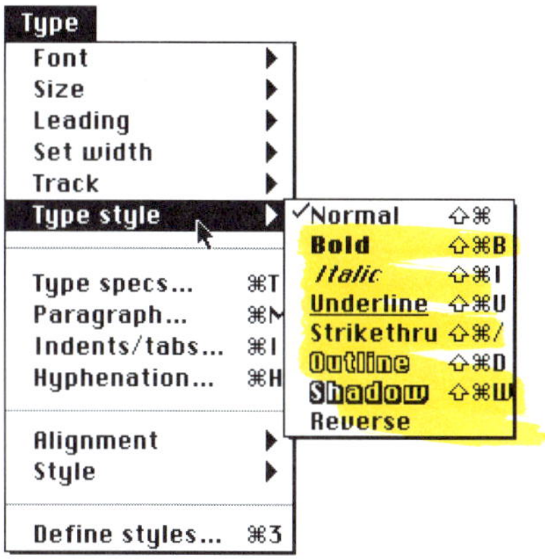

TYPE SPECIFICATIONS

Figure 16. The *Type specs* command combines all the choices of the six commands above it in the **Type** menu, plus additional features. This command and its associated dialog box (Figure 17) let you apply multiple commands at one time to highlighted text.

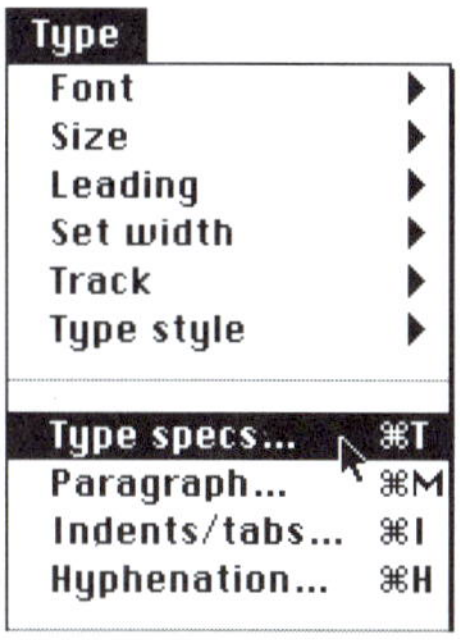

Figure 17. The *Type specifications* dialog box contains *Font, Size, Leading, Set width*, and *Track* options. They provide similar pop-up menus to those described above in Figures 10 through 14. The *Type style* selections at the bottom of the box are the same as those in the *Type style* submenu (Figure 15). Figures 18 through 20 show the other options you have in this dialog box.

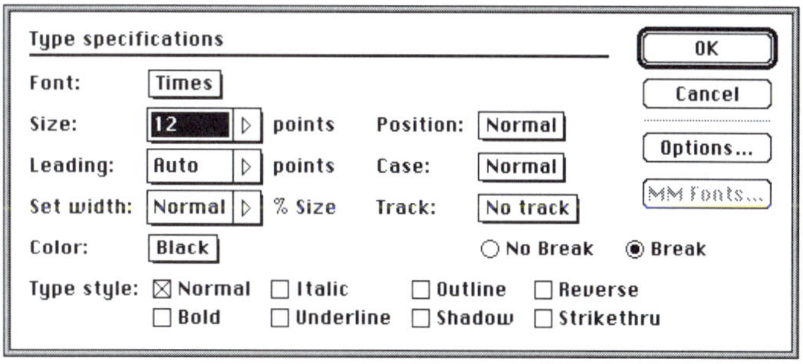

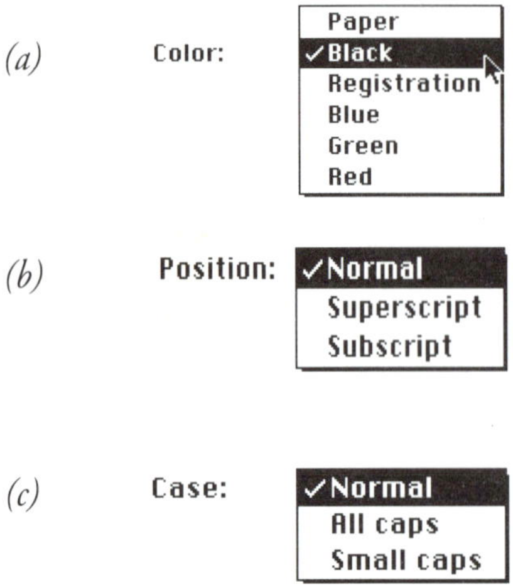

Figure 18. Three additional pop-up menus from the *Type specifications* dialog box are shown here. You can apply *Color* to text as shown in (a). (See Chapter 12, **Using Color** for more information on color.) The *Position* list (b) lets you super/subscript characters. The *Case* list (c) allows you to convert text to ALL CAPS or SMALL CAPS.

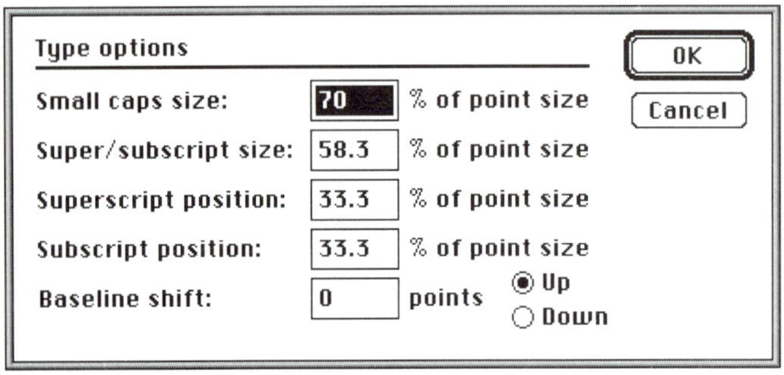

Figure 19. Clicking on *Options* in the *Type specifications* dialog box opens the *Type options* dialog box. Here you can adjust the size of small caps and super/subscript characters, super/subscript positions, as well as the baseline position of highlighted text.

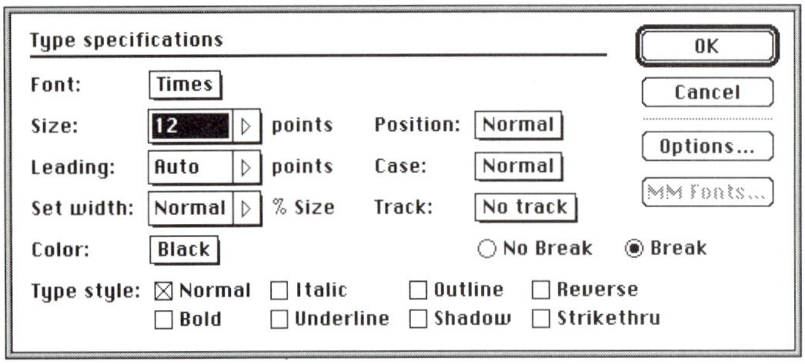

Figure 20. The *No break* option prevents selected text from wrapping from one line to the next. You can use *No break* to force PageMaker to keep words on one line. The *Break* option uses PageMaker's normal rules for flowing text from one line to another.

PARAGRAPH SPECIFICATIONS

Figure 21. You get the *Paragraph* specifications dialog box by choosing the *Paragraph* command. This dialog box contains a range of options that let you affect whole paragraphs rather than individual words. The options in this dialog box affect the selected text or the text containing the insertion point.

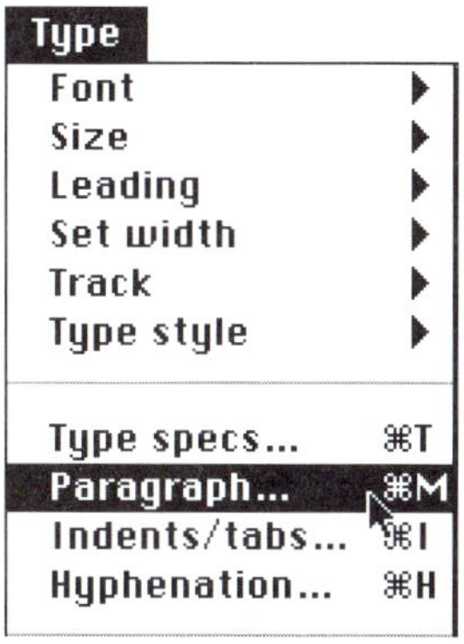

INDENTS AND PARAGRAPH SPACE

Figure 22. In the *Paragraph specifications* dialog box, the five options at the top are *Indents* (*Left* applies to the entire paragraph; *First* applies to the first line only; and *Right* applies to the right of the entire paragraph), and *Paragraph space* (controls the amount of space before and after your paragraph).

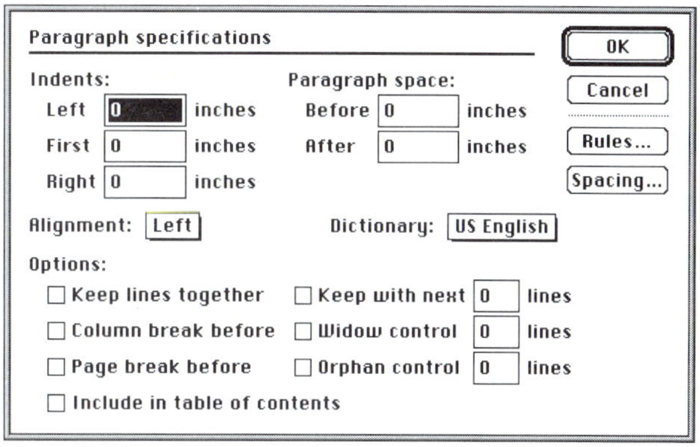

ALIGNMENT

Figure 23. Open the *Alignment* pop-up menu by holding the mouse button down with the cursor on the *Alignment* box. This list is identical to the one you open with the *Alignment* command in the **Type** menu. You can change the alignment of the whole paragraph by selecting a different option.

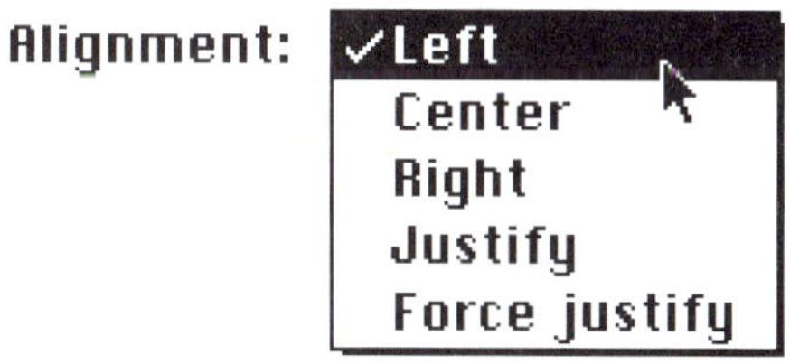

Figure 24. PageMaker uses the *Dictionary* when checking spelling and hyphenation. You open it by clicking to the right of the currently displayed dictionary. Select your choice from the pop-up menu that appears, if any others are available.

OPTIONS

The *Keep lines together* option in the Paragraph specifications dialog box ensures that a selected paragraph is not separated by a page or column break.

The *Column break before* option ensures that the selected paragraph begins a new column.

The *Page break before* option ensures the selected paragraph begins a new page.

When you select the *Include in table of contents* option, the selected text is added to your table of contents. For more information on this command, see Chapter 15.

Keep with next x lines makes sure that a selected paragraph moves with 1 to 3 lines of the next paragraph. This stops subheadings from appearing on their own at the bottom of a column.

Use the *Orphan control* option to set how many lines at the end of a paragraph start a new page or column. You have the option of leaving 1 to 3 lines here.

The *Widow control* command works in a similar way to the *Widow control* command. The difference is that *Orphan control* decides how many lines at the start of a paragraph remain at the bottom of a column or page. To ensure consistency throughout your document and to save time, you can preset these options before placing large documents.

PARAGRAPH RULES

Figure 25. The *Paragraph rules* dialog box appears after you click on the *Rules* button in the *Paragraph specifications* dialog box. These options let you place lines above and below your text. You can set the above and below rules separately, and you can have one without the other. Enable these rules by clicking inside the *Rule above paragraph* and the *Rule below paragraph* selection boxes.

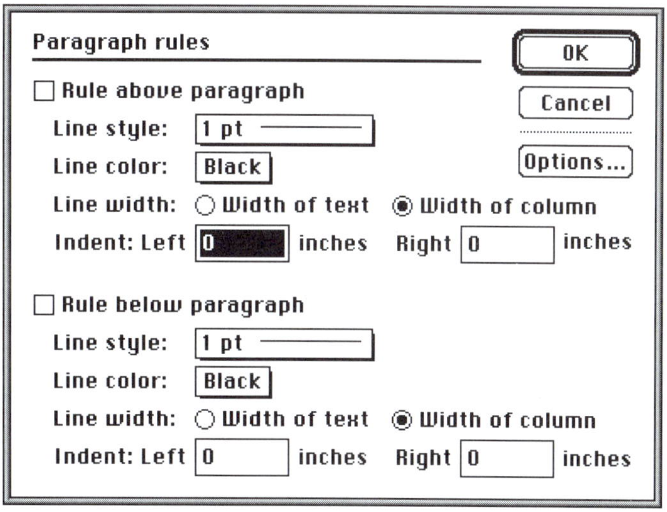

Figure 26. Click or hold the mouse down on the arrow to the right of the *Line style* box in the *Paragraph rules* dialog box. A pop-up menu appears. Use the mouse to select the line thickness you require.

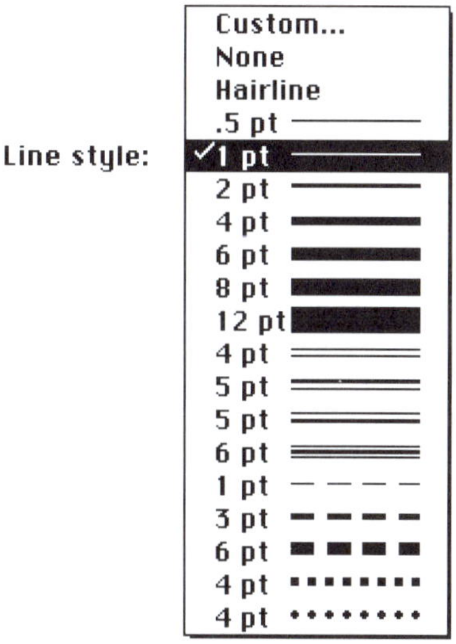

Figure 27. If you're working with a color screen, you can apply a color to the lines above and below your text through the *Paragraph rules* dialog box. Use this pop-up menu in the same way that you use the *Line style* pop-up menu.

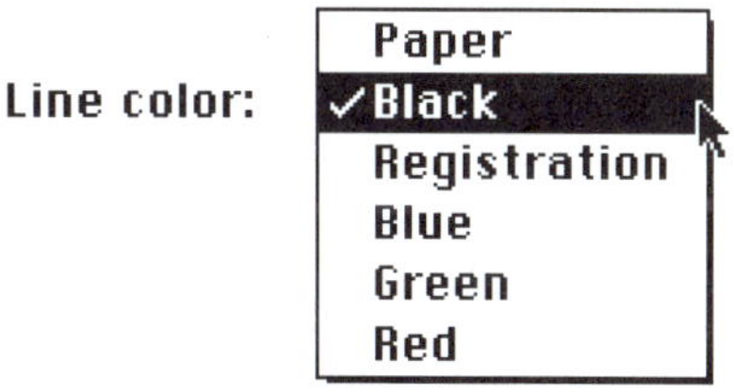

You have two choices in the *Line width* option. Choose either the *Width of text* or *Width of column* option.

You can apply indents to the rules if you do not want the rules to be exactly the width of the text or the column.

You have the same options for the *Rule below paragraph* as you do for the *Rule above paragraph*.

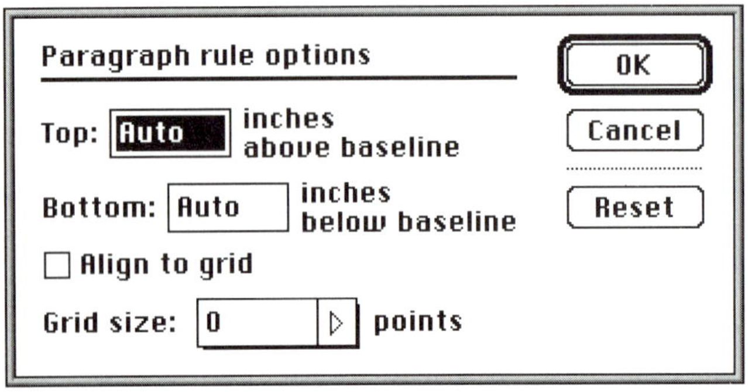

PARAGRAPH RULE OPTIONS

Figure 28. You get the *Paragraph rule options* dialog box by clicking on the *Options* button in the *Paragraph rules* dialog box shown above. The *Top* and *Bottom* options let you position the rules relative to the text. Double-click in the relevant box and type in the desired value.

The *Align to grid* option in the *Paragraph rule options* dialog box ensures that the body text on your page aligns horizontally. When using this option, the grid size should reflect the leading size of the text. This option does not work when you have applied Autoleading to the text.

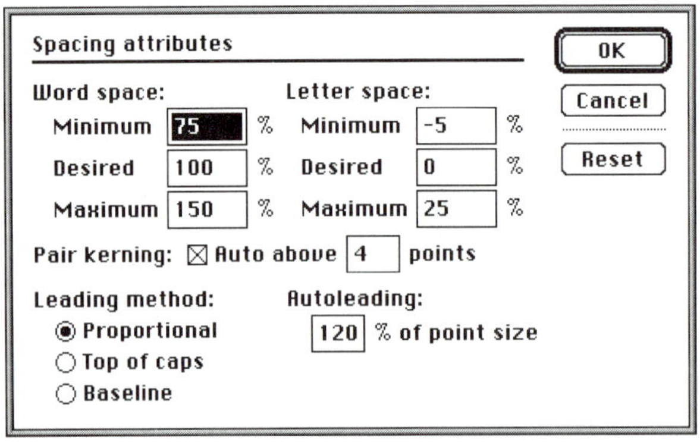

SPACING ATTRIBUTES

Figure 29. Open the *Spacing attributes* dialog box by clicking on the *Spacing* button in the *Paragraph specifications* dialog box shown in Figure 22.

The *Word space* values in the *Spacing attributes* dialog box affect the spacing between your words. The percentages here are based on normal text. The possible settings for each option can range from 0% to 500%. Increasing or decreasing these figures increases or decreases the word spacing respectively.

Letter space affects the spacing between characters. The range available for *Minimum* and *Maximum* is -200% to +200%. The *Desired* must be between the minimum and maximum settings. Again, increasing and decreasing the settings here will change the letterspacing of the selected text.

Pair kerning varies the amount of space between two adjacent characters. By default, *Auto above x points* is selected.

The *Leading method* selection should nearly always be *Proportional.* You can use the *Top of caps* method for special design effects. Use the *Baseline* option when you wish to align leading from the baseline of the text — used in traditional typography.

The *Autoleading* option in the *Spacing attributes* dialog box represents a proportion of the point size. Changing this figure affects the line spacing of the text.

INDENTS/TABS

Figure 30. Selecting the *Indents/tabs* command from the **Type** menu brings up the *Indents/tabs* dialog box.

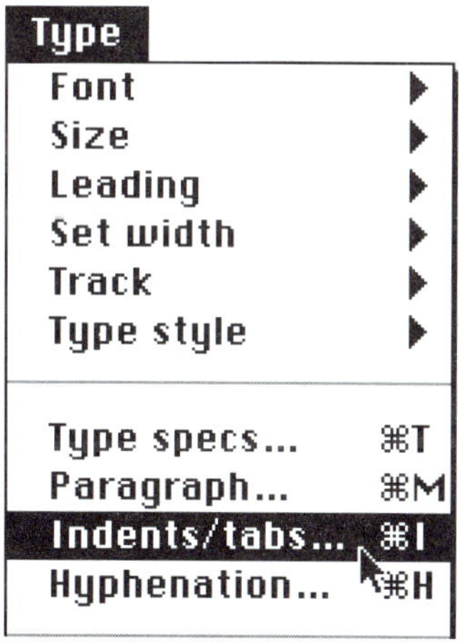

Figure 31. To start with, there are four tab options at the left of this dialog box. These are (a) left tab, (b) centered tab, (c) right tab and (d) decimal tab.

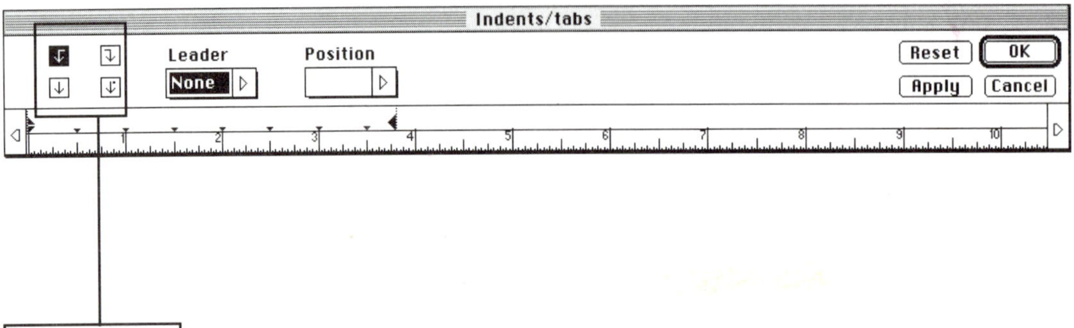

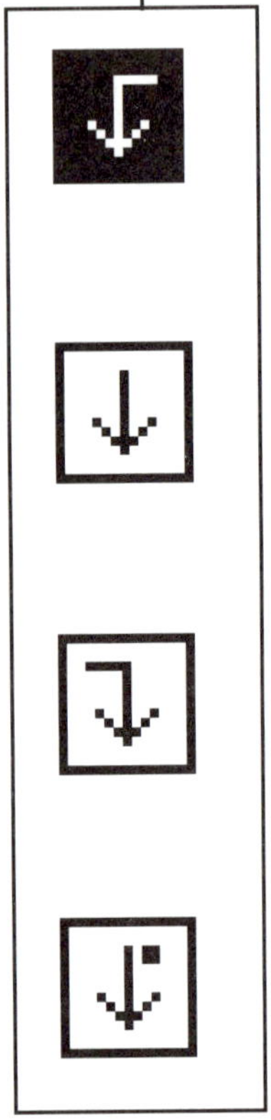

(a) The left tab left aligns the selected text at the tab point.

(b) The centered tab center aligns the text around the tab point.

(c) The right tab right aligns the selected text at the tab point.

(d) When working with figures, use the decimal tab to vertically align all decimal points in the selected text, as shown here.

456.56
34.45
1.23
123.45

Figure 32. If you want a character repeated between tabs, such as the leader dots found in a table of contents, use the *Leader* option. The associated pop-up menu, which you activate by clicking the arrow, gives you five options. The *Custom* option lets you type in your own preferred character to be used as your tab leader.

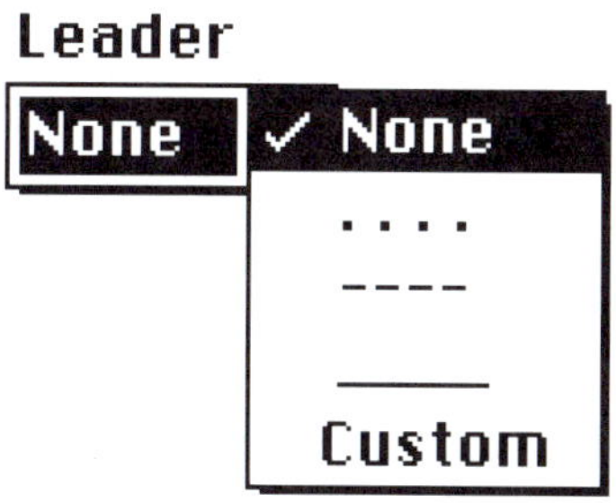

Figure 33. The *Position* option displays the position on the ruler of the currently selected tab. It also has a pop-up menu that lets you add, delete, move, and repeat tabs.

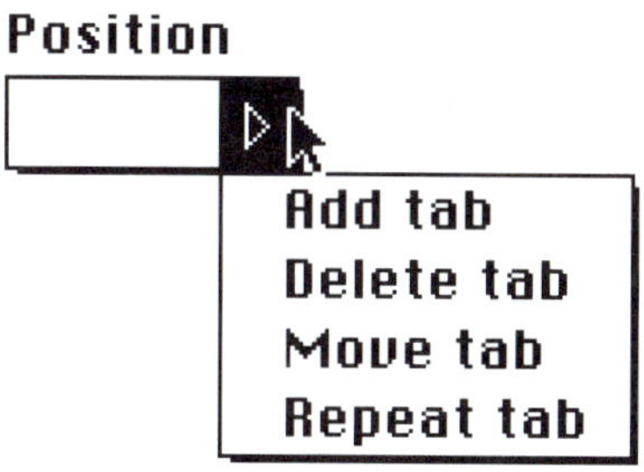

Figure 34. When you open the *Indents/tabs* dialog box, the zero point of the ruler indicates the beginning of the selected text or the beginning of the text block containing the insertion point.

You can move this dialog box around the page by holding the mouse down on the title bar and dragging it to a new position.

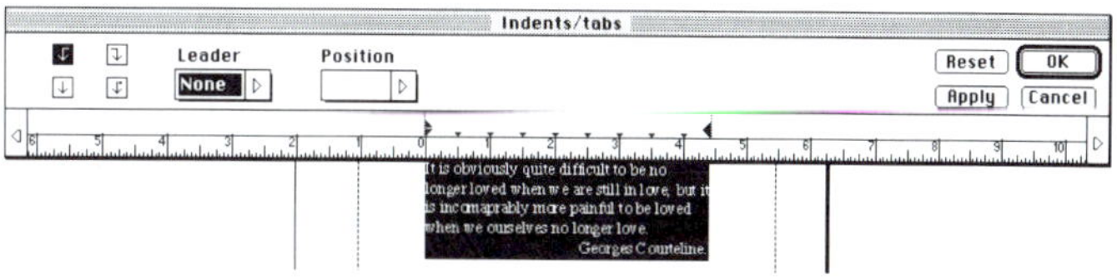

Figure 35. The ruler has two markers that start at the zero point. The top marker represents the first line indent of the selected paragraph. Moving this marker with the mouse alters the position of the first line of your selected text.

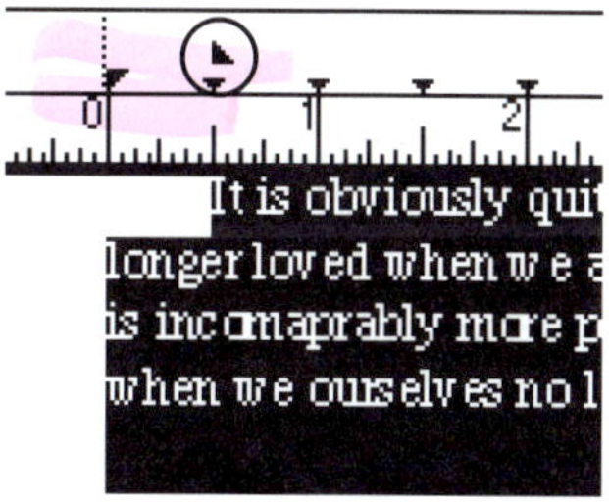

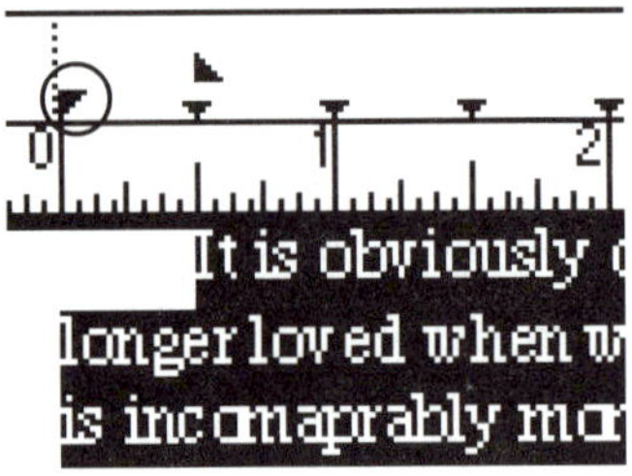

Figure 36. The bottom marker (◤) identifies the left indent of the whole paragraph; all selected text moves to reflect the amount you have moved the marker with the mouse.

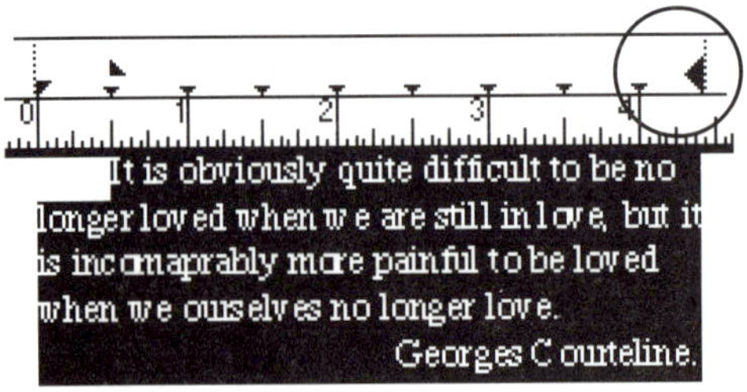

Figure 37. The right indent marker (◀) sits on the ruler at the right margin of the selected text block.

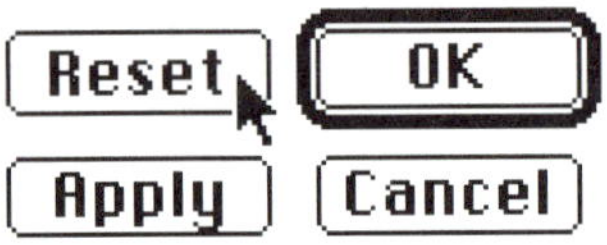

Figure 38. The *Reset* button in the *Indent/tabs* dialog box removes all tabs you have placed yourself and returns the dialog box to the default settings.

HYPHENATION

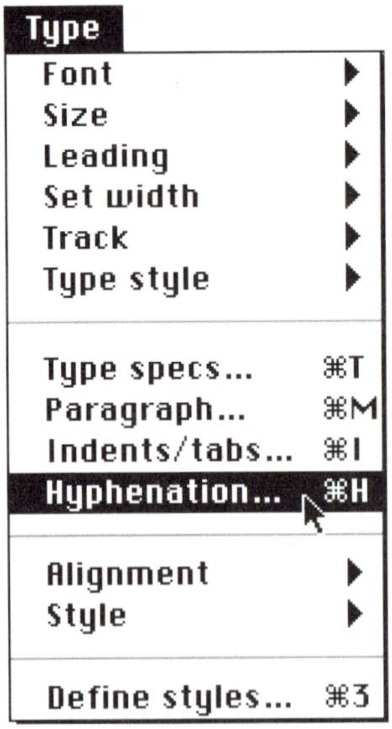

Figure 39. The next command in the Type menu is *Hyphenation.*

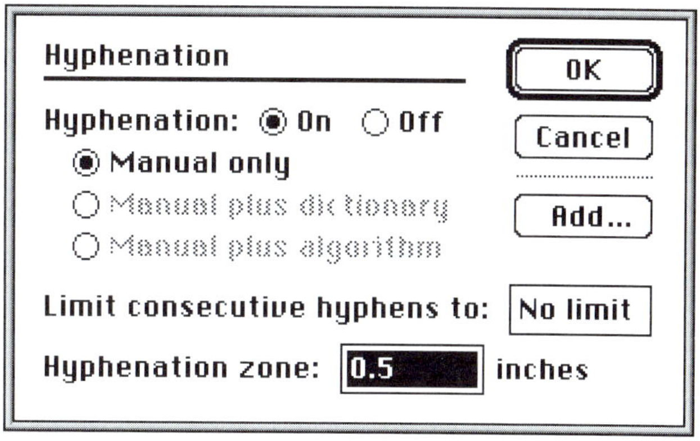

Figure 40. This command brings up the *Hyphenation* dialog box. By default, the hyphenation is on.

If you select the *Manual only* option, PageMaker hyphenates only where you have placed discretionary hyphens (Command+-). The hyphen appears only when the manually hyphenated word falls at the end of a line. PageMaker splits the word to fit the paragraph correctly in the text block.

If you select the *Manual plus dictionary* option, PageMaker uses all discretionary hyphens plus the hyphens that appear in PageMaker's dictionary.

If you select the *Manual plus algorithm* option in the *Hyphenation* dialog box, PageMaker hyphenates any word whether it appears in the PageMaker dictionary or not. If a word falls at the end of a column, PageMaker hyphenates the word in what it calculates to be the most suitable place.

The *Limit consecutive hyphens to* option lets you set a maximum number of consecutive hyphens you would like to appear (from 1 to 255 or No limit) in the selected text.

The *Hyphenation zone* option affects the amount of space before hyphenation occurs. The larger the figure you put in this box (up to 2 inches), the less hyphens that occur.

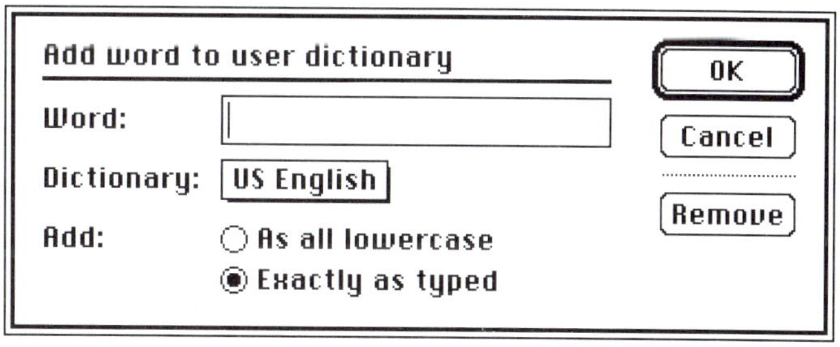

Figure 41. Clicking on the *Add* button in the *Hyphenation* dialog box opens a dialog box where you can add words to your dictionary and select your preferred place of hyphenation.

You can also change the position of hyphens in words that already exist in the dictionary. Put one tilde (~) in a word where you would prefer to split the word. Add two tildes for your second choice and three for your third choice. For example: Hyph~en~~a~~~tion.

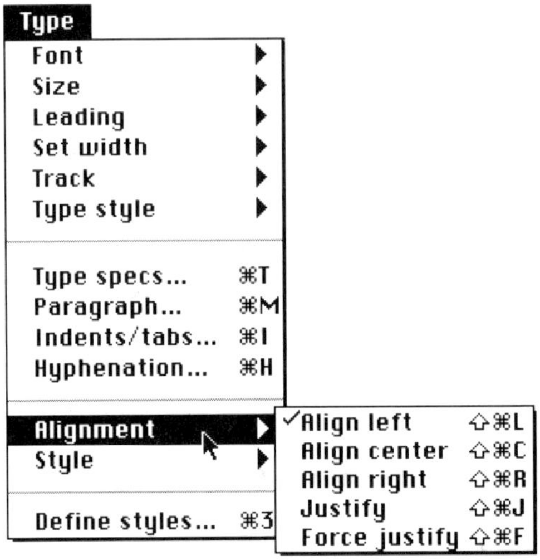

Figure 42. You have the same set of alignment choices in the *Alignment* submenu as in the *Paragraph specifications* dialog box (see Figure 23).

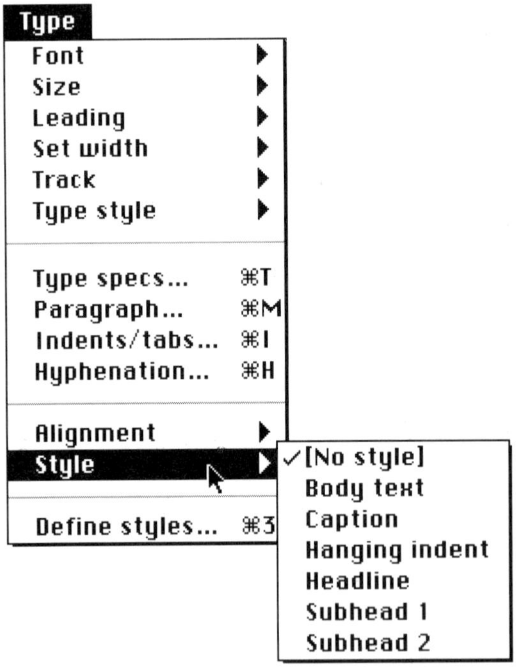

Figure 43. The *Style* and *Define styles* commands are explained in Chapter 11.

Exporting Text

You can export text from PageMaker to a file through the *Export* command in the **File** menu.

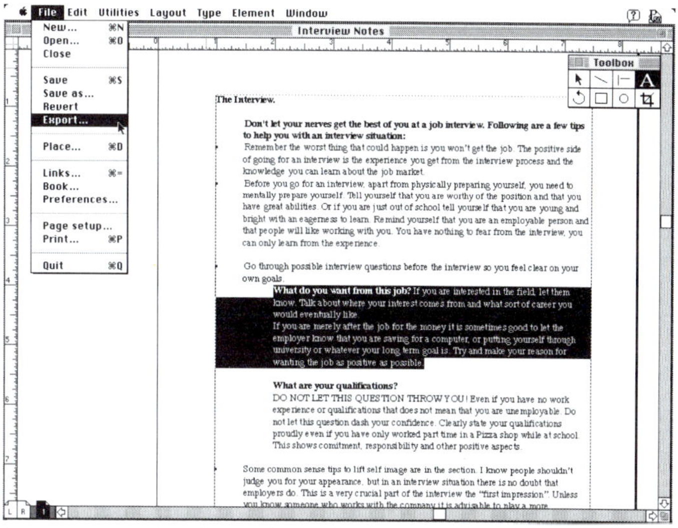

Figure 44. Before choosing the *Export* command, highlight the text that you would like to export. If you want to export the whole story, put the insertion point anywhere in the text.

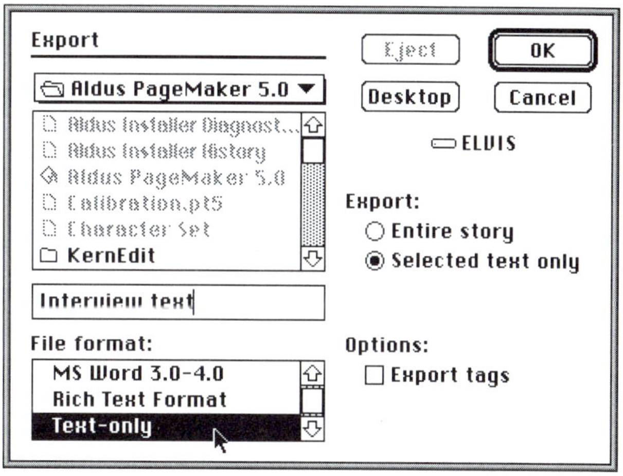

Figure 45. In the *Export* dialog box, give the file a name and select the drive or folder where you want to save it.

You can either export the entire story or just the selected text.

Select *Export tags* if you also want to export the styles you created for your text in PageMaker.

When you export a file, the *File format* pop-up menu in the *Export* dialog box lets you select the format from the export filters you installed. Click on the format you require. After you have set up the *Export* dialog box, click on *OK*.

The Control Palette and Text

You can use the Control palette as a quick way of formatting text and applying styles; it is as an alternative to using the menu commands in the **Type** menu. Nearly every option in the Control palette has an equivalent menu command. See the section on the *Type specs* command earlier in the chapter for more information.

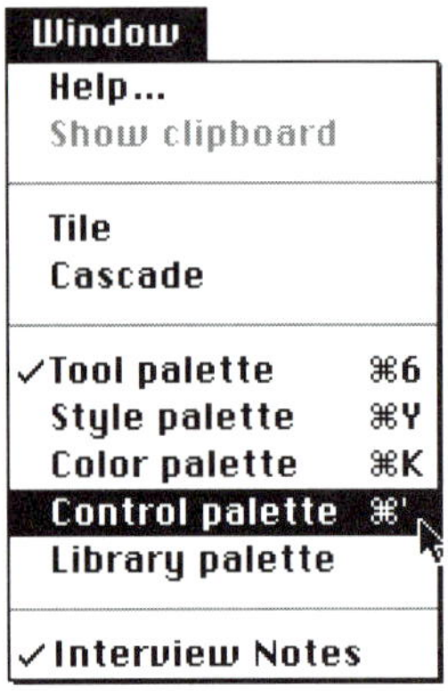

Figure 46. You can get the Control palette through the **Window** menu.

Figure 47. This figure shows how the Control palette looks on screen when you have nothing selected and the pointer tool is active. The *X* and *Y* coordinates show the position of the mouse.

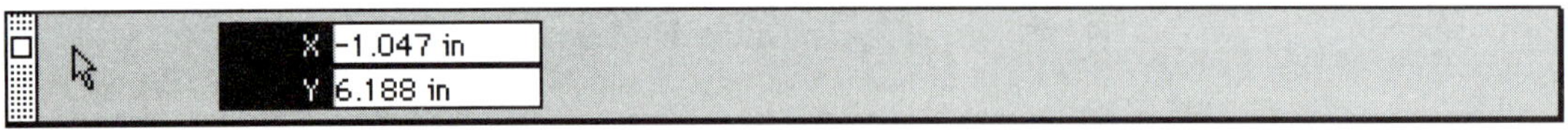

THE TEXT PALETTE

CHARACTER VIEW

Figure 48. When you select the text tool, the Control palette changes to the one shown below—the Text palette. PageMaker uses Character view by default. You use Character view to apply text attributes to selected text.

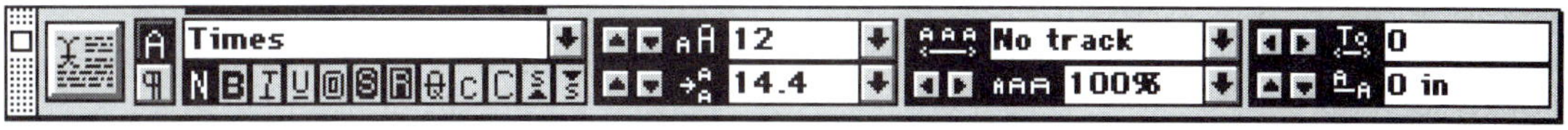

Figure 49. In this figure, we have labeled the different parts of the Text palette in *Character view.*

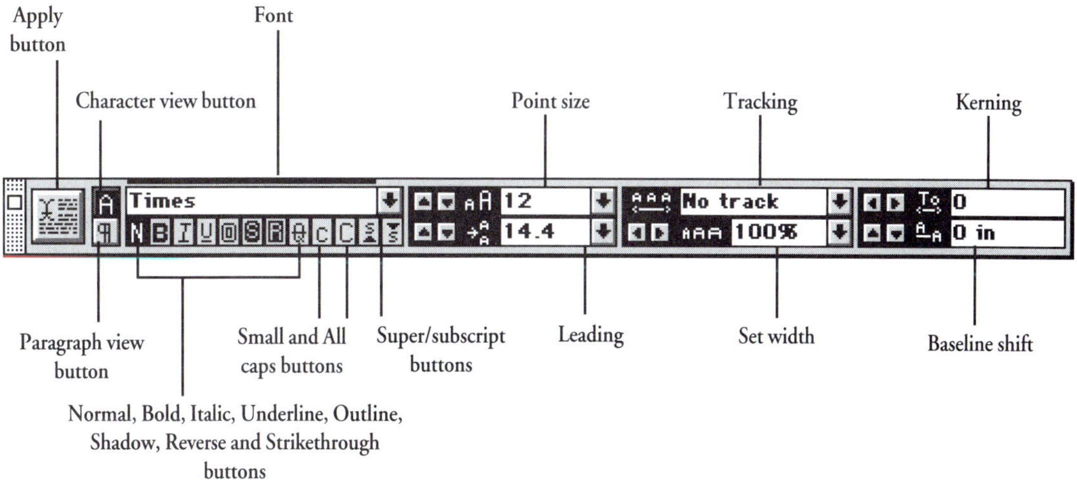

APPLY BUTTON

Figure 50. Use the *Apply* button in the Control palette to display changes you have made to selected text using the Control palette. (Some changes appear automatically.)

Pressing the Tab key moves you to the next option in the Control palette.

PALETTE VIEW BUTTONS

Figure 51. Click on the appropriate button to switch between Character view and Paragraph view.

FONT

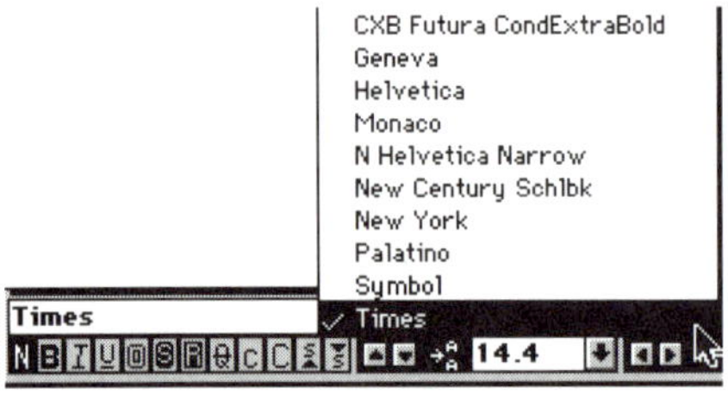

Figure 52. Use the *Font* pop-up menu to change the font of selected text. Click on the down arrow to display the pop-up menu and click on the desired font.

TYPE STYLE, CASE, AND SUB/SUPERSCRIPT BUTTONS

Figure 53. Use these buttons to change the style of highlighted text. To turn a style off, click on the button of the relevant type style. (Do not confuse these styles with paragraph styles.)

POINT SIZE OPTION

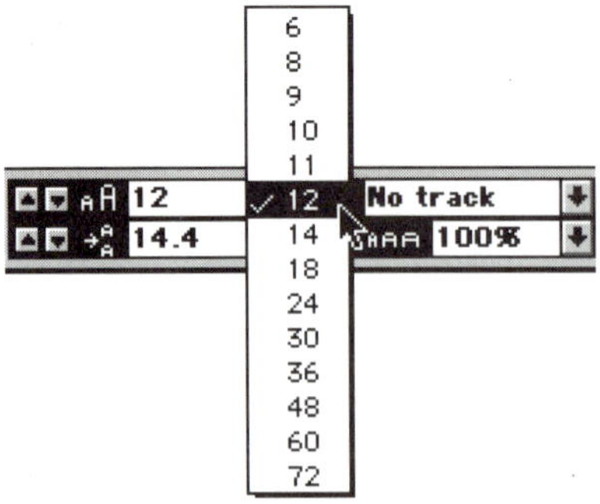

Figure 54. The *Point size* text box lets you either change the point size from the pop-up menu, or type the size into the text box to change the size of highlighted text.

The nudge buttons to the left let you increase or decrease the point size by 0.1 of a point. Holding down the Command key while clicking on a nudge button increases or decreases the point size by 1 point. You can set the nudge amount in the *Preferences* dialog box.

LEADING OPTION

Figure 55. The *Leading* text box lets you set the leading value for highlighted text. Choose from the pop-up menu or type a value into the text box. Use the nudge buttons to increase or decrease the leading size by 0.1 of a point.

Holding down the Command key while clicking on a nudge button increases or decreases the leading by 1 point.

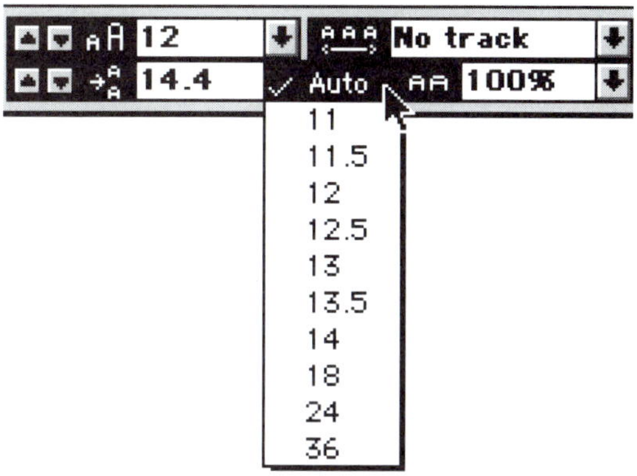

TRACKING OPTION

Figure 56. Use the *Tracking* option to set the tracking (letter space) for selected text.

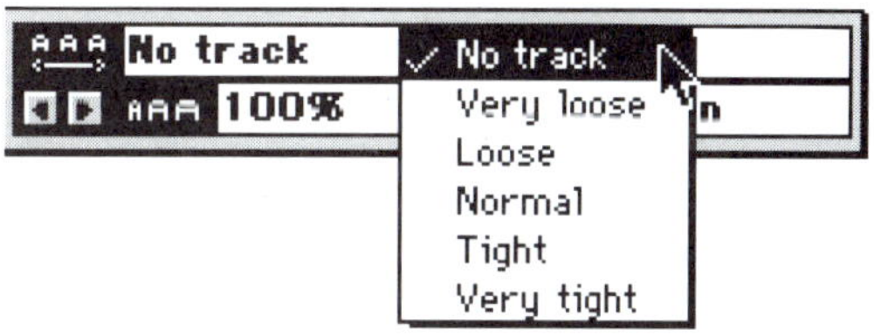

SET WIDTH OPTION

Figure 57. Use the *Set width* option to change the horizontal width of the selected characters. Use the nudge buttons to increase or decrease the width by 1%. Holding down the Command key while clicking on a nudge button increases or decreases the width by 10%.

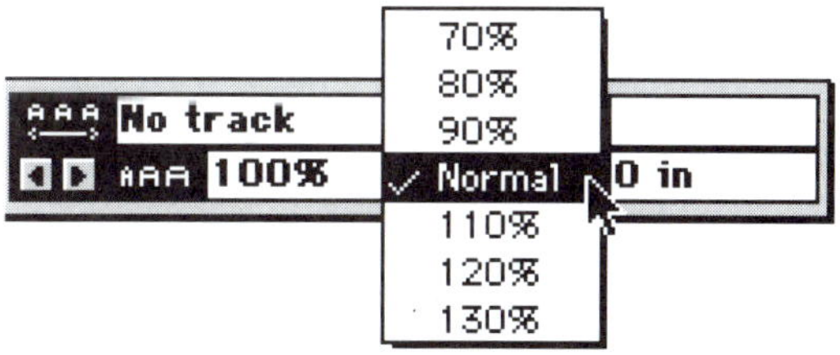

KERNING OPTION

Figure 58. Change the *Kerning* option to modify the space between the letters of highlighted text. Use the nudge buttons to increase or decrease the space by 0.01 em. Holding down the Command key while clicking on a nudge button increases or decreases the space by 0.1 em.

BASELINE OPTION

Figure 59. You can modify the baseline of highlighted text by changing this option. The default unit of measure used for the baseline is the unit of measure used for the vertical ruler (specified in the *Preferences* dialog box). Use the nudge buttons to raise or lower the text from the baseline by the nudge amount specified in *Preferences.* Holding down the Command key while clicking on a nudge button increases or decreases the baseline by 10 times that amount.

PARAGRAPH VIEW

Figure 60. When you click on the *Paragraph view* button, the Control palette changes.

Figure 61. You use *Paragraph view* to apply paragraph styles to text. You can also modify and create styles in *Paragraph* view (see Chapter 11, for more information).

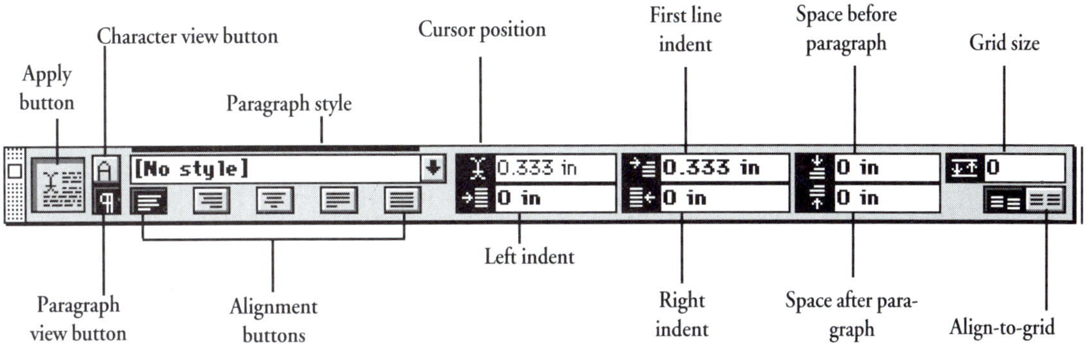

APPLY BUTTON

See Figure 50 in this chapter.

PALETTE VIEW BUTTONS

See Figure 51 in this chapter.

PARAGRAPH STYLE

Figure 62. Use the *Paragraph style* pop-up menu to apply a style to selected text. To create a new style, format some text with the attributes of the style you wish to create, select it, and type a new style name in the text box (see Chapter 11, for more information).

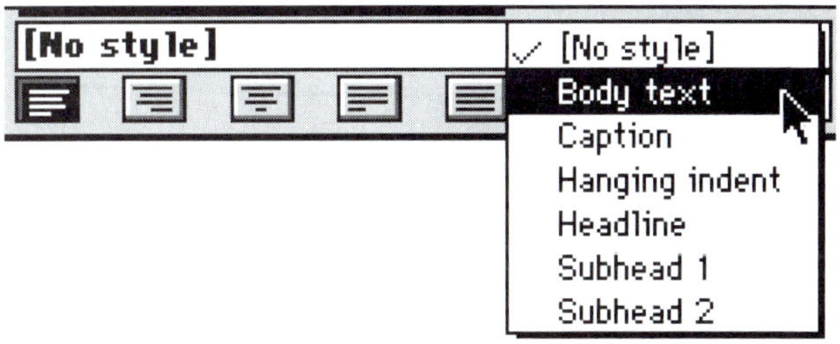

ALIGNMENT BUTTONS

Figure 63. Use the *Alignment* buttons to change the justification of highlighted text.

CURSOR POSITION INDICATOR

Figure 64. The *Cursor position* indicator displays the position of the cursor on the page in relation to the left side of the text block, as opposed to rulers or margins.

INDENT OPTIONS

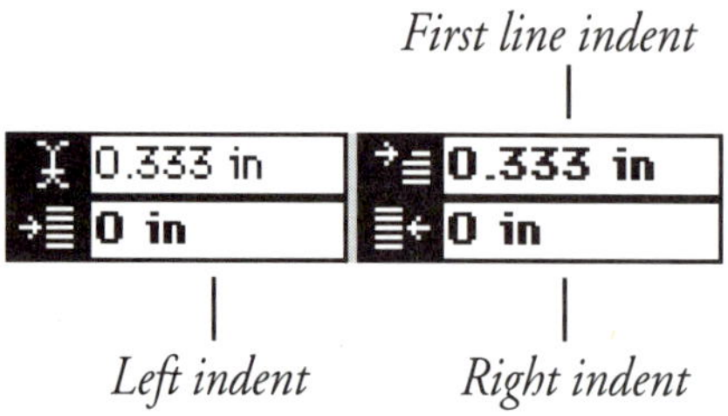

Figure 65. You can insert values in the *Indent* option text boxes to apply left, right and first-line indents to highlighted text. Indents are measured from the left and right sides of the text block.

SPACE BEFORE AND SPACE AFTER OPTIONS

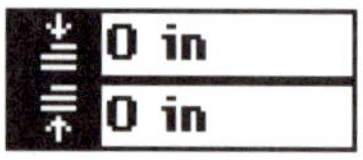

Figure 66. Use the *Space before* and *Space after* text boxes to insert space above and below paragraphs.

GRID SIZE OPTION

Figure 67. The value you type in the *Grid size* text box relates to the text grid size when you use the *Align-to-grid* option. The leading value of your text is the best value to key into this option, in this case 13.

ALIGN-TO-GRID OPTION

Figure 68. If you have set your vertical ruler measurement to points, you can use the *Align-to-grid* option to ensure that adjacent columns of text remain aligned. Click on the right button to turn the grid align feature on.

USING THE CONTROL PALETTE

Figure 69. You can apply any options in the Control palette simply by highlighting some text and changing an option. You will notice that after you highlight some text and click on an option in the Control palette (as shown here) that the highlighted text becomes surrounded by a box rather than remaining highlighted. Here we are changing the font of the selected text from Times to Futura Condensed Bold.

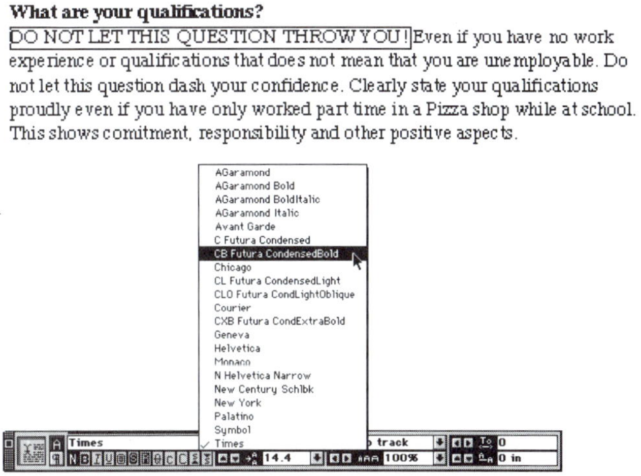

Figure 70. The changes occur immediately, and are reflected in the text and in the Control palette.

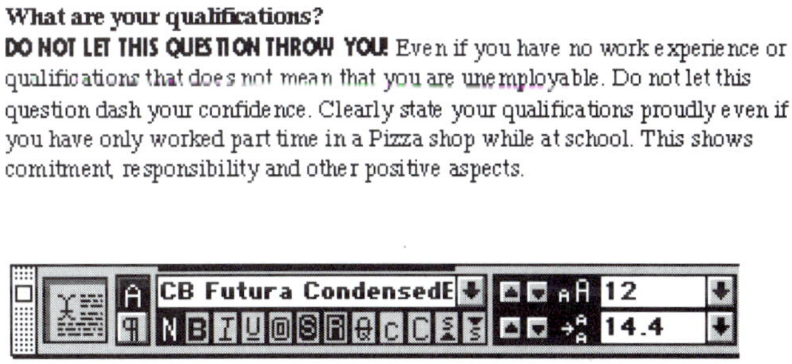

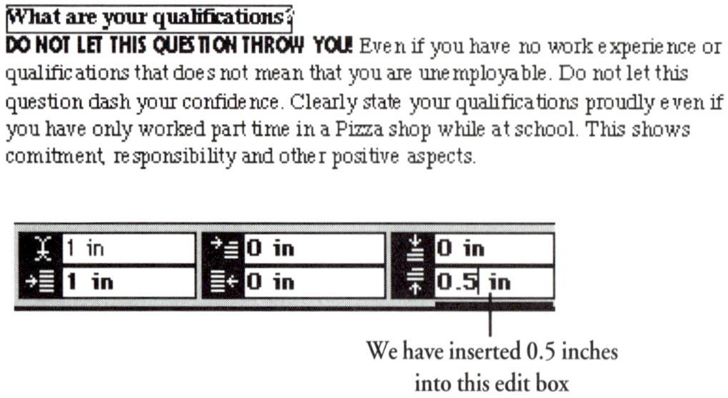

Figure 71. In this figure, we have switched to *Paragraph view*, and have inserted space in the text box of the *Space after* option to apply to the selected text. As in this case, some options which require you to type in a value do not affect the text automatically.

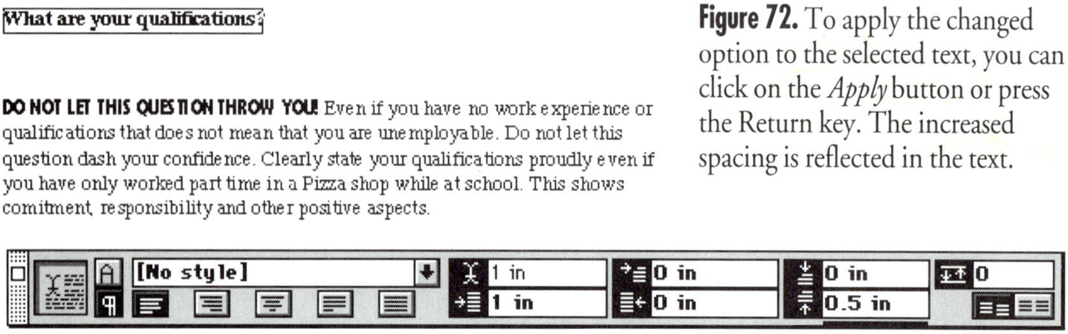

Figure 72. To apply the changed option to the selected text, you can click on the *Apply* button or press the Return key. The increased spacing is reflected in the text.

Figure 73. Use the nudge buttons by clicking on a right, a left, an up or a down button to increase or decrease the value in the connected text box. Nudge buttons occur in pairs of up and down and left and right. As with all the other options, you must have some text selected before you can make any change.

Keyboard Shortcut	Result
Command+'	Displays or hides Control palette.
Tab/Shift+Tab	Moves to next option/moves to previous option.
Return/Tab	Applies change to selected text.
Spacebar	Turns the current button on or off.

Figure 74. This table displays a number of keyboard shortcuts and their results.

Story Editor

Figure 75. Story editor, which provides the word processing features in PageMaker, puts a separate text window on top of layout view. The menus are slightly different and all of the text in a story is in one continuous block. You can scroll through the text if you can't see it all. You can resize and move the window around the screen if you need to.

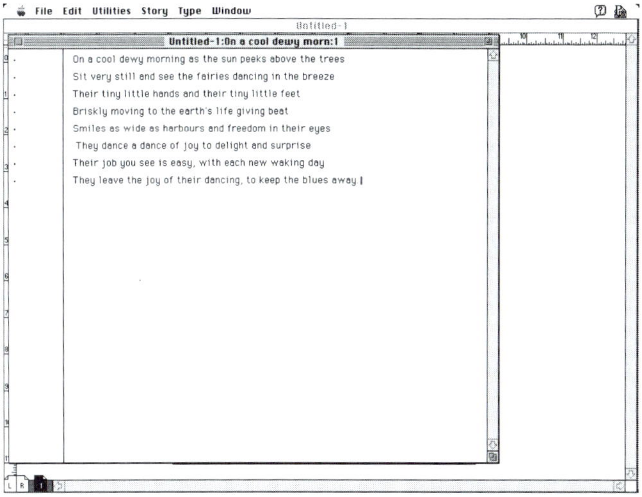

PageMaker automatically names a story window with the first few words of the text file. You can list paragraph styles at the left of the story window by choosing *Display style names* from the **Story** menu.

Figure 76. You can open Story editor in a variety of ways. Clicking the insertion point in a story and choosing *Edit story* from the **Edit** menu is one way. You can also triple-click on a text block with the pointer tool.

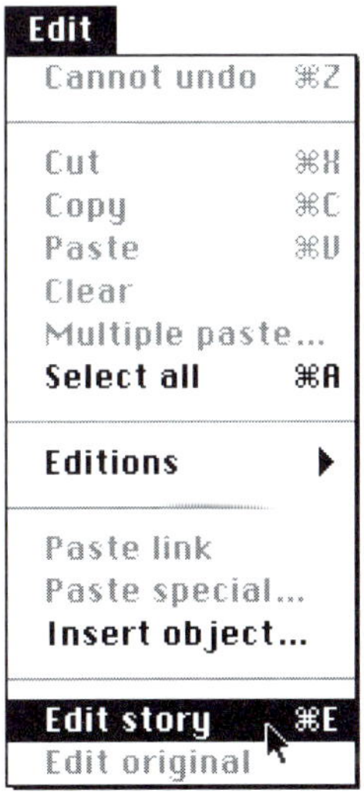

The difference between a story and a text block is that a story is a combination of text blocks that are threaded together as part of the same text file. A text block that you select with the pointer tool may only be a part of a story.

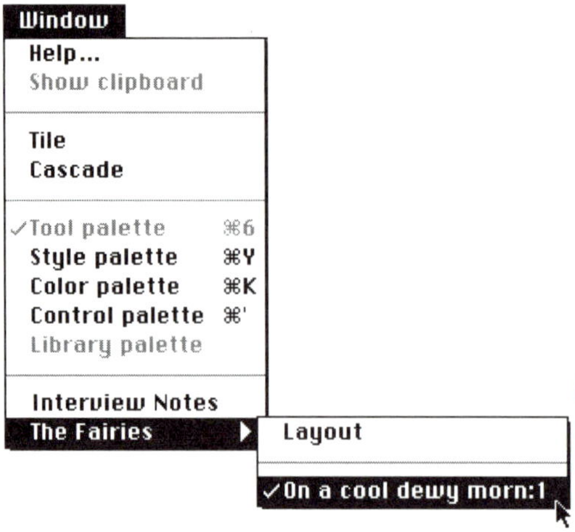

Figure 77. To move between Story editor and layout view, use the **Window** menu to select the window you want to view. You can also triple-click with the pointer tool on text to move automatically into Story editor. Clicking on an exposed part of an open story window also moves you into Story editor view.

If you have no text on screen, select the *Edit story* command and the story window appears ready for you to enter a new story.

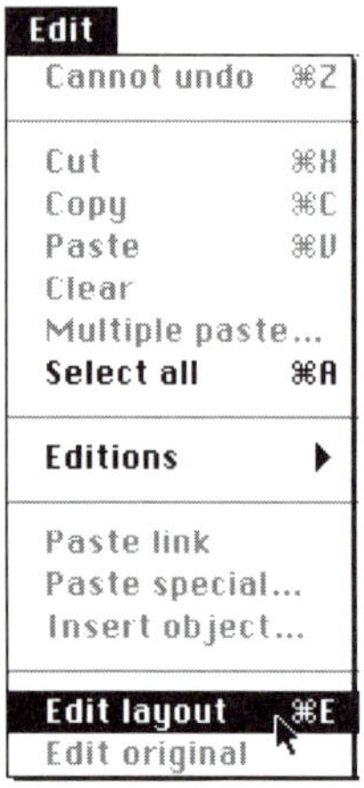

Figure 78. To return to layout view from Story editor, you can click in the close box in the story window, choose *Close story* from the **Story** menu, choose *Edit layout* from the **Edit** menu, choose *Layout* from the file's submenu in the **Window** menu, or click on an exposed part of the publication. The latter three options keep the Story editor window open but it moves behind the layout window.

Figure 79. If you have not yet placed your story (e.g. if you opened Story editor to type in a text file), PageMaker gives you the option of placing this text or discarding it when you select the *Close story* command.

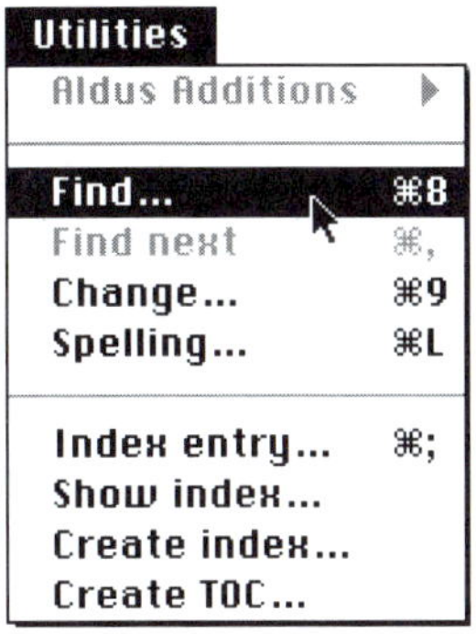

Figure 80. The *Find* command from the **Utilities** menu in Story editor lets you search for text while in Story editor.

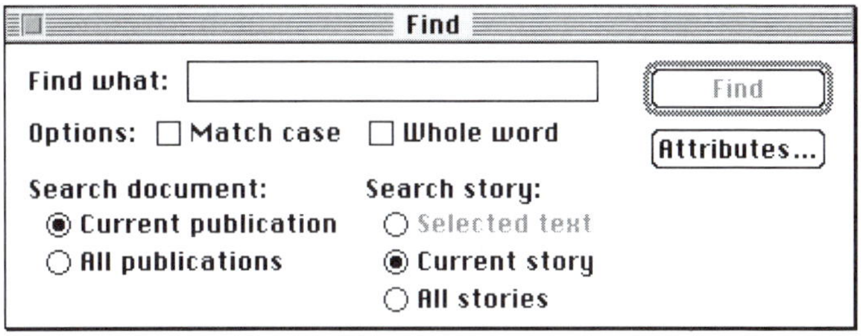

Figure 81. The *Find* dialog box lets you insert the text to search for. You can search selected text, the current story, all stories, or even all publications. The *Attributes* button brings up a further dialog box where you can search for a certain paragraph style, font, size or type style.

To close this or any similar dialog box in Story editor, click on the close box in the top-left corner of the dialog box or click outside the dialog box.

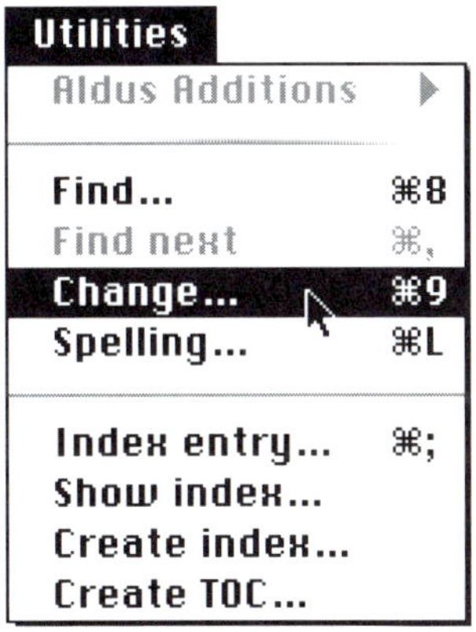

Figure 82. Use the *Change* command from the **Utilities** menu in Story editor to search for and replace found text with new text.

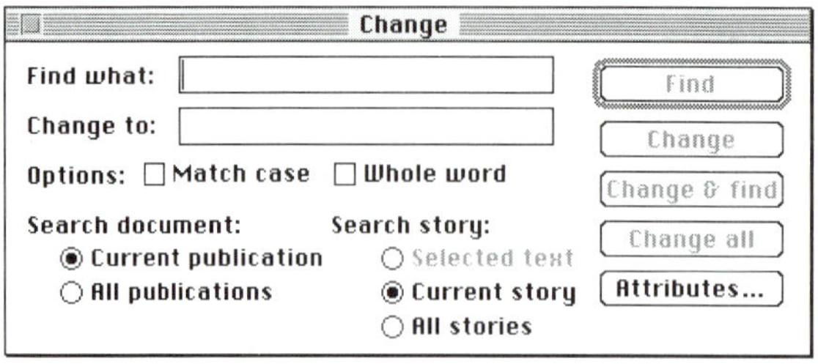

Figure 83. Insert the appropriate text in the *Find what* and *Change to* text boxes. The *Match case* option lets you search for words in upper and lower case , exactly as you have typed them. The *Whole word* option lets you search for the whole word as you have typed it, and not as part of another word.

You have a number of choices throughout this process which include *Find, Change, Change & find* and *Change all.* If you want to search for formatting features applied to text, and replace these attributes with others, click on the *Attributes* button.

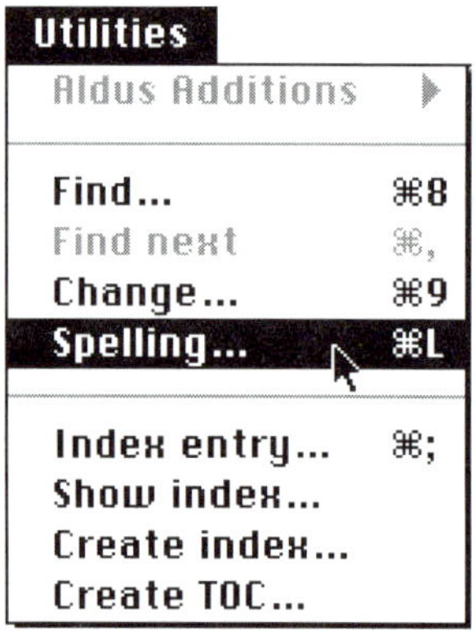

Figure 84. You can check the spelling of your text in Story editor by choosing *Spelling* from the **Utilities** menu.

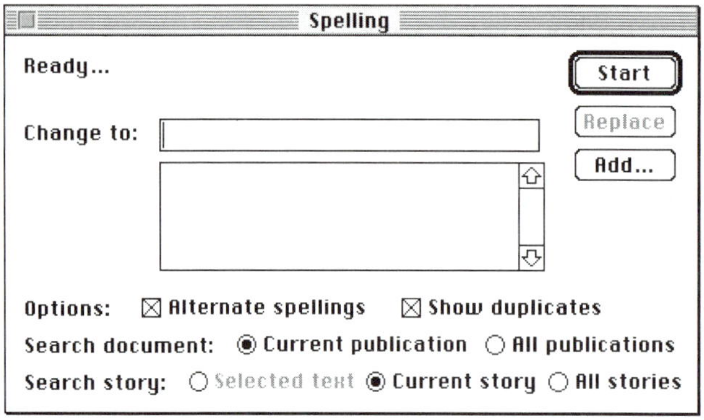

Figure 85. Click on *Start* in the *Spelling* dialog box to start the spell check. When PageMaker detects a word that isn't in its dictionary, it displays it in the dialog box, as well as possible alternatives in the bottom rectangle (if you have the *Alternate spellings* option selected).

The *Show duplicates* option detects when you have typed the same word twice. When PageMaker detects an error, you can select a PageMaker suggestion, type in your own correct spelling, or ignore the selected word altogether by using the *Ignore* button that appears.

The *Place* command from the **File** menu lets you import text and graphics into the story window.

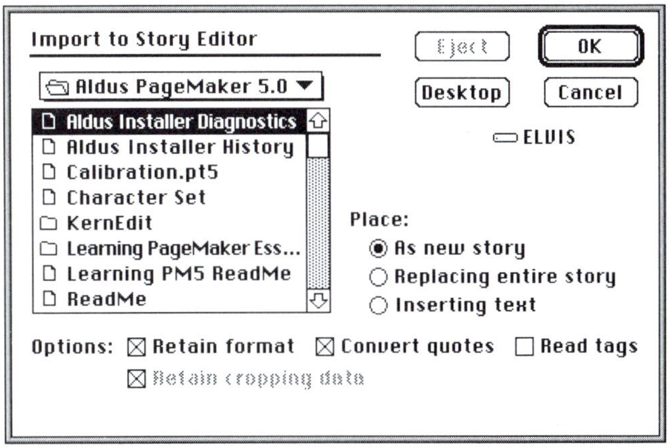

Figure 86. The *Import to Story Editor* dialog box lets you choose the file you want to import.

You have the option of importing graphics only as inline graphics in Story editor. These graphics will not appear as graphics in Story editor, but as small markers. See Chapter 7 for more information on inline and independent graphics.

STORY EDITOR AND THE CONTROL PALETTE

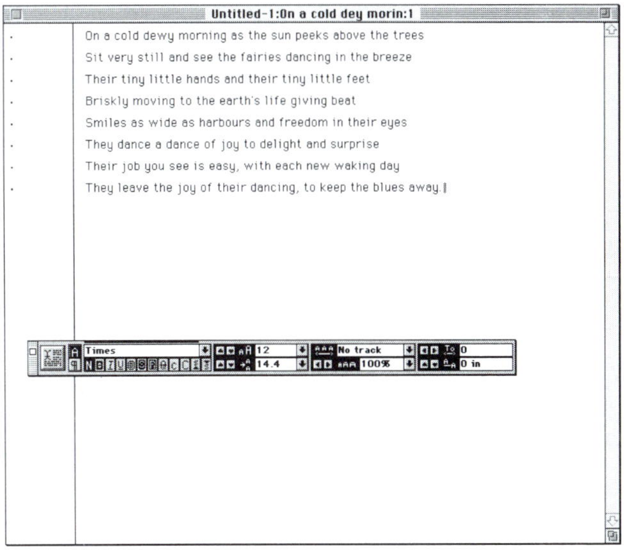

Figure 87. You can use the Control palette in Story editor exactly as you do in layout view (see Figures 46 through 74 for information on the Control palette). You will not, however, see most of the changes until you switch back to layout view.

MANIPULATING TEXT BLOCKS

MOVING TEXT BLOCKS

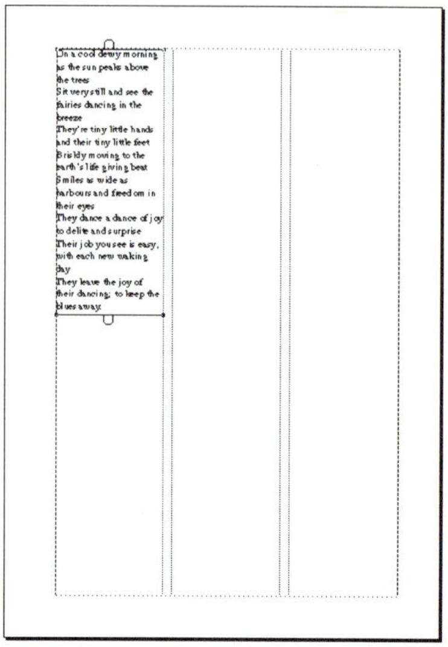

Figure 88. When PageMaker loads text into a publication, it does so in segments called text blocks. You can manipulate these text blocks using the pointer tool in a variety of ways. This figure shows text placed into one column of a three-column page.

You now look at different ways to manipulate this text block.

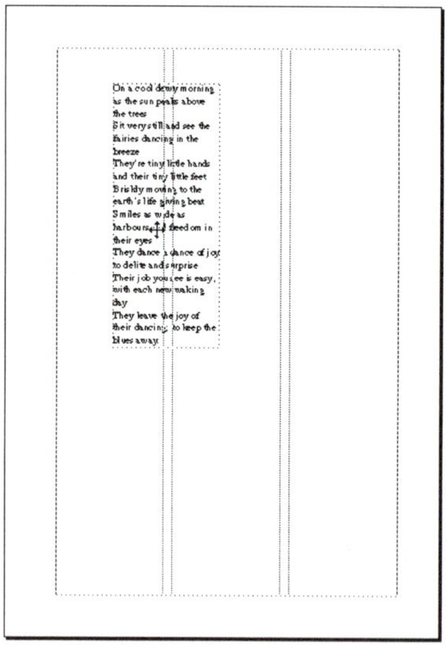

Figure 89. By using the pointer tool, you can hold the mouse button down with the pointer on the text block and move it anywhere on the page. In this figure, we held the mouse button down for a few seconds and then moved the mouse to the right. This moves the text block. You release the mouse button when the text block is in the desired position.

If we had held our mouse button down and immediately moved the mouse, only a boxed outline of the text would move. The result, however, is the same—you move the text block to a new location.

RESIZING TEXT BLOCKS

Figure 90. As well as repositioning text blocks, you can also adjust their size horizontally, vertically and diagonally. This figure shows the various handles of a selected text block that you use for resizing.

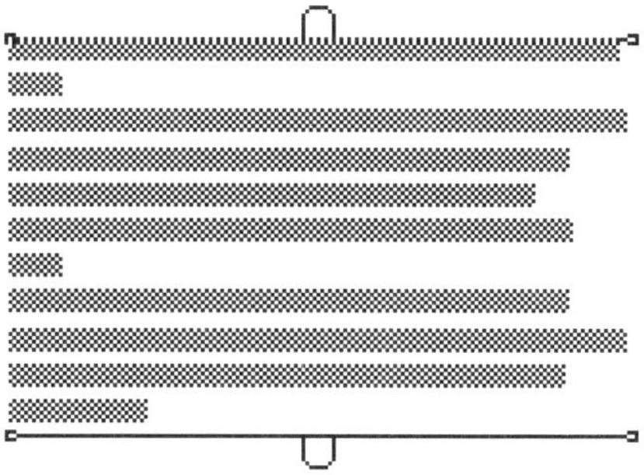

Figure 91. The corner squares of the selected text block let you resize a block in any direction. You simply grab the corner handle with the pointer tool, and move it in any direction you like. You can resize the text block horizontally, vertically and diagonally using this method. If you enlarge the text block, additional text (assuming more text is available) appears.

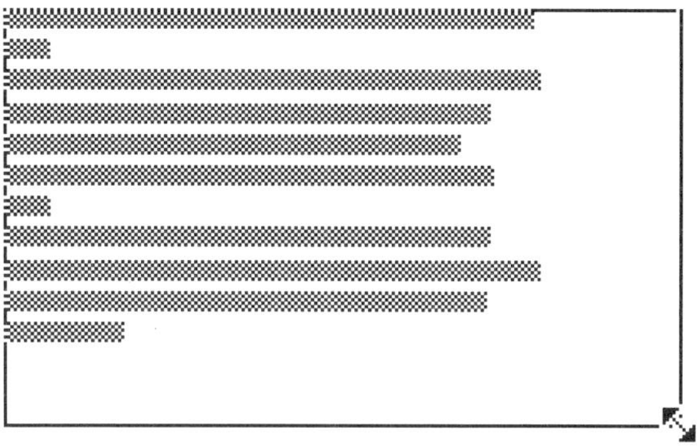

Figure 92. If a selected text block appears with windowshade handle that has a  symbol in it, then more text is available to flow onto the page. Holding the mouse down on this handle with the pointer tool active and pulling it downwards resizes the block vertically and reveals the text that belongs to this particular text block.

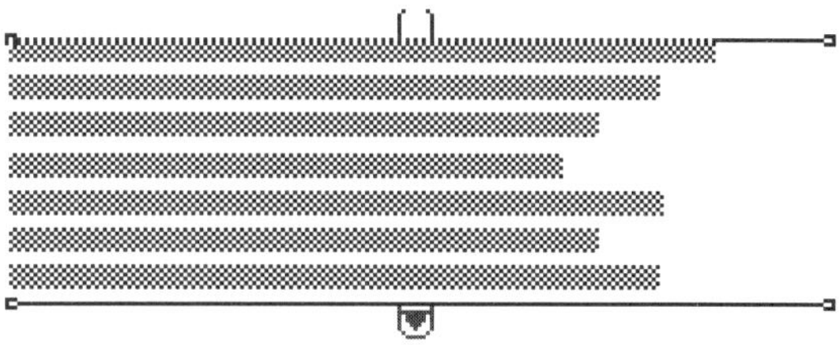

ADJUSTING TEXT BLOCKS

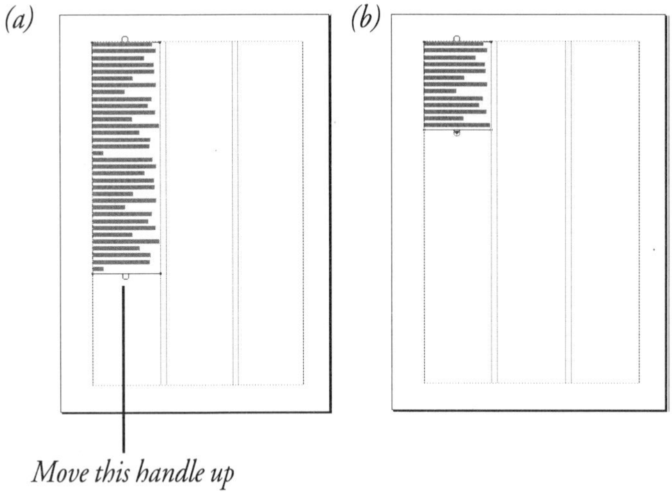

Figure 93. Here there is a text block that was placed in column 1 (a). No further text is in this story. If you want to break this text block into three parts and put parts of it in columns 2 and 3 as well, select the block with the pointer tool and move the bottom windowshade handle up to approximately one-third down the second column (b).

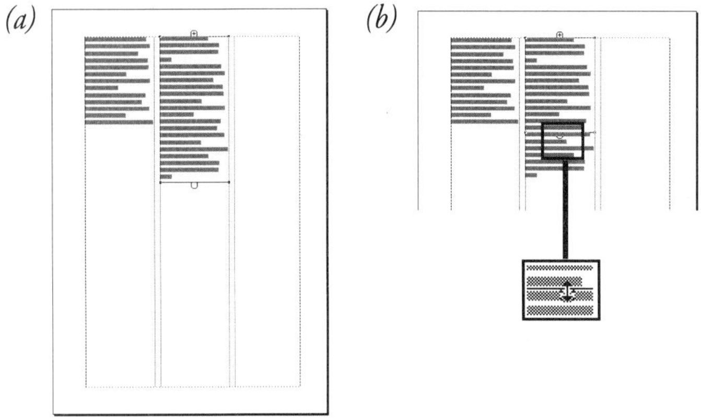

Figure 94. Click once on the bottom windowshade handle in Figure 93(b) and put the loaded text cursor at the top of the middle column. Click at the top of the middle column to place the text (a). Now drag the bottom windowshade handle and drag it up. Release it at approximately one-third of the way up the column (b).

(a)

(b)

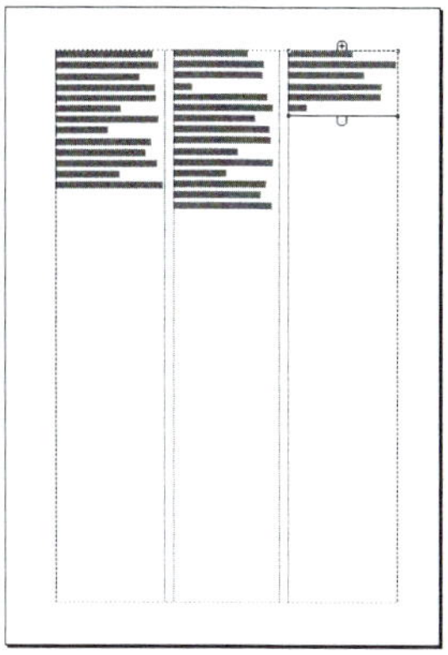

Figure 95. Click once on the bottom windowshade handle from Figure 94(b) and place the loaded text cursor at the top of column 3 (a). Click here to place the text down this column (b). You have now broken the text into three separate blocks.

CAN YOU LOSE TEXT?

When you are manipulating and placing text, you cannot lose text that is part of a text block, unless you delete it. You can manipulate text blocks in PageMaker in a variety of ways. For example, you could remove the middle text block of Figure 95 by simply grabbing the bottom windowshade handle and pulling it up to the top. Then, if you click anywhere on the page, you remove this block without losing text. The text from the middle block flows into column 3. The size of the block in column 3 changes to accommodate the extra text.

So far, you have seen the manipulation of text blocks which are all part of the same story. Sometimes you may need to take some text from the original text block and make it an independent text block. This is called *unthreading* text. The reverse process, *threading* text, allows you to join independent text blocks to create one text block.

UNTHREADING TEXT

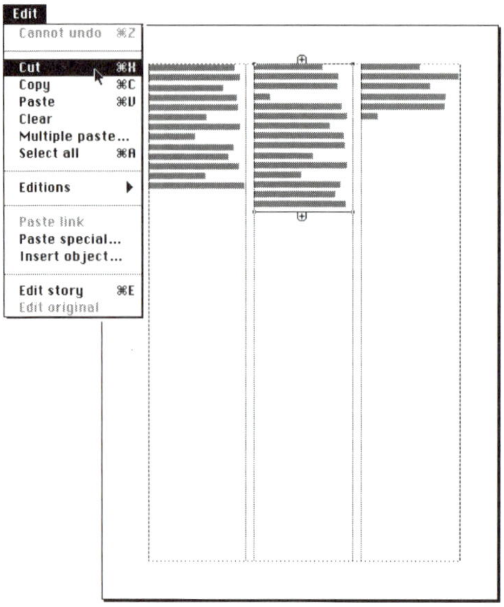

Figure 96. Let's say you want to unthread the text block in the middle column of this figure. Select it with the pointer tool and choose *Cut* from the **Edit** menu.

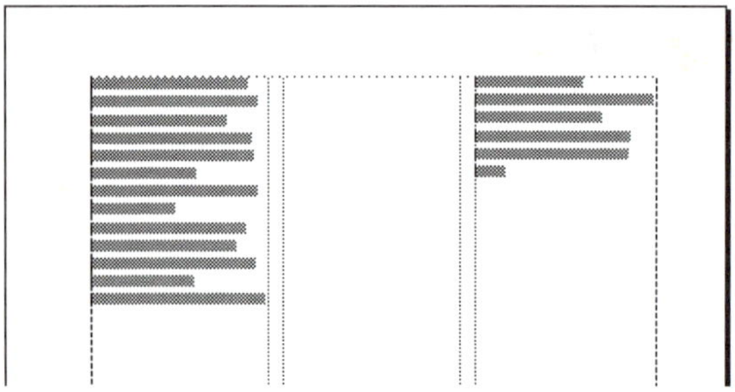

Figure 97. The selected text block is removed from the page.

Figure 98. To bring the deleted text block back as a separate independent story, select *Paste* from the **Edit** menu.

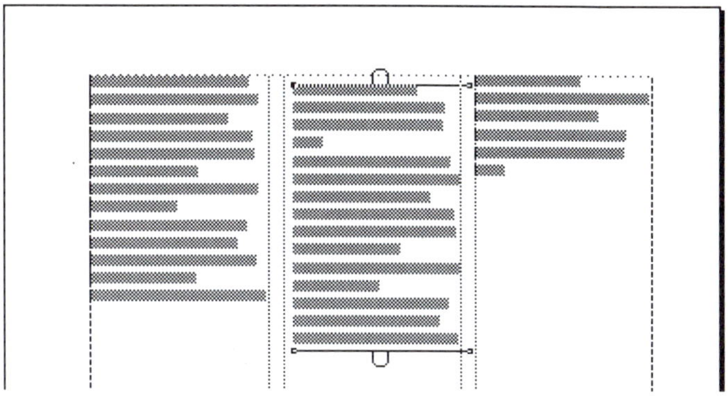

Figure 99. The *Paste* command puts the text block back into the middle column. However, this text block is no longer part of the original story. The empty windowshade handles at both the top and bottom of the middle text block indicate this. You can change, edit, and modify the block without affecting the other two columns. You will probably notice that PageMaker pastes the text block back slightly offset from its original position.

THREADING TEXT

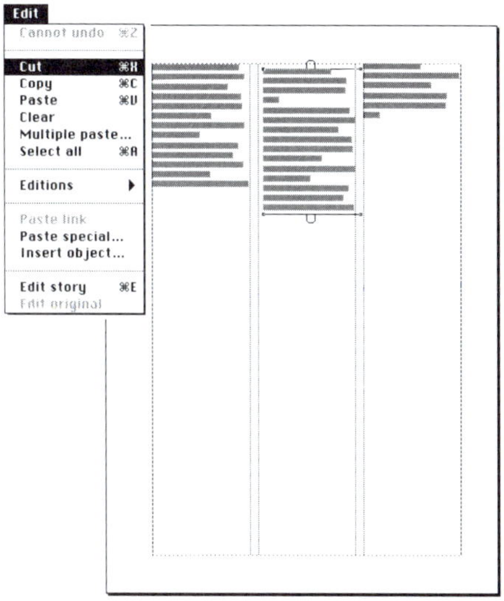

Figure 100. To rethread the text block of Figure 99 back into the original story, select this block with the pointer tool and choose *Cut* from the **Edit** menu.

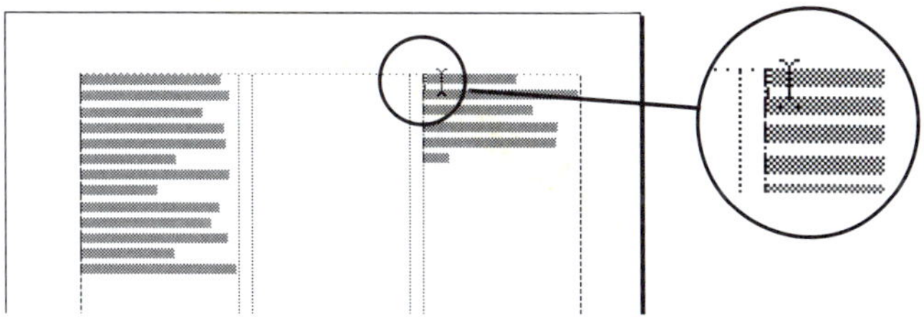

Figure 101. You have removed the text block from the page. Next, select the text tool and click to put an insertion point in the text where you want the deleted text to appear.

Figure 102. Now choose *Paste* from the **Edit** menu to put the text back into the original text block.

TRANSFORMING TEXT

You can rotate, skew and reflect selected text blocks using the rotation tool and the Control palette. These features are described in this section.

ROTATING TEXT

THE CONTROL PALETTE

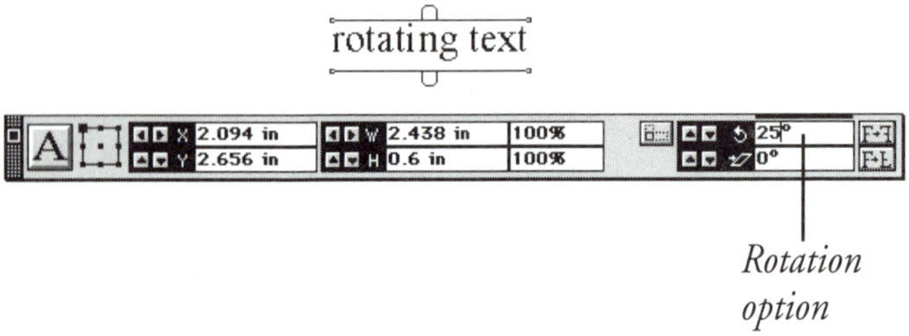

Figure 103. You can rotate text in PageMaker by 360 degrees at 0.01 degree intervals. Select *Control palette* from the **Window** menu to activate the Control palette. Select the text block with the pointer tool and select a reference point in the Proxy. This determines the point that the selected object rotates around. Type a value into the *Rotation* text box (in this case 25°) and click on the Apply button.

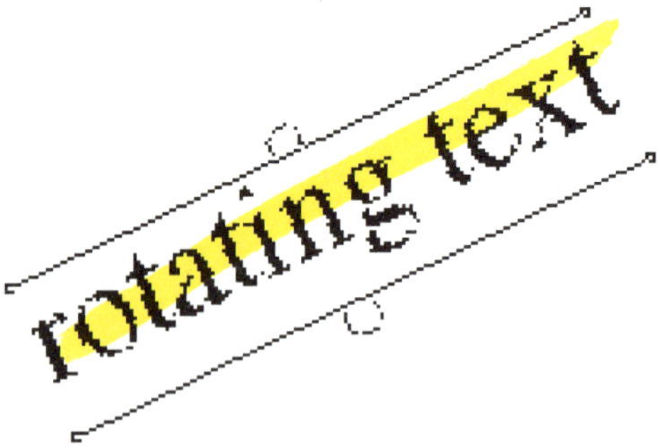

Figure 104. Once you select a reference point and insert a rotation value, press the Return key to make the changes. The results can be seen here. Note that you can also rotate longer text blocks in this fashion.

USING THE ROTATION TOOL

Figure 105. Select the text block with the pointer tool, then activate the rotation tool.

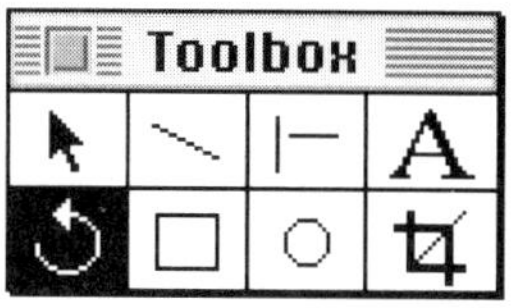

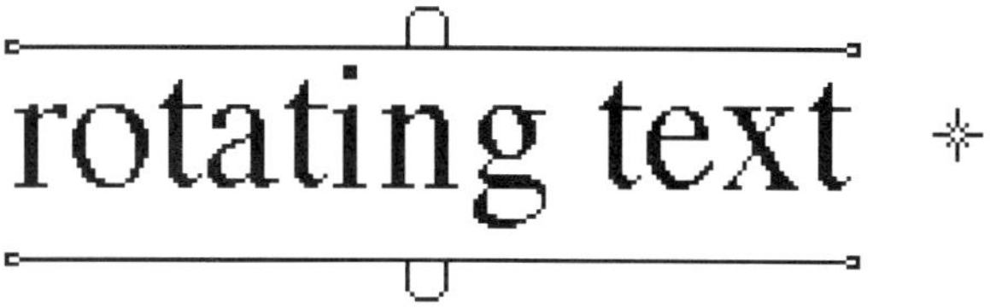

Figure 106. Put the starburst cursor on the text block or anywhere on the page. Drag the mouse in the opposite direction to which you want to rotate the text. The rotation lever that appears gives you control over the amount of rotation. The further you drag the starburst cursor away from the fixed point, the more control you have.

Use the Shift key while you are rotating the object to constrain the rotation to 45 degree angles.

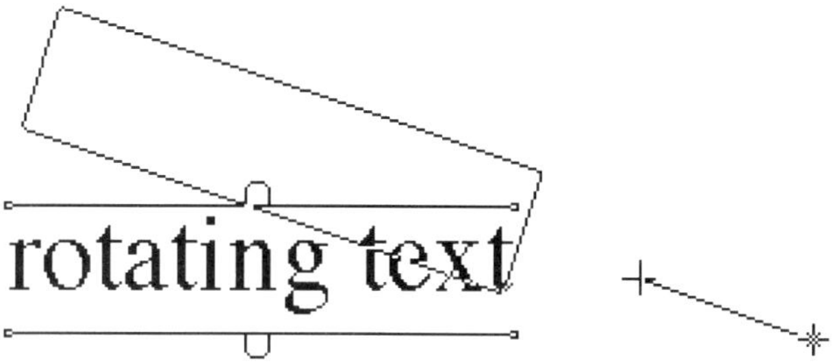

Figure 107. When you release the mouse button, the rotated text reformats on the screen as seen here. If you have the Control palette on screen while you are rotating an object, the total amount of rotation is reflected in the *Rotating* option text box, even if you have rotated the object more than once.

SKEWING TEXT

Use the Control palette to skew text horizontally by + or - 85 degrees at 0.1 degree increments.

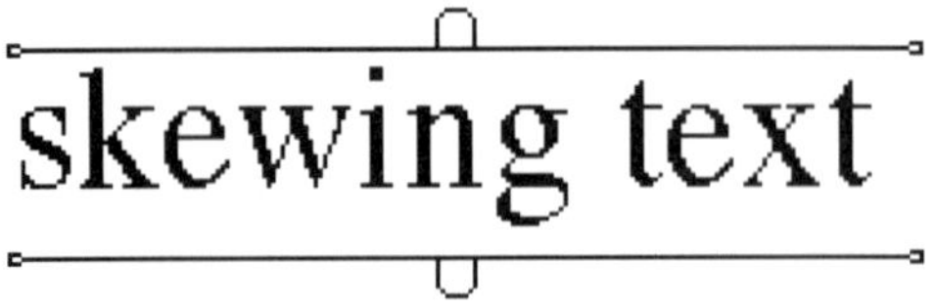

Figure 108. To skew a text block, first select it with the pointer tool.

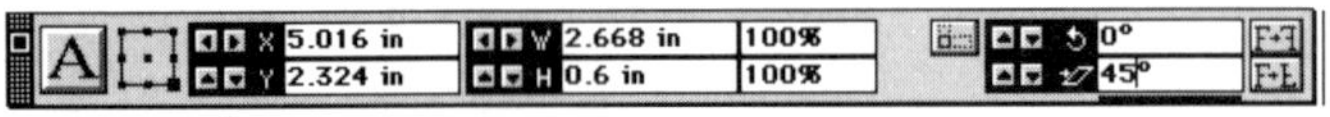

Figure 109. Select a reference point on the Proxy. The equivalent point of the selected text block remains stationary when you skew the text. (If you click twice on a reference point, it becomes a resizing reference point, which looks like a two-headed or a four-headed arrow. The equivalent point of the selected text block moves as you skew it in this case.)

Specify a skewing angle in the *Skewing* text box in the Control palette. A positive angle moves the top-edge to the right and a negative angle moves it to the left.

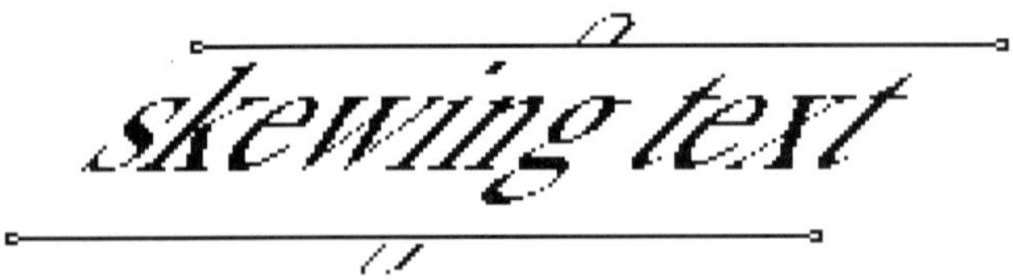

Figure 110. Press the Return key or click on the Apply button to view the skewing changes.

REFLECTING TEXT

Figure 111. Use the Control palette to reflect text or other objects. First, select the text block with the pointer tool. Then, select a point on the Proxy and click on one of the reflecting buttons in the Control Palette.

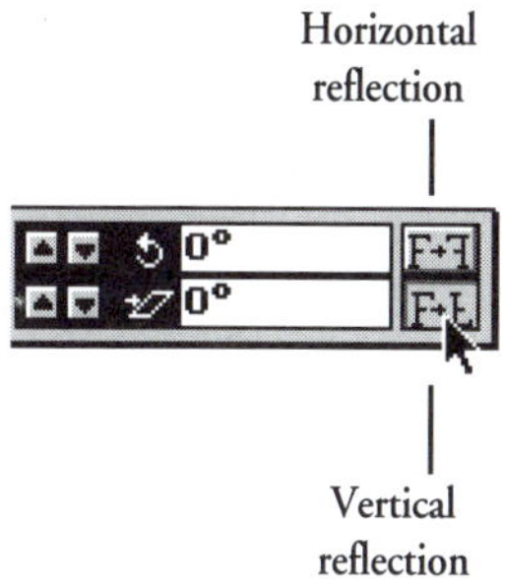

Figure 112. Clicking on one of the reflecting options affects the selected text immediately.

Note: Reflecting an object horizontally is the same as reflecting it vertically and rotating it 180 degrees. When you do this, PageMaker adds 180 degrees to the object's rotation value in the Control palette.

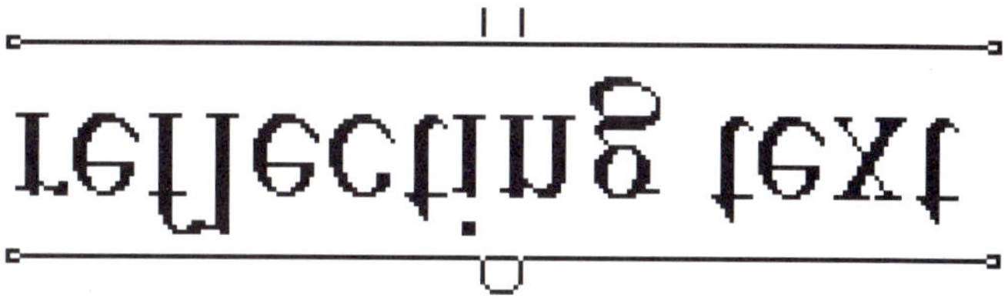

REMOVING TRANSFORMATIONS

Figure 113. To restore any transformed object (rotated, reflected or skewed) to its original state, select the object and select *Remove transformation* from the **Element** menu.

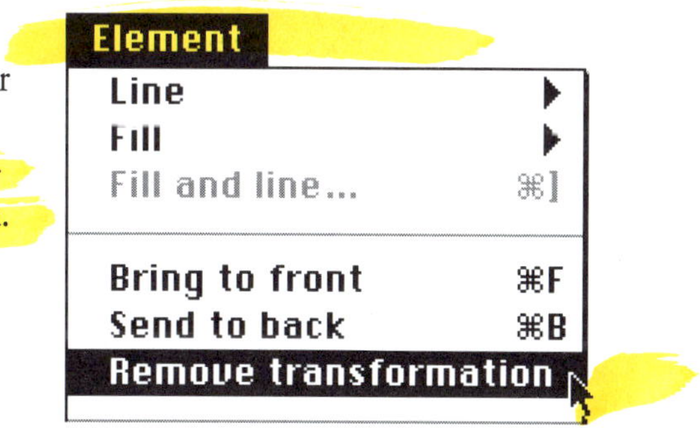

MASTER PAGES 5

MASTER PAGE CONCEPT

Every PageMaker publication has a master page. The master page stores information that you want to appear on every page of a publication. How the master page or pages are set up is determined by how you define your document in the *Page setup* dialog box; a double-sided document has two master pages, a single-sided document only one.

Figure 1. The L and R icons to the left of the numbered page icons represent the master pages. If you set up a single-sided document, only the R icon shows.

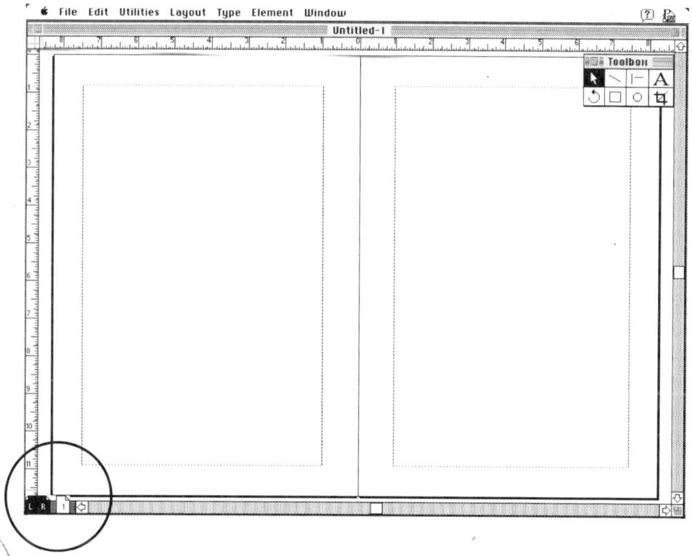

Figure 2. The left and right master pages are identical to all other PageMaker pages, except for some important considerations. First, you cannot print the contents of the master pages directly. Second, anything (text or graphics) you include on a master page appears on all other pages in your publication. This is useful if you have items such as headers, footers, or a company logo that you want to include on every page in your document.

Simply put these objects on the left or right master page and they appear on every left or right page in your publication unless you turn them off.

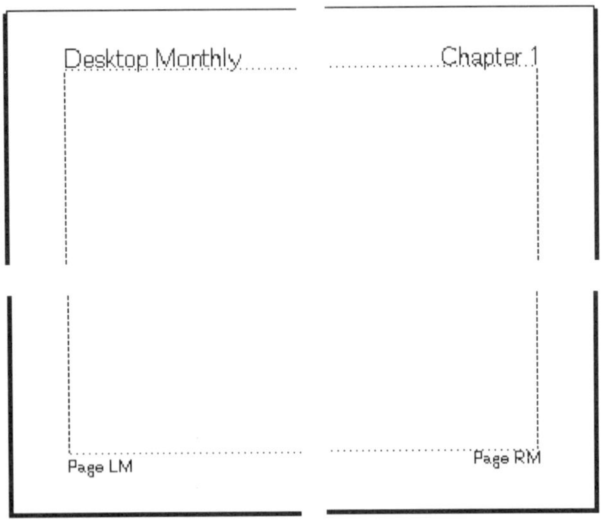

Automatic Page Numbering

Figure 3. Here we have enlarged the four corners of the left and right master pages. The top-left and right corners include a header each, and the bottom left and right corners include a page number as a footer. You insert the page number on the master pages by pressing Command+Option+P with the insertion point at the required locations. The page numbers, appearing as LM and RM on the left and right master pages, automatically update to reflect the correct number on every page. The headers, like the page number, also appear on every page.

(a)

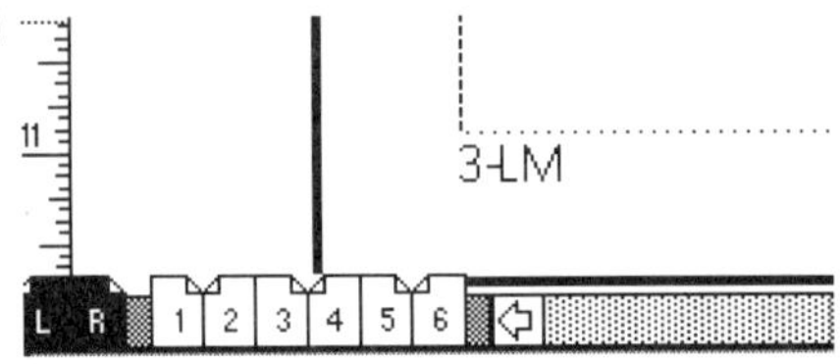

(b)

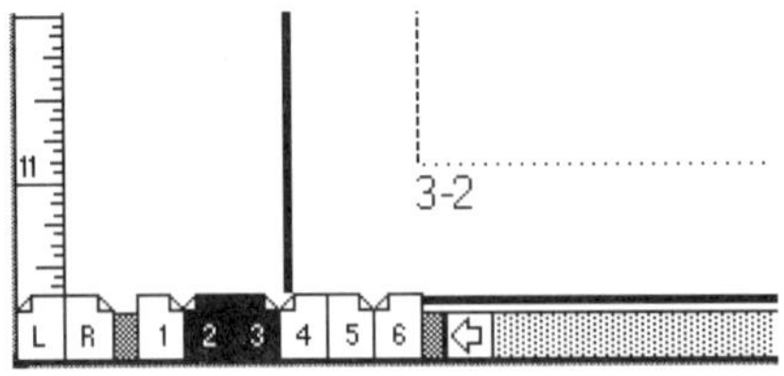

Figure 4. You can put fixed wording on the master page in front of the page number. This fixed wording, in our case “3” (to show this is part of Chapter 3), now appears on every page as part of the page numbering system.
(a) The fixed character “3” on the master page denotes the whole publication is Chapter 3.
(b) Page 2 of the publication reflects the numbering format as “3-2”, being page 2 of Chapter 3.

Figure 5. The automatic page number on a page is the same as the number inside the icon representing that page in the bottom left-hand corner of the screen. You can alter the page number, as shown here, by adjusting the *Start page #* box in the *Page setup* dialog box from the **File** menu.

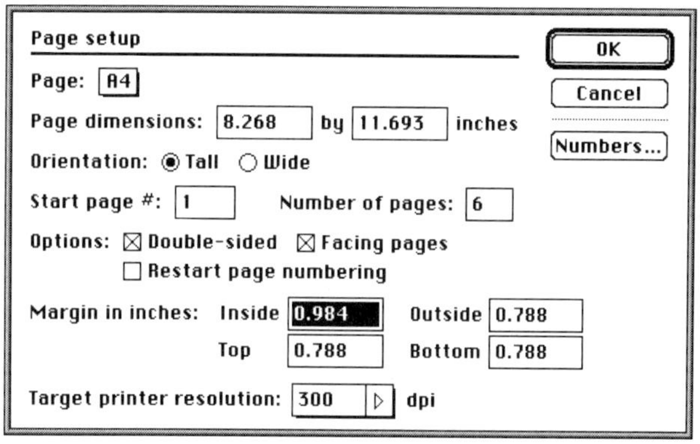

Figure 6. The *Page numbering* dialog box, which you get by clicking on the *Numbers* button in the *Page setup* dialog box, gives you a choice of numbering systems. You can choose from the different options shown in this dialog box.

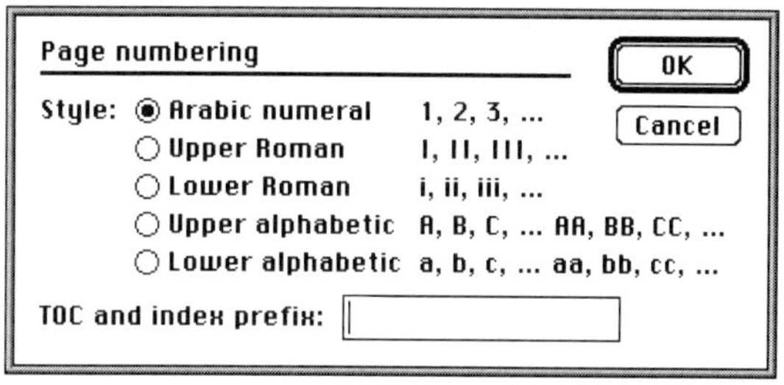

Guides on Master Pages

Figure 7. Apart from headers, footers and page numbers, you can use the master pages to set up column guides, ruler guides and other constant information, such as a company logo.

Here we have set up, through the *Column guides* command, three columns on both master pages. We have included two headers and one footer per page, and a logo. These now appear on all pages of the publication (unless you turn them off on a particular page).

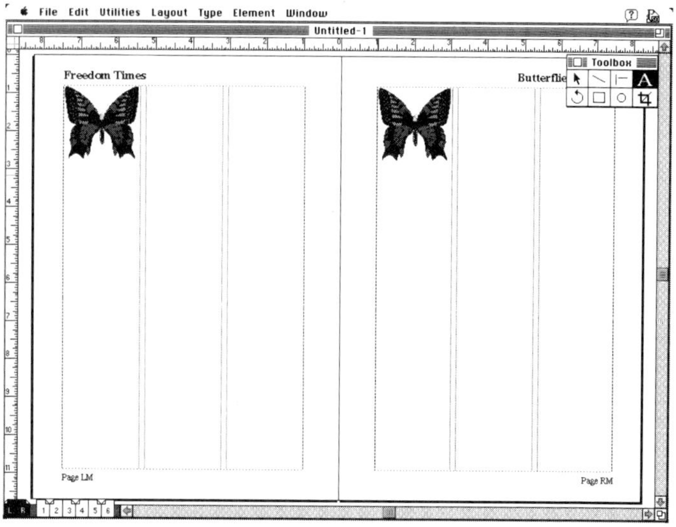

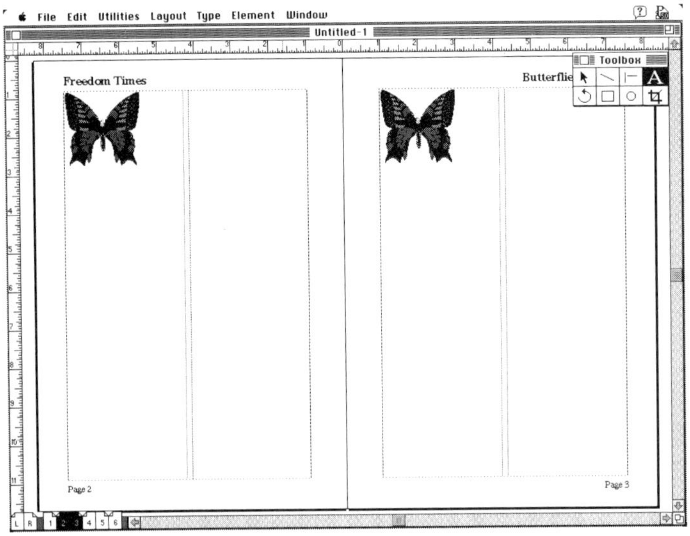

Figure 8. This figure shows pages 2 and 3. All items from the master pages show exactly as we positioned them on the master pages.

Removing Master Page Items

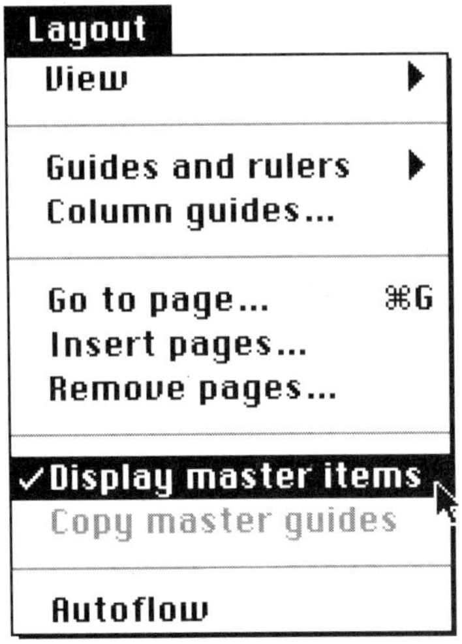

Figure 9. You can't select or delete text and graphics created on master pages in the normal way. You can select and manipulate master page text and graphics only on the master pages. To delete all master page items from the currently active page or pages, select *Display master items* from the **Layout** menu.

Figure 10. After you deselect the *Display master items* command, the current pages do not have the master page items on them.

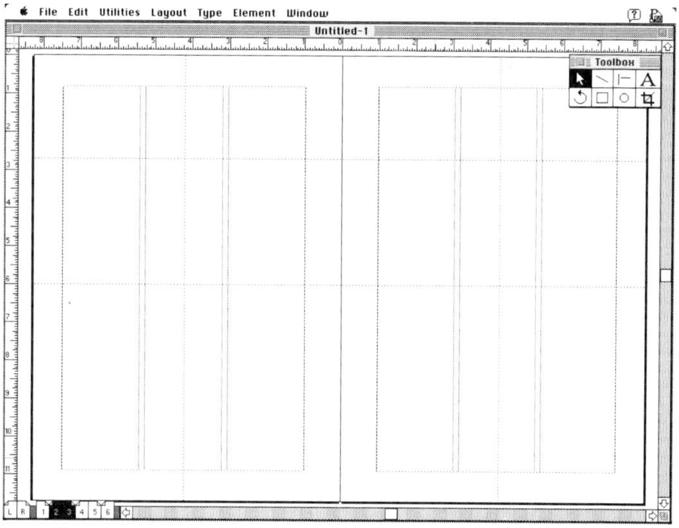

Figure 11. If you want to delete only certain master page items on a particular page, simply draw a box with a paper fill over them. In this case, we drew a box over the top-left header on page one, to stop it from printing. You can do this for any number of master page items you want to hide. (To create a box to hide elements, apply *Fill: Paper* and *Line: None* from the **Element** menu to a selected rectangle.)

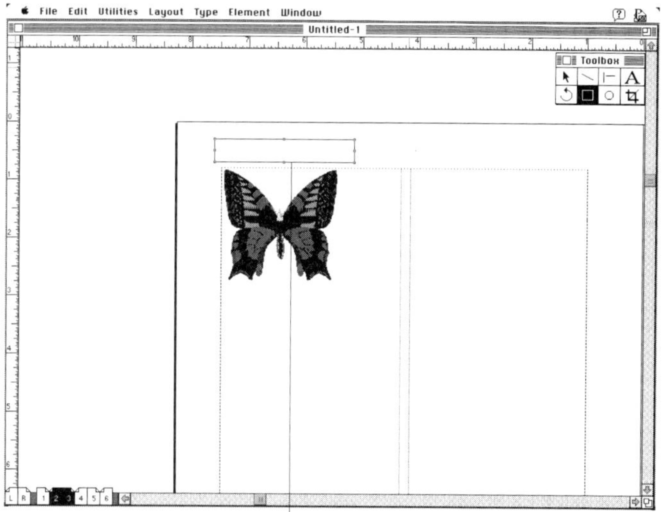

Selected white box hiding a master page item at the top left of page 2

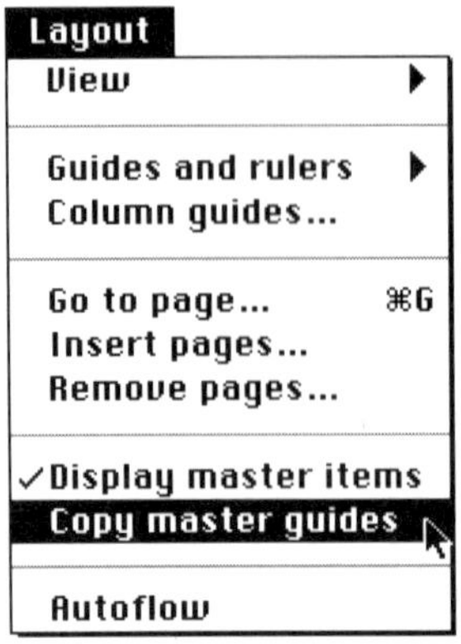

Figure 12. You can adjust column, ruler, and margin guides on any page, even though you may have created them on the master pages. If you wish to revert to the original nonprinting guides as they appear on the master pages, choose *Copy master guides* from the **Page** menu.

Creating Graphics

6

The Drawing Tools

PageMaker's drawing tools in the toolbox let you draw graphic objects in PageMaker.

Figure 1. The toolbox has the drawing tools you use to create and manipulate internal graphics.

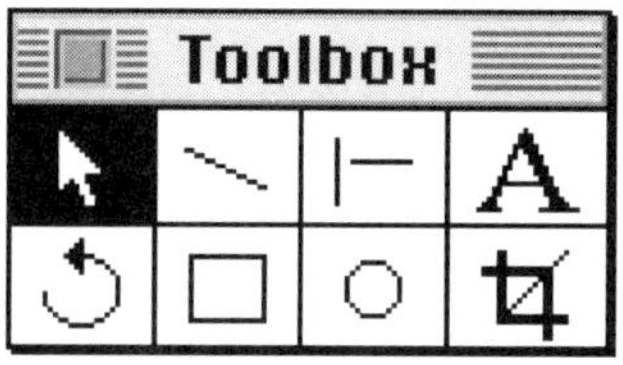

(a) Use the line tool to draw straight lines at any angle.

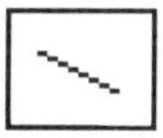

(b) Use the constrained line tool to draw lines at 45 degree angles.

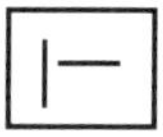

(c) Use the rotation tool to rotate objects on the page.

(d) Use the rectangle tool to draw squares and rectangles.

(e) Use the ellipse tool to draw circles and ellipses.

DRAWING GRAPHICS

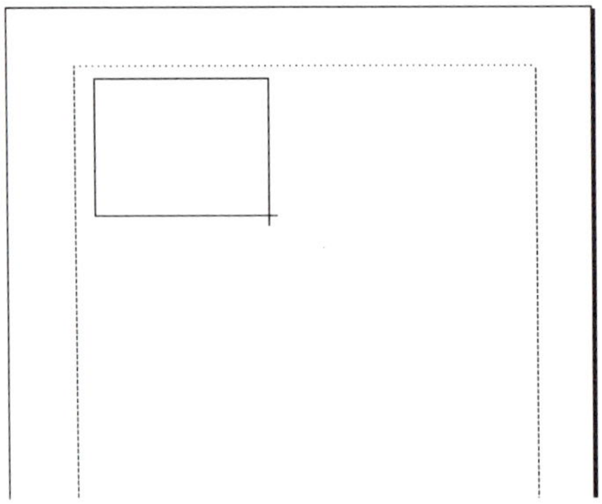

Figure 2. To draw a graphic, select the appropriate tool, and drag it across the page. You can drag in any direction.

(a)

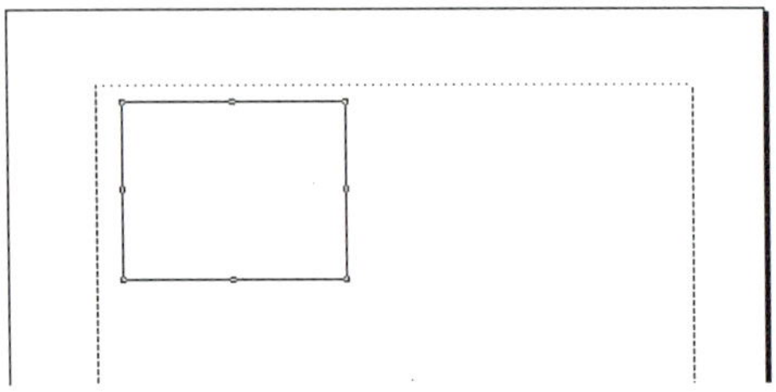

Figure 3. Release the mouse button when you finish. PageMaker automatically selects the graphic. (Note the eight small square dots or handles around the edge of the graphic shown in (a).) You can draw many types of different graphics in PageMaker (b).

(b)

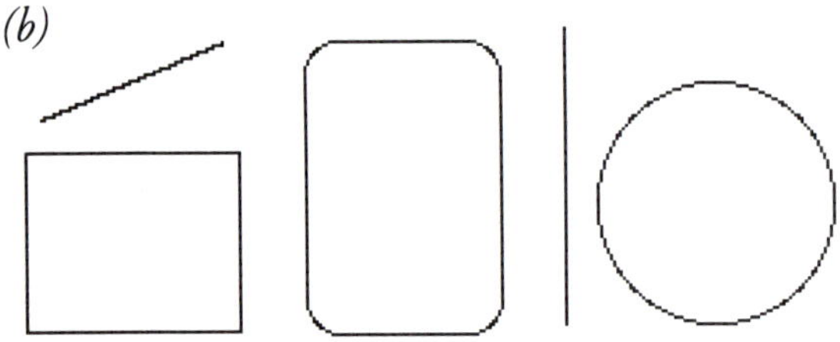

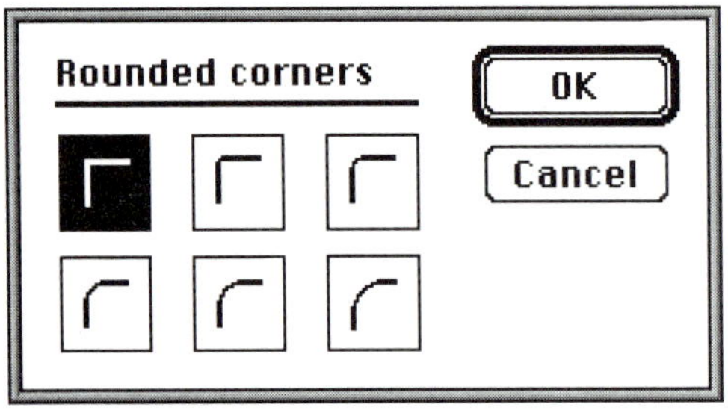

Figure 4. The *Rounded corners* dialog box (from the **Element** menu) gives you a choice of various radii for drawing rectangles or squares with the rectangle-drawing tool.

Figure 5. Graphics are automatically selected after you have drawn them. If you choose another tool from the toolbox, this deselects the graphic. To re-select a graphic, click on its edge with the pointer tool or drag over the graphic with the pointer tool selected.

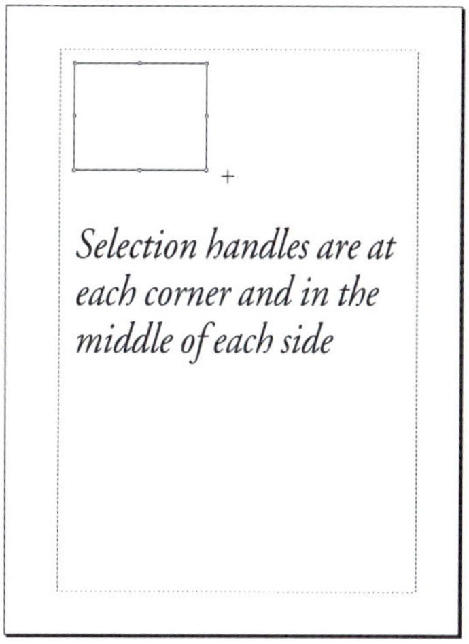

SELECTING MULTIPLE GRAPHICS

Figure 6. You can select multiple graphics by selecting each graphic while pressing the Shift key or by choosing *Select all* from the **Edit** menu.

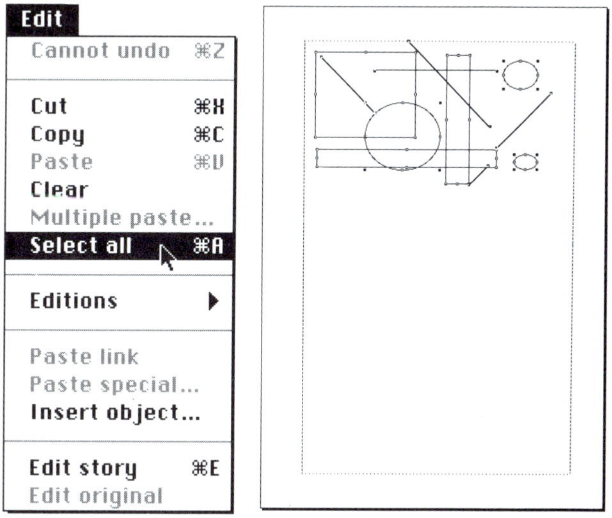

Figure 7. You can also drag a selection rectangle around all graphics with the pointer tool.

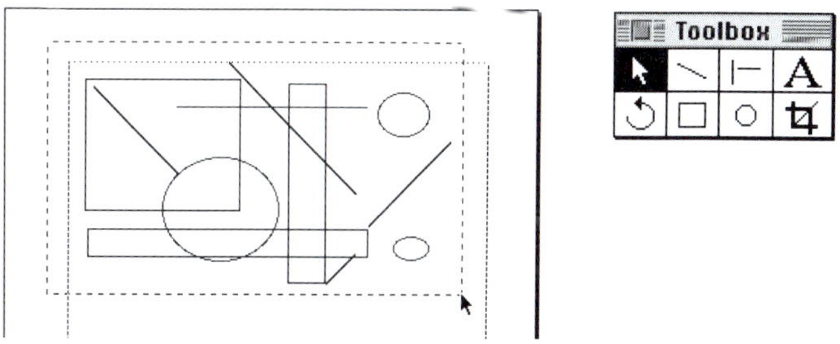

Moving and Resizing Graphics

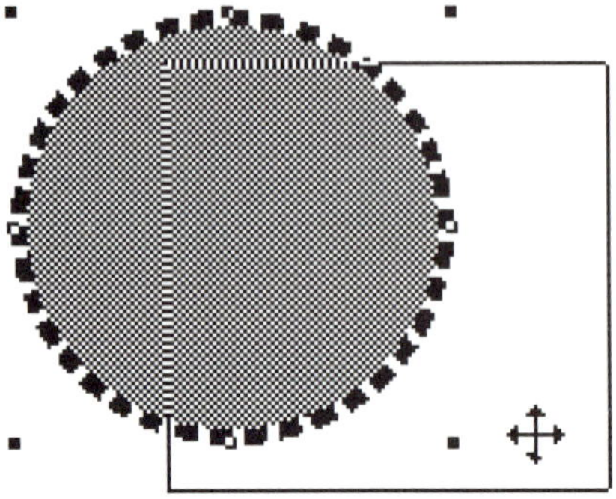

Figure 8. To move a graphic, hold down the mouse button on the border of the graphic if it is hollow, or anywhere within the graphic if it has a fill pattern, and move the mouse. Note in this figure, the cursor changes to a four-headed arrow.

If you drag the graphic immediately, the original graphic stays in position and an outline or rectangle moves with the mouse, as the example shows in this figure. If you hold the mouse button down for a few seconds before dragging it, the actual object moves with the mouse.

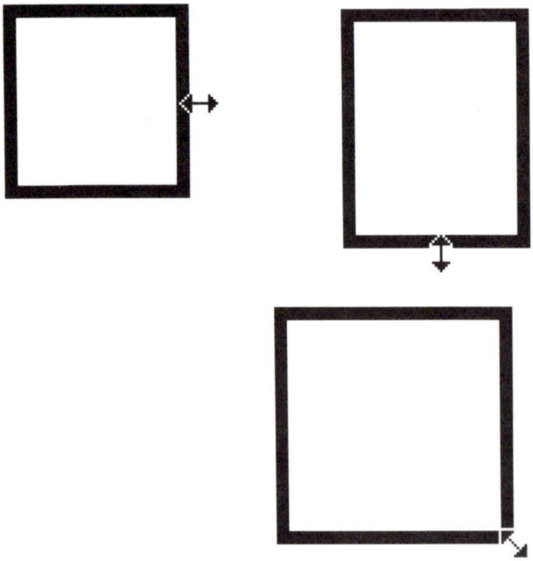

Figure 9. You can resize a selected graphic by grabbing one of the small black handles on its edge and dragging the mouse horizontally, vertically or diagonally.

See the section in this chapter on **The Control Palette and Graphics** for more information on moving and resizing graphics.

Altering the Appearance of Graphics

Figure 10. The **Element** menu includes *Line, Fill,* and *Fill and line* commands that you can use to change the appearance of graphics.

Figure 11. To use the *Line* command from the **Element** menu, choose a line thickness or style from the submenu.

In this figure, we are choosing a *4 pt* line thickness.

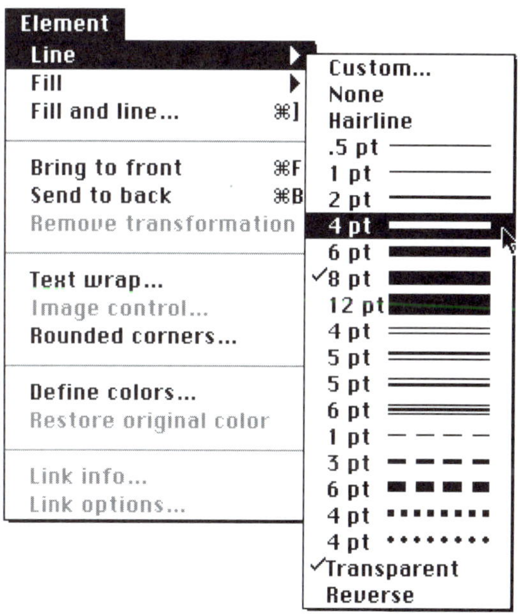

Figure 12. The graphic now adjusts to the new line thickness we selected in the previous figure.

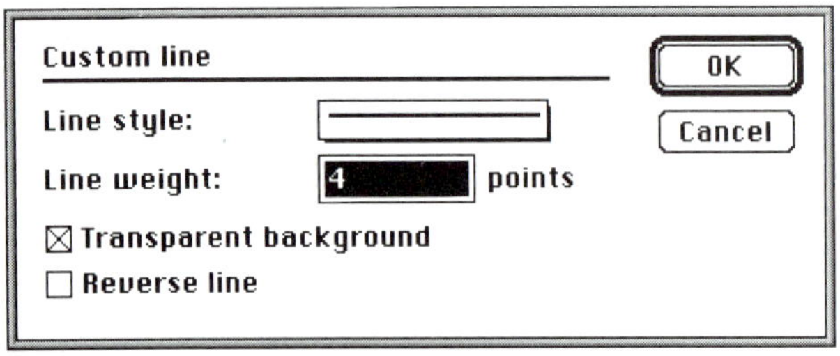

Figure 13. Choosing *Custom* from the *Line* submenu gives you the *Custom line* dialog box. Here you can specify a line weight (line thickness) from 0 to 800 points, and you can select a line style from the *Line style* pop-up menu.

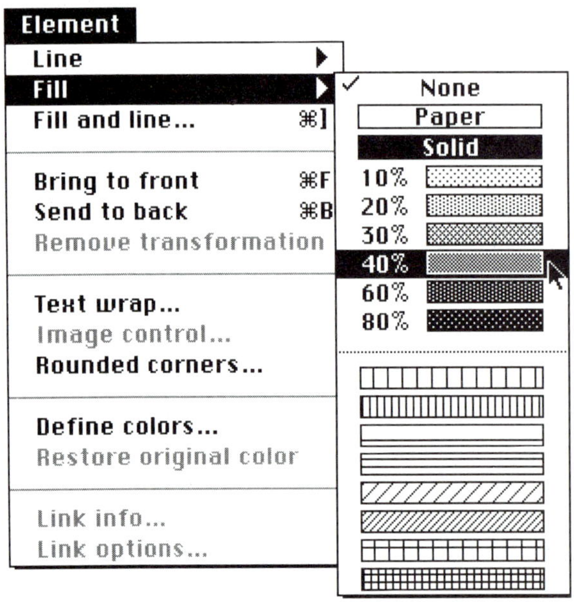

Figure 14. To change the fill of a graphic, select it, then go to the **Element** menu and choose the *Fill* command. When the submenu appears, select the fill pattern you want.

In this figure, we have chosen a 40% fill.

Figure 15. The selected graphic reflects the new pattern or shade chosen in the previous graphic.

Figure 16. Select *Fill and line* from the **Element** menu and you get the *Fill and line* dialog box.

Figure 17. In this dialog box, you can select fill, line and color attributes together to apply to a selected graphic. See Chapter 12 for information on the *Overprint* option. Use the *Reverse line* option to draw a white line on a colored or black background. If you have no graphic selected, the choices you make in this dialog box become the default settings.

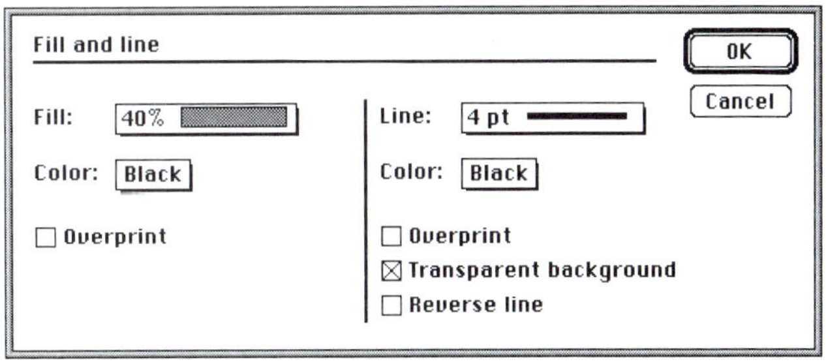

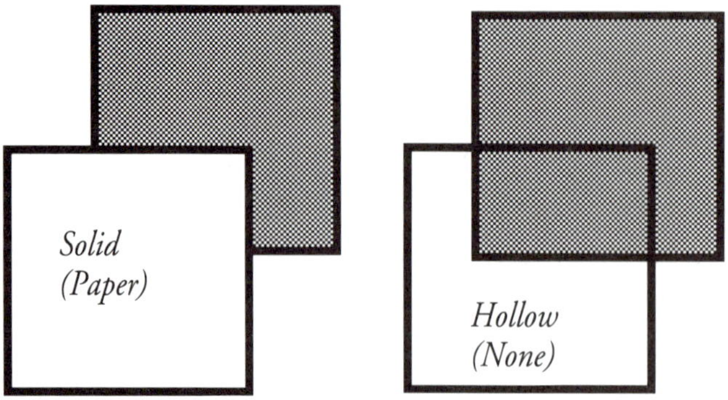

Figure 18. You can give a graphic on screen a hollow or a solid fill.

You apply a hollow fill by choosing *None* from the *Fill* submenu. You apply a solid fill by choosing *Solid* or *Paper* from the *Fill* submenu.

LAYERING OF GRAPHICS

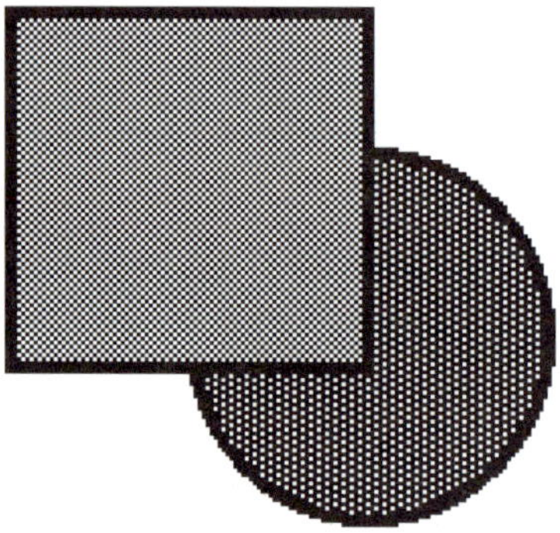

Figure 19. These two graphics overlap each other. The square is on top and the circle on the bottom. We now want to reverse this.

Figure 20. Select the top graphic and choose *Send to back* from the **Element** menu.

Figure 21. PageMaker puts the circle on top.

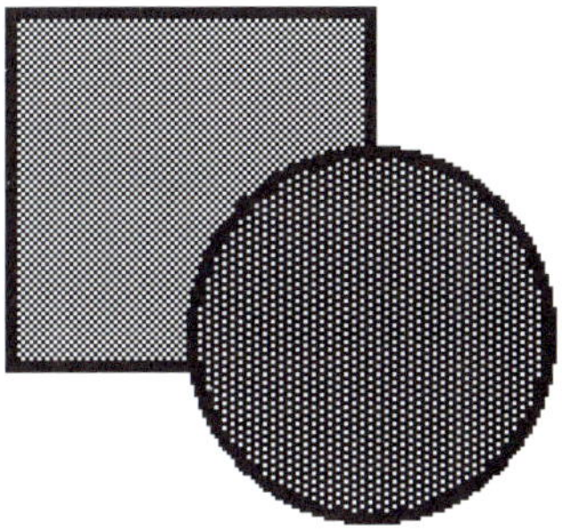

Editing Graphics

Cut, Copy, and Paste

Figure 22. In the **Edit** menu, *Cut* removes a selected graphic from the screen to the Clipboard; *Copy* copies the selected graphic to the Clipboard and leaves the original graphic on screen; *Paste* transfers whatever is in the Clipboard back to the screen; *Clear* deletes a selected graphic from the screen without transferring it to the Clipboard; *Multiple paste* positions and pastes a specified number of copies; and *Select all* selects all objects (graphics and text) on the screen.

Multiple Paste

Figure 23. Use the *Multiple paste* command from the **Edit** menu if you want to paste multiple copies of an object from the Clipboard onto your publication page. In the *Multiple paste* dialog box, you can specify the number of pasted copies and where they appear on the page.

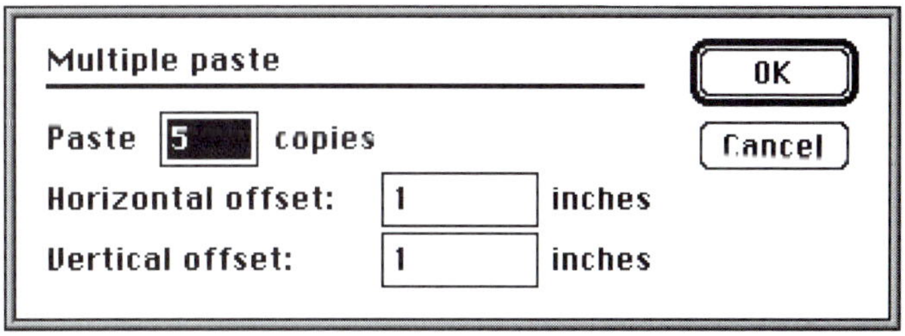

We have specified 5 copies, with a 1 inch horizontal and vertical offset. See the results in the next figure.

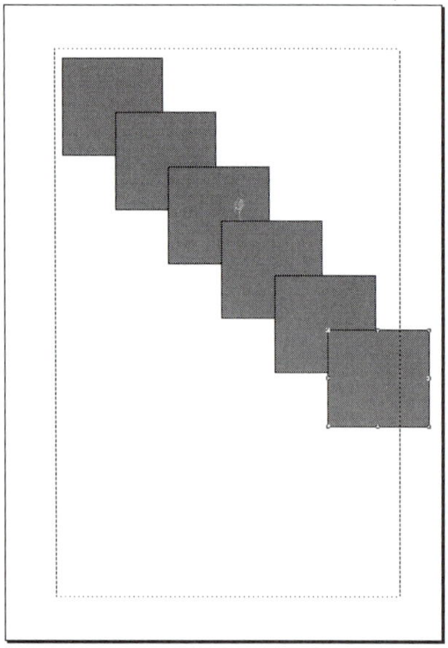

Figure 24. PageMaker has pasted the object copied to the Clipboard as we defined in the *Multiple paste* dialog box.

To duplicate objects without the *Multiple paste* dialog box, press the Option key while selecting the *Multiple paste* command. Objects are duplicated using the values you last entered for each option.

Setting Graphic Defaults

Figure 25. Choosing the *Line* or *Fill* command from the **Element** menu with the pointer tool (with no graphic selected) causes the particular *Line* or *Fill* selection to be the new default setting. This means that every new graphic you draw on the page has these line and fill settings as their attributes.

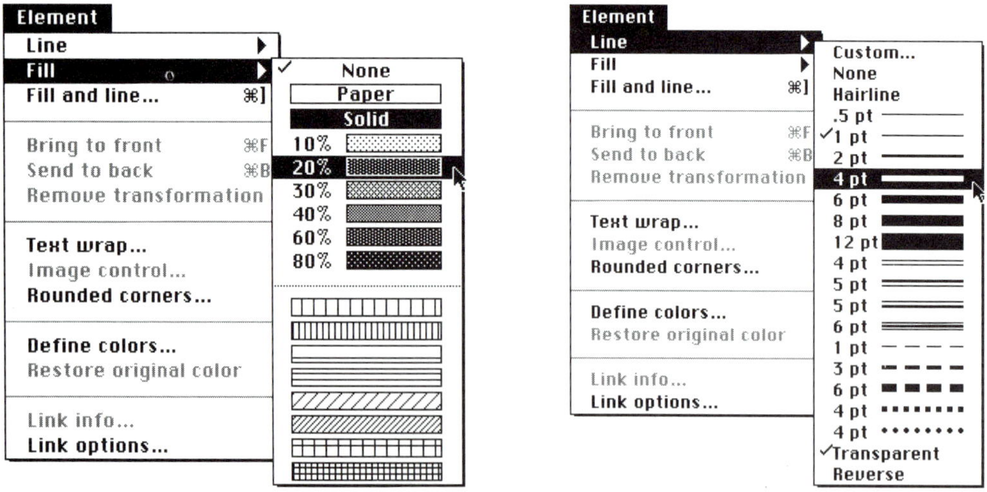

Figure 26. You can also define the default settings in the *Fill and line* dialog box. As well as setting the default for the line and fill attributes, you can also specify a default color for the line and fill.

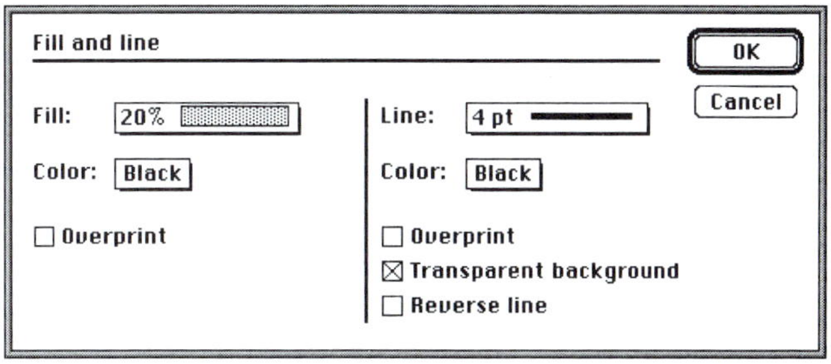

Constraining Graphics

Figure 27. You can constrain graphics by holding the Shift key while drawing them. When you press Shift with the rectangle or ellipse tool this constrains the object to a square or a circle, respectively. When you use the Shift key with the line tool, a line can be drawn at 45 degree intervals, which is the same as using the constrained line tool.

Square drawn with the Shift key held down

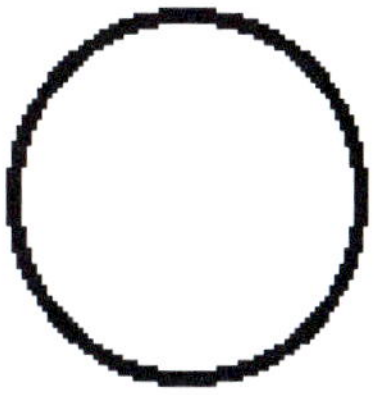

Circle drawn with the Shift key held down

THE ROTATION TOOL

Figure 28. Use the rotation tool to rotate selected graphics on the page. Select the graphic with the pointer tool and then select the rotation tool.

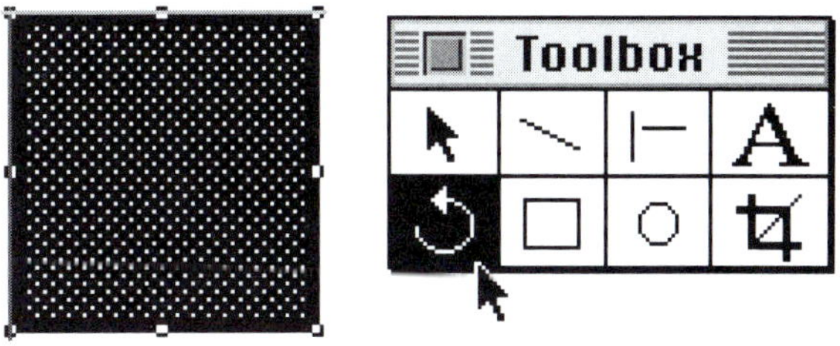

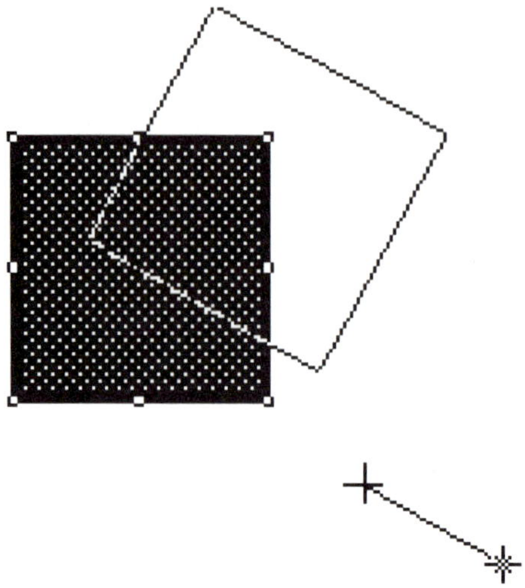

Figure 29. Position the starburst cursor anywhere on the page and click. This becomes the point that the graphic rotates around. Hold the mouse button down and drag the mouse in the direction you want to rotate the object.

The rotation lever helps you control the amount of rotation. The further you drag the mouse away from the graphic, the more control you have.

Hold down the Shift key while rotating the object to constrain the rotation to 45 degree increments.

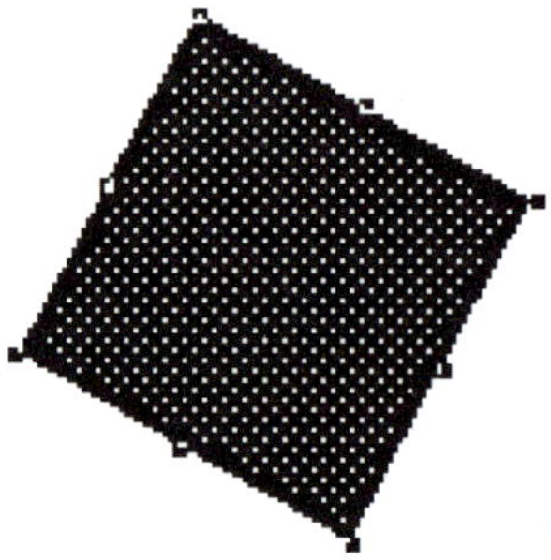

Figure 30. Release the mouse when you have rotated the graphic to the position you want.

If the Control palette is on screen, it displays the total rotation in degrees of the selected graphic in the *Rotation* option text box. See Figure 42 for more information.

The Control Palette and Graphics

You can use the Control palette as a quick, precise way of manipulating graphics as an alternative to using the toolbox or menu commands. If you would rather use the mouse to edit objects, the Control palette still displays an immediate response to any changes you make to a graphic in its text boxes.

Figure 31. Bring up the Control palette through the **Window** menu. This is how the Control palette looks on screen when you have nothing selected. The *X* and *Y* coordinates change to reflect where you move the mouse.

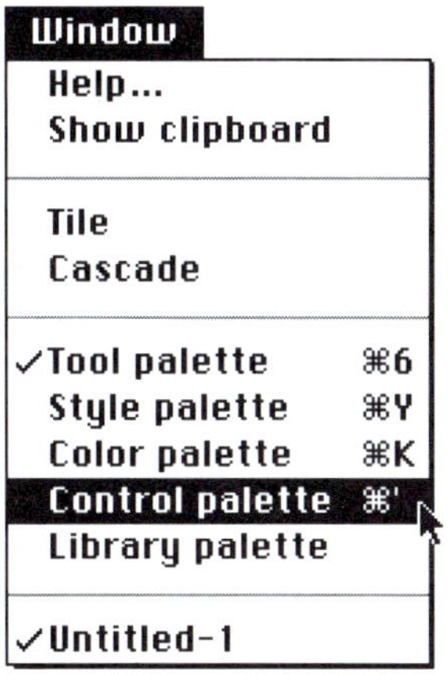

Figure 32. When you select or draw a graphic, the Control palette changes as shown below. The first example shows the options you get in the Control palette for ellipses and rectangles, and the second, for graphics drawn with the line tools.

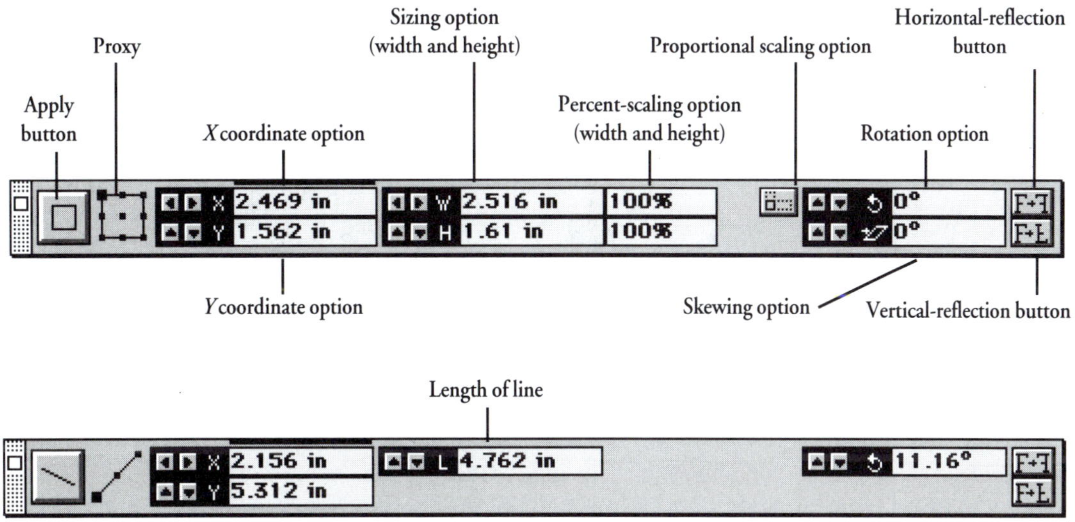

APPLY BUTTON

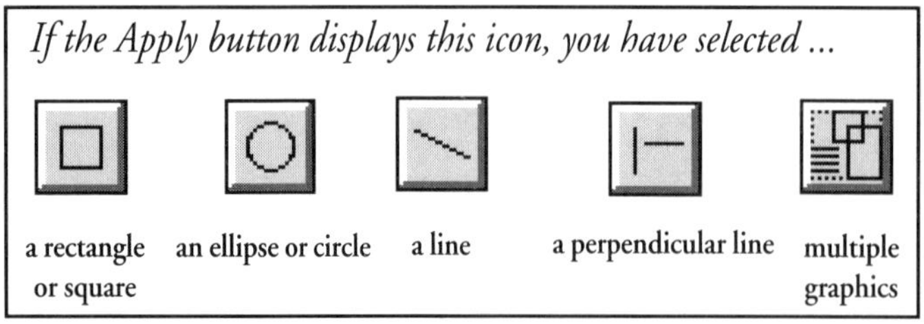

Figure 33. Use the Apply button to display changes you have made to selected graphics with the Control palette. Note that the Apply button icon changes depending on what type of graphic object you select.

THE PROXY

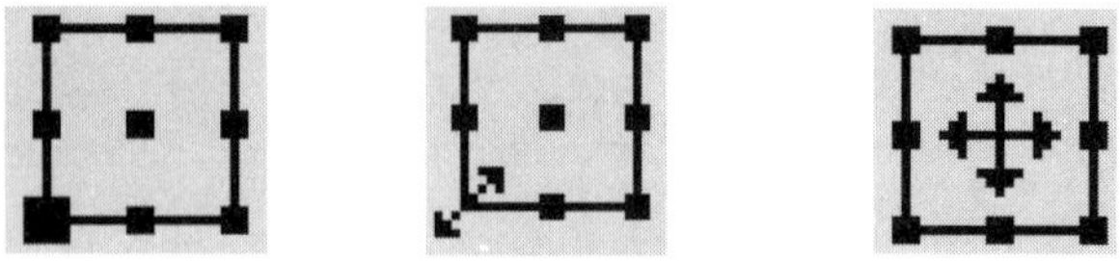

Click on a handle for a moving reference point

Double-click on a handle for a resizing reference point

Figure 34. The Proxy on the Control palette lets you select a reference point so you can change objects. Click on a black handle on the Proxy to select the reference. This becomes the reference point for all objects you select until you choose a new reference point.

Note: When you resize a graphic with the mouse, the corresponding reference point where you place the mouse on the object, automatically changes the reference point on the Proxy.

If you click on a reference point once, the selected point becomes a moving reference point, indicated by a larger black box. The corresponding point of the selected graphic remains stationary when you are modifying the graphic.

If you double-click on a reference point, it becomes a resizing reference point, indicated by a double-headed arrow, or a four-headed arrow on the center point. This corresponding point on the selected graphic moves when you are modifying the graphic.

POSITION OPTION

Figure 35. You can modify the *X* and *Y* coordinates to move and resize a selected object. For more information on resizing and moving objects, see Figures 38 through 41. Use the nudge buttons to increase or decrease the width or height by increments of 0.01 inch.

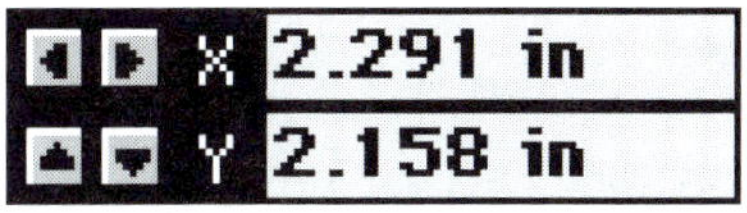

By holding down the Command key while clicking on the nudge button you can increase or decrease values by increments of 0.1 inch.

SIZING AND PERCENTAGE SCALING OPTION

Figure 36. You can change the width and the height of a graphic by specifying values in the *W* and *H* text boxes. See Figures 38 through 41 for more information. Use the nudge buttons to increase or decrease the width or height by increments of 0.01 inch.

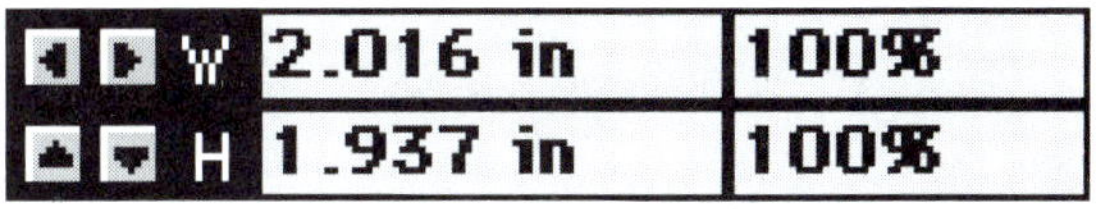

By holding down the Command key while clicking on the nudge button you can increase or decrease the value by increments of 0.1 inch.

You can type in a percentage to increase or decrease the size of the selected object.

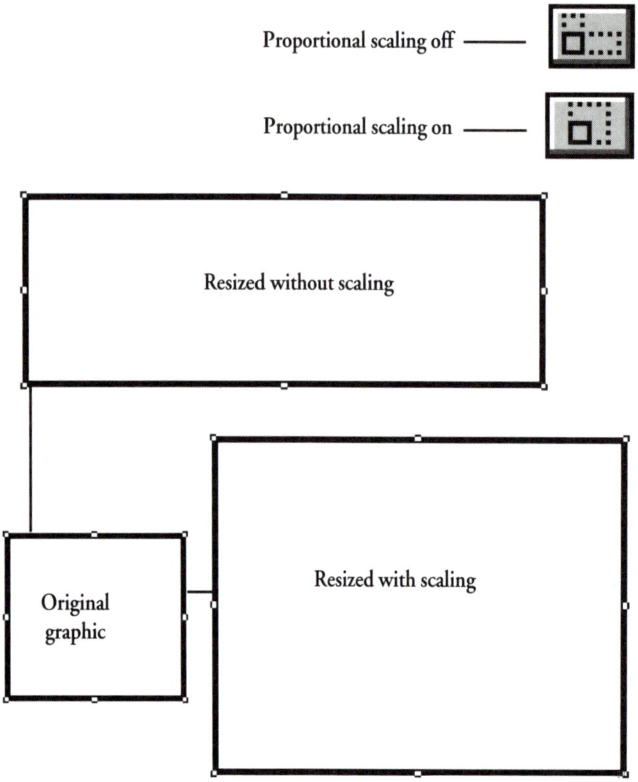

PROPORTIONAL SCALING OPTION

Figure 37. Click on the Proportional scaling button to turn the proportional scaling on or off. If you have the scaling button turned on, when you change the height (for example) of a selected graphic using the *H* text box, then PageMaker also scales the width of the graphic in proportion to the original size. The scaling option does not affect a graphic if you resize it directly with the mouse.

TRANSFORMING GRAPHICS

MOVING AND RESIZING GRAPHICS

Figure 38. If you are using the Control palette to move an object, select the object and then select a referenc point on the Proxy. Click on the reference point once for a fixed reference point (a). Change either the *X* or the *Y* value depending on where you want it to move and ther press the Return key.

Here, we have moved the rectangl 1 inch to the right (b).

You can also click on the nudge buttons to the left of the *X* and *Y* text boxes to move the object in small increments. If you click on the graphic again you can use any of the directional arrow keys on the keyboard to move the selected graphic in increments of 0.01 inch in the direction of the chosen arrow.

By holding down the Command key while clicking on the nudge button you can move the graphic in increments of 0.1 inch.

(a)

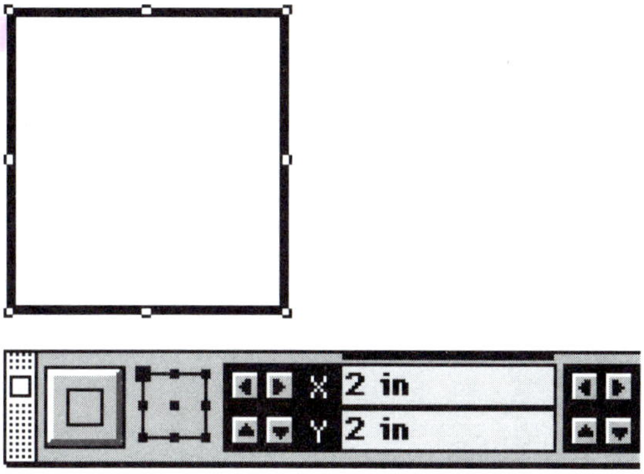

(b)

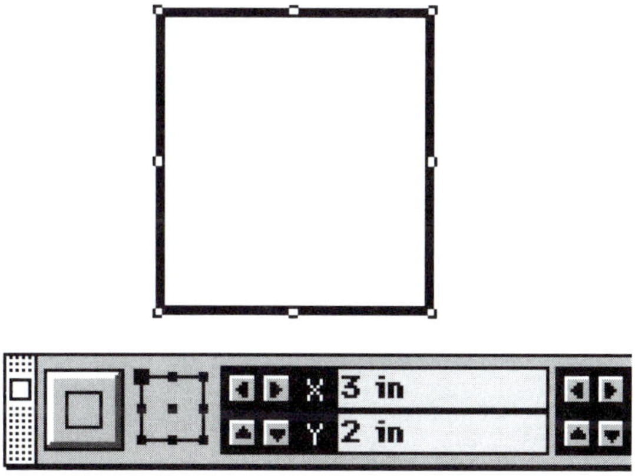

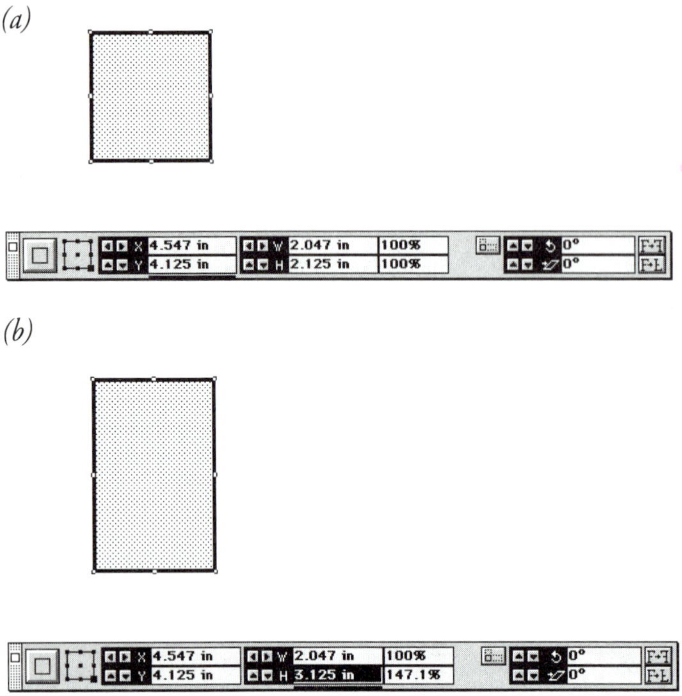

Figure 39. To resize an object with the Control palette, select the object with the pointer tool and click twice on a reference point in the Proxy. You may also like to alter the proportional scaling option (see Figure 37) as required (a).

When you change either the *X* or *Y* values, the object resizes accordingly. Here, we have resized the rectangle 1 inch taller by changing the *Y* value (b).

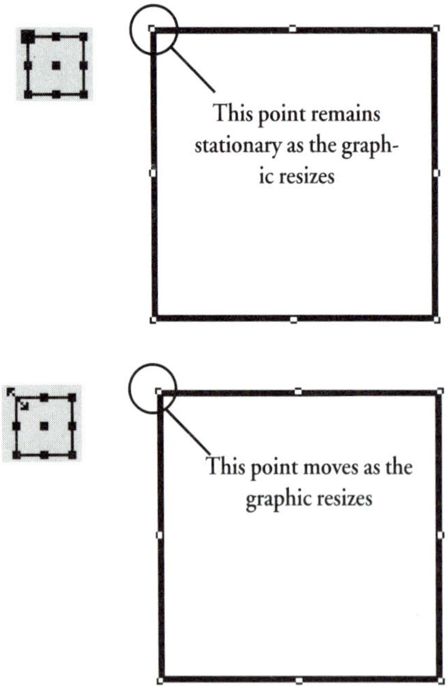

Figure 40. When you use the *W* and *H* text boxes to resize a graphic, again you must select the graphic and then a reference point on the Proxy. If you click once on a reference point, the selected point remains stationary when you change a value.

If you click twice on a reference point, this point moves as the graphic resizes. You can insert new values into the *W* and *H* text boxes and you can apply them by pressing the Return key or clicking on the Apply button.

Figure 41. A third way you can resize graphics using the Control palette is to use the *Percent-scaling* option. Select the required graphic and change the width and height value if proportional scaling is not turned on, or just the width or the height (if the scaling option is on). In this example, we have turned proportional scaling on and changed the *H* value to 1 (a).

Press the Return key or click on the Apply button to see the results. Because the proportional scaling option is on, the circle is proportionally scaled (b).

(a)

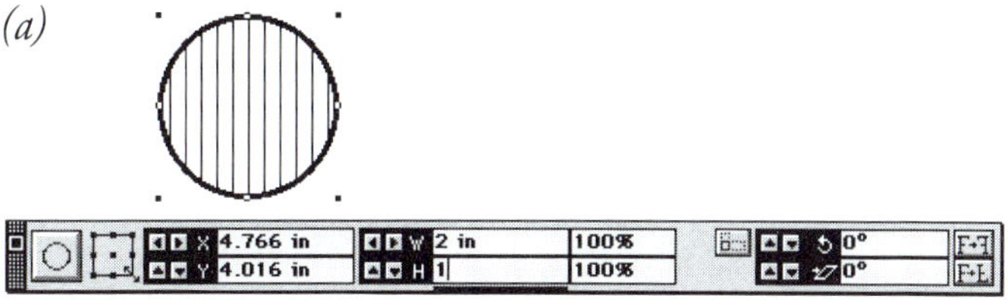

(b)

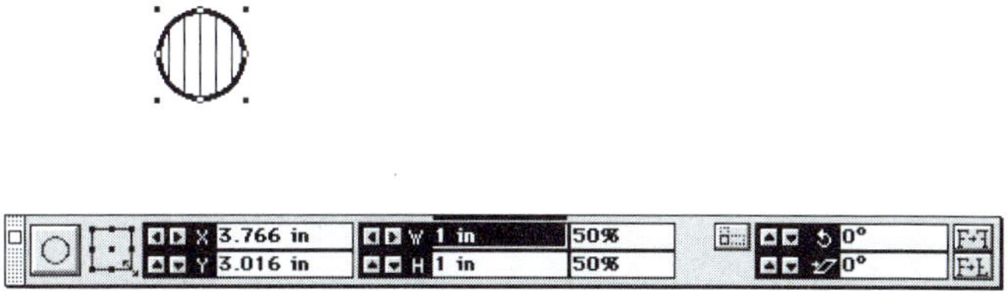

ROTATING GRAPHICS

Figure 42. You can rotate objects within PageMaker by 360 degrees at 0.01 degree intervals. Select the object with the pointer tool, choose a reference point on the Proxy (this determines the point that the object rotates around), and type a value into the *Rotation* option text box (a).

After pressing the Return key or clicking on the Apply button, the object rotates (b). For clockwise rotation, use - angles; for counterclockwise rotation, use + angles.

(a)

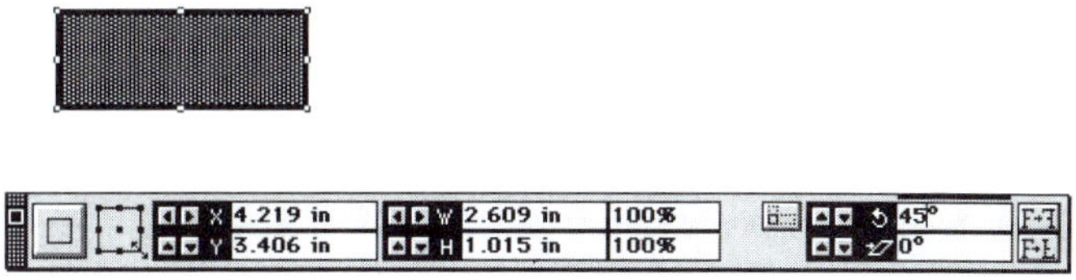

(b)

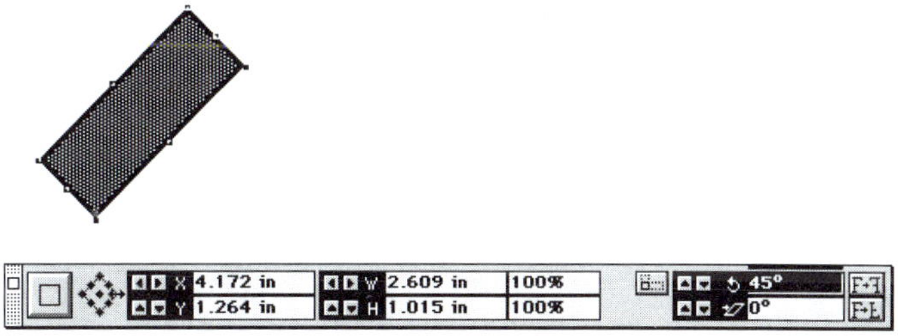

SKEWING GRAPHICS

Figure 43. You can skew objects horizontally by + or - 85 degrees at 0.01 degree increments. Select the object with the pointer tool and select a fixed point on the Proxy. Specify a skewing angle in the *Skewing option* text box (a), and press the Return key or click on the Apply button to apply the skew (b).

(a)

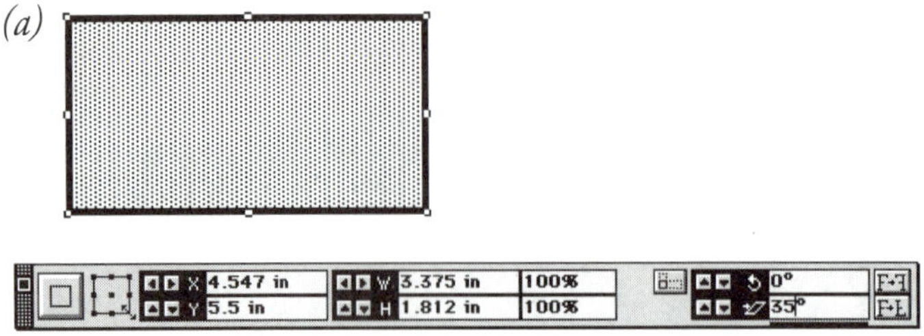

(b)

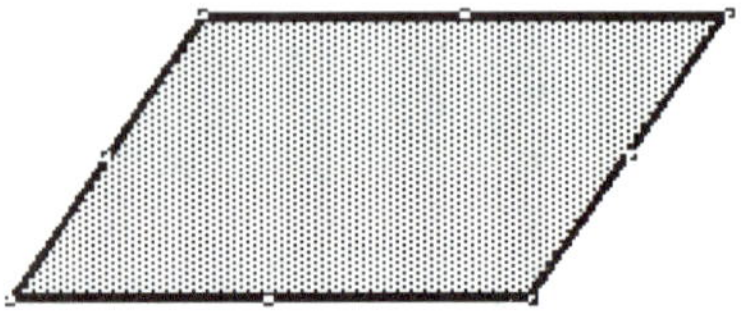

REFLECTING GRAPHICS

Figure 44. Select the object with the pointer tool and select a point on the Proxy. PageMaker reflects the object around this point. Click on the *Horizontal* or *Vertical* reflection button (a) and you will see the change immediately (b).

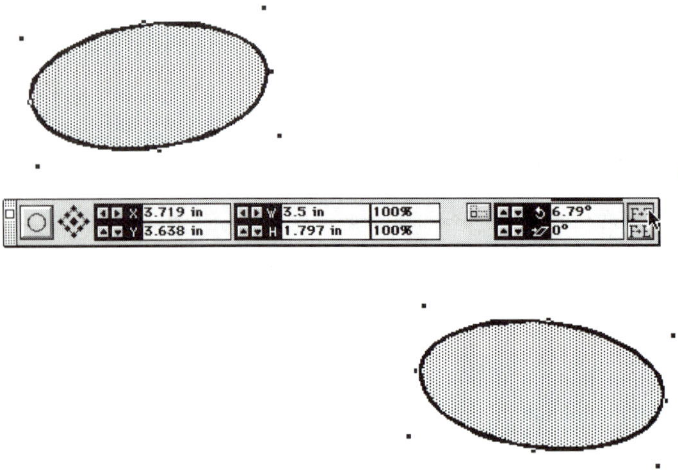

REMOVING TRANSFORMATIONS

Figure 45. To remove the transformations you have applied to an object (rotated, reflected or skewed), select the object and select *Remove transformation* from the **Element** menu.

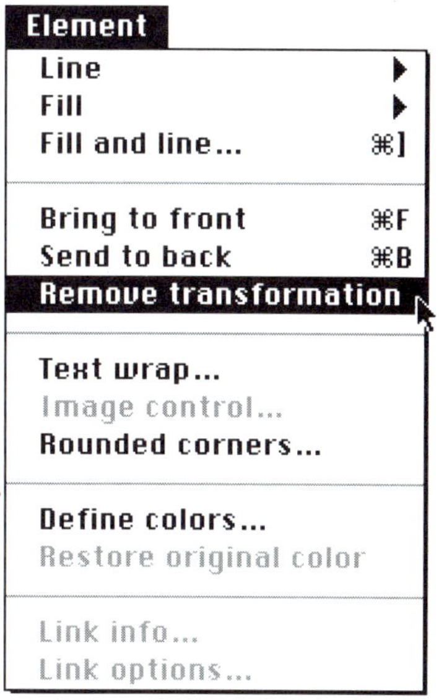

IMPORTED GRAPHICS

7

THE FORMATS PAGEMAKER SUPPORTS

PageMaker can import a wide variety of graphic files. These include bitmap files and scanned images (these can be paint or TIFF graphics), object-oriented or vector graphics, EPS files (PostScript-coded files).

PageMaker accepts a variety of files according to what format they are in. Figures 1 through 5 provide examples of some of the different types of graphics you can place in PageMaker.

Figure 1. A bitmap graphic from a paint program.

Figure 2. A PICT graphic.

Figure 3. An EPSF graphic.

Figure 4. A TIFF graphic.

Figure 5. This is a scanned image which has been saved as a TIFF file.

Loading Graphics

Figure 6. Use the *Place* command in the **File** menu to import all types of graphics into PageMaker. This opens the *Place document* dialog box, shown in Figure 6. You can use this command to:

- place a new graphic, or
- replace an existing graphic.

Graphics you place in your document can be part of your text—an inline graphic—or totally independent of the text—an independent graphic.

Figure 7. To add a new graphic to your document, choose the name of the file from the list of files to the left.

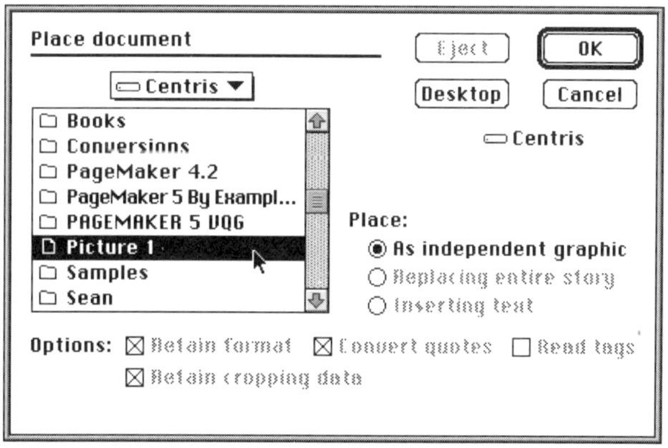

Figure 8. Depending on the type of graphic you are importing, the mouse cursor takes on one of the following four shapes:
(a) paint graphic
(b) scanned or TIFF graphic
(c) draw graphic
(d) encapsulated PostScript graphic

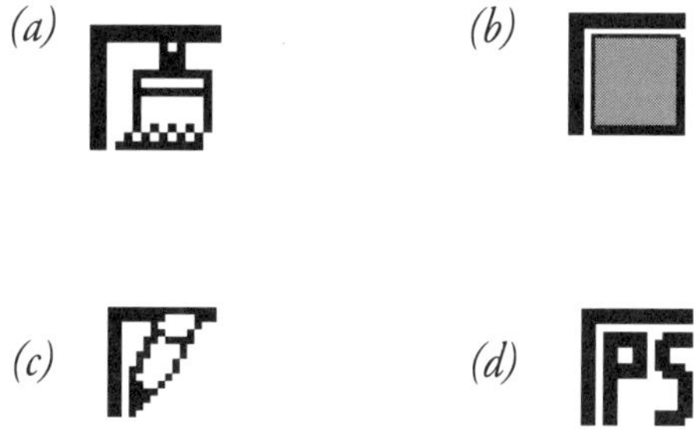

Figure 9. You can place a graphic onto the page in two ways. One way is to position the mouse cursor anywhere on screen and click once. By using this method, you load the graphic onto the page at its original size, which is often very difficult for you to pre-determine.

Figure 10. Another way to place a graphic is to drag the mouse until the selection rectangle is the size you would like the graphic to be. This is known as *drag-placing.*

Figure 11. Once you release the mouse button, the graphic fills the area of the box. To resize the graphic proportionally, hold down the Shift key and select one of the corner handles to resize. The graphic snaps to its true proportions.

REPLACING EXISTING GRAPHICS

Figure 12. To replace an existing graphic, including any resizing and cropping that you have applied, select the graphic on the page, select the graphic file in the *Place document* dialog box and choose *Replacing entire graphic.*

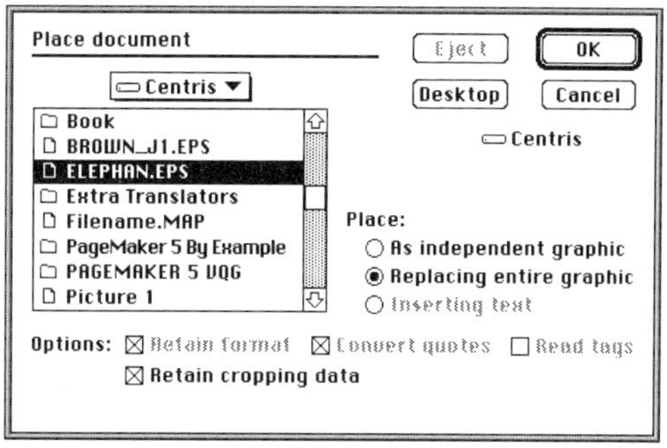

Figure 13. If you put the insertion point in any text before you select the *Place* command, you have the option of placing the graphic as an inline graphic. Figures 28 through 33 explain this procedure.

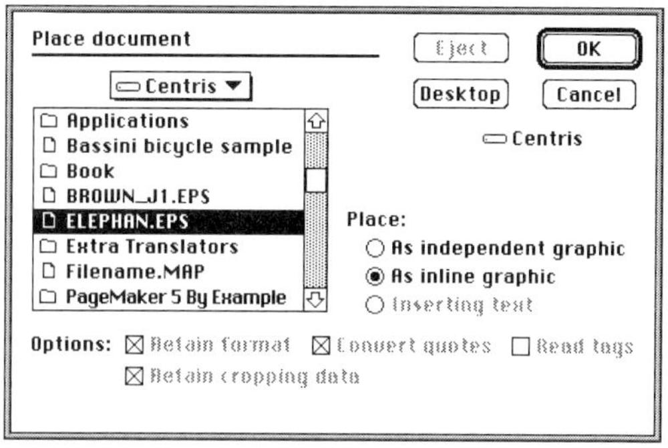

Figure 14. Turn the *Retain cropping data* option on if you have cropped an imported graphic and you wish to update (replace) the link with the original graphic (see the **Cropping graphics** section in this chapter). You can also access this option in the *Link info* dialog box.

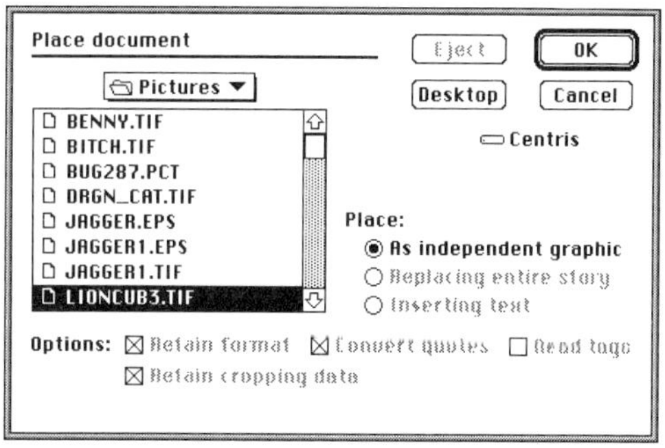

You need apply this option only if you wish to replace or relink graphics using PageMaker's linking options—PageMaker automatically retains cropping information for hotlinked files, OLE-linked or embedded files, and editions (see Chapter 3 for more information on links).

Cropping Graphics

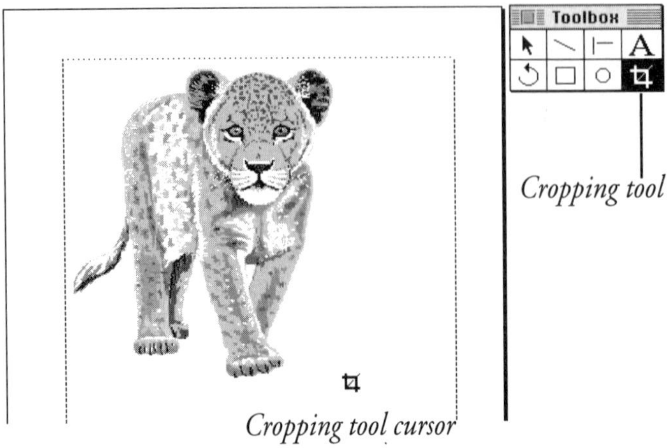

Figure 15. Use the cropping tool to crop imported graphics. Note that when you select the cropping tool, the cursor changes to the same icon as the cropping tool.

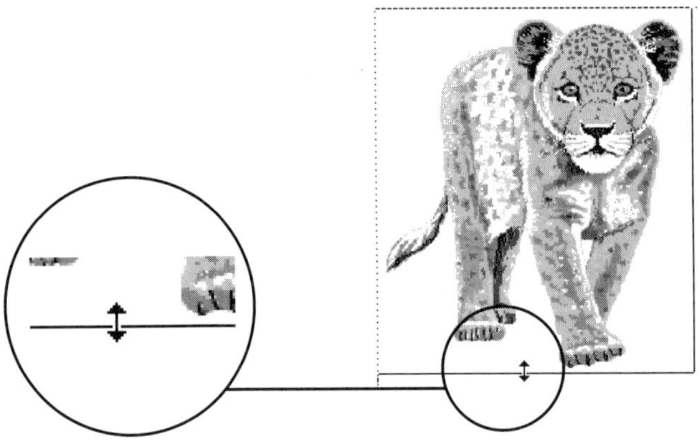

Figure 16. Select the graphic with the cropping tool and position it over one of the selection handles. Once the cursor changes to a two-headed arrow, move the mouse pointer towards the center of the graphic. You will find this is similar to resizing a graphic, but in this case you hide part of the graphic. You can crop graphics both horizontally and vertically.

Figure 17. When you have cropped a graphic, you still have access to any part of the graphic you want to bring into view. To move the graphic inside the window, hold the cropping tool down inside the graphic and drag it.

WRAPPING TEXT AROUND GRAPHICS

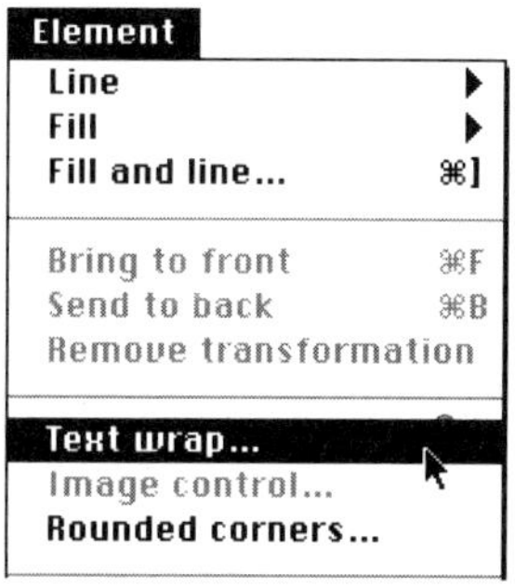

Figure 18. You can flow text around imported graphics in a variety of ways, using the *Text wrap* command and its associated dialog box. Select a graphic before choosing this command, unless you want the choices you make in the *Text wrap* dialog box to become the default settings.

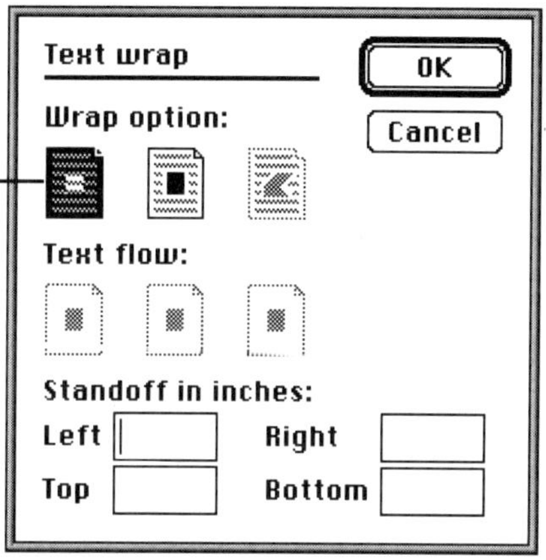

Figure 19. Select *Wrap off* if you want text to flow through the graphic.

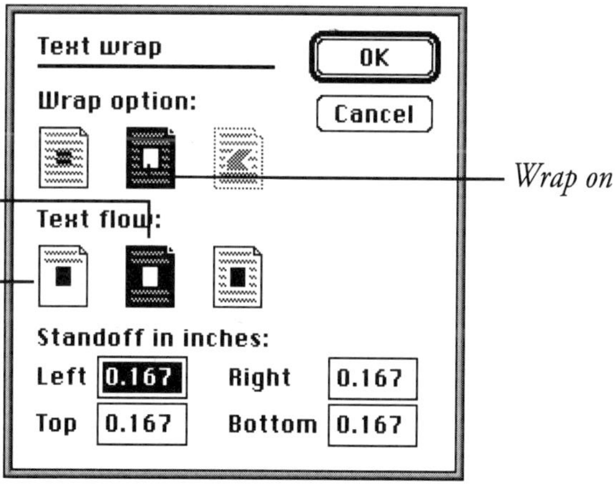

Figure 20. Select *Wrap on* and *Jump over* if you want text to jump right over the graphic with no text flowing down either side.

If you select *Column break*, text stops when it reaches the graphic.

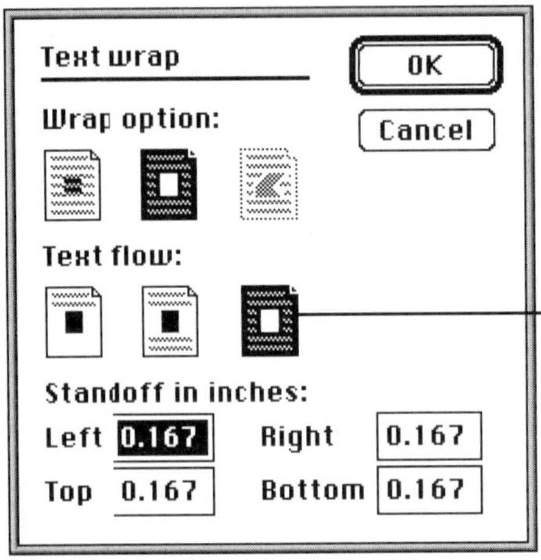

Figure 21. Select *Wrap on* and *Wrap all sides* if you want text to flow regularly around a graphic, including down both sides. See the example shown in Figure 22.

Wrap all sides

Figure 22. This is an example of text flowing regularly around a graphic using the Text wrap settings in Figure 21.

IRREGULAR WRAP-AROUNDS

Figure 23. Set up the *Text wrap* dialog box with *Wrap on* and *Wrap all sides* to get an irregular wrap-around.

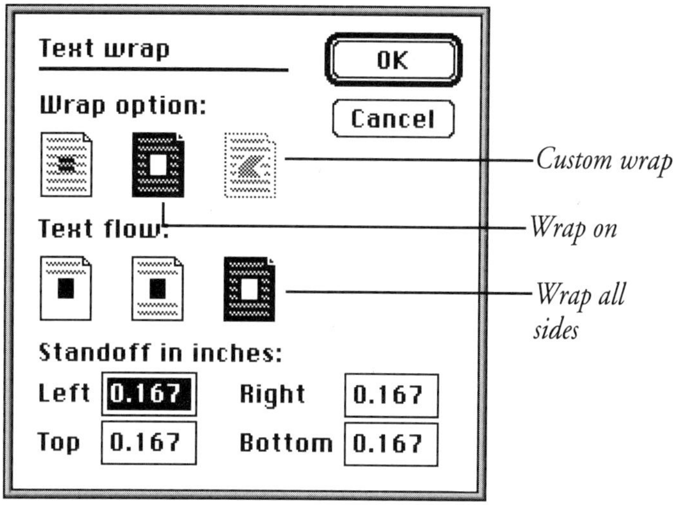

As soon as you begin to manipulate the irregular text wrap border around the graphic, PageMaker automatically selects *Custom wrap* in the *Text wrap* dialog box.

Figure 24. These settings give you two sets of handles around the graphic. The inside handles resize the picture. The outside handles adjust the text wrap to any shape.

Figure 25. You can move the outside handles with the mouse to adjust the shape of the wrap-around, as we have started to do. You can add extra handles to create more bends simply by clicking anywhere on the dotted lines with the mouse.

Figure 26. We created extra handles by clicking on the vertical dotted line and moved these handles toward the graphic. See how the text moves as you move the handles. If you find it irritating having to wait for the text to reflow as you move each handle, move multiple handles while holding down the Spacebar. The text will not reflow until you release the Spacebar.

Figure 27. A finished irregular wrap-around.

Inline Graphics

Inline graphics are graphics that become part of the text. As you move the text, inline graphics move with it.

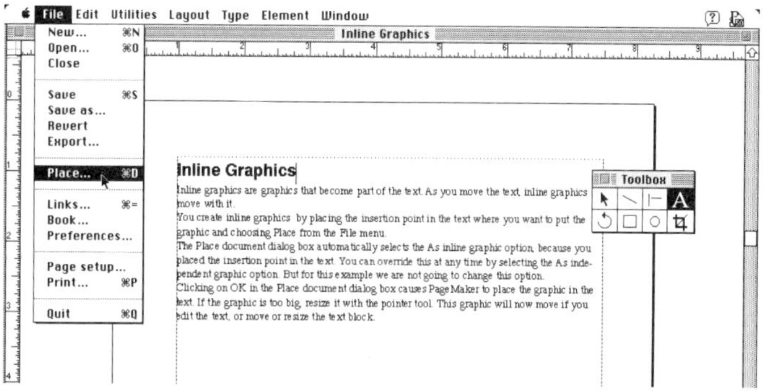

Figure 28. You create inline graphics by placing the insertion point in the text where you want to put the graphic and choosing *Place* from the **File** menu.

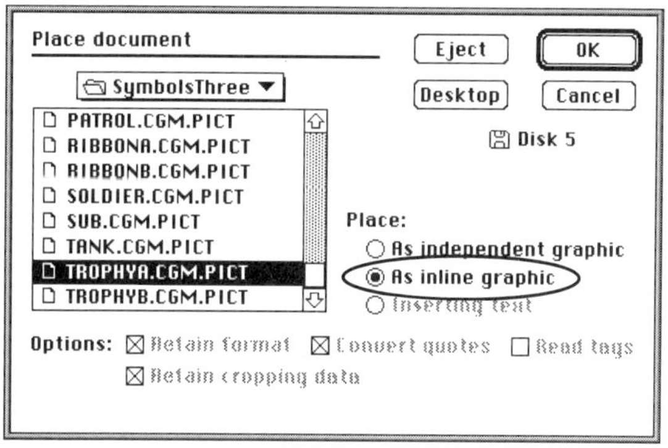

Figure 29. The *Place document* dialog box automatically selects the *As inline graphic* option, because you placed the insertion point in the text. You can override this at any time by selecting the *As independent graphic* option. But for this example we are not going to change this option.

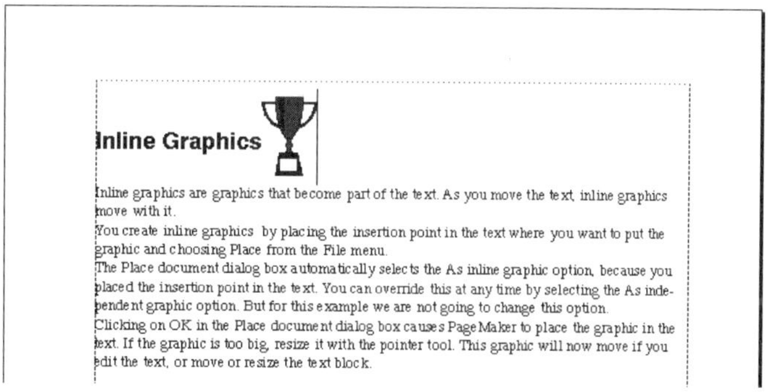

Figure 30. Clicking on *OK* in the *Place document* dialog box makes PageMaker put the graphic in the text. If the graphic is too big, resize it with the pointer tool. The graphic now moves if you edit the text, or move or resize the text block.

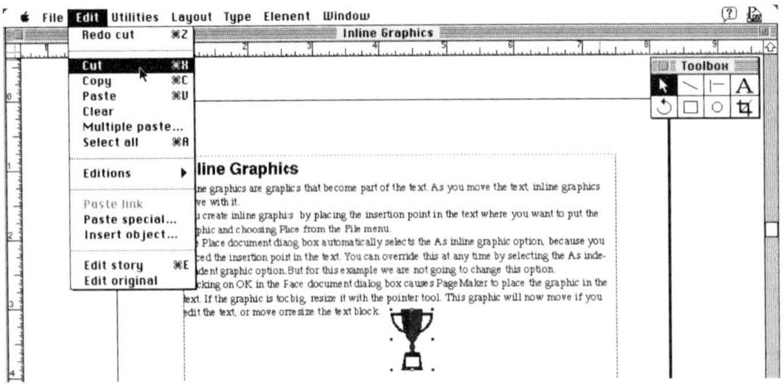

Figure 31. You can turn an independent graphic into an inline graphic in your text as follows:

Select the graphic with the pointer tool and choose *Cut* from the **Edit** menu.

Put the insertion point where you want the graphic in the text and choose *Paste* from the **Edit** menu.

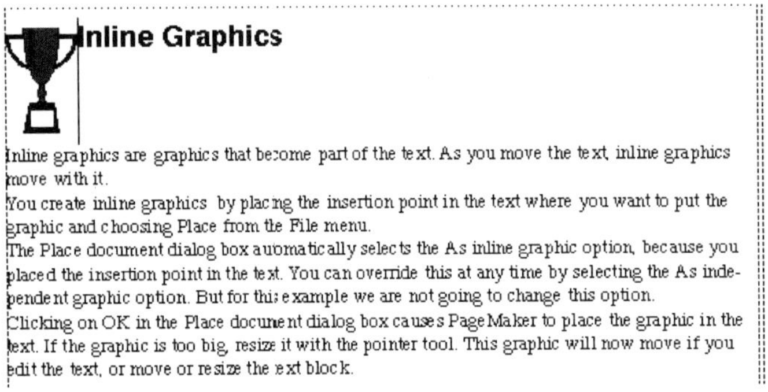

Figure 32. We put the insertion point in the text and pasted the removed graphic in. It now becomes an inline graphic.

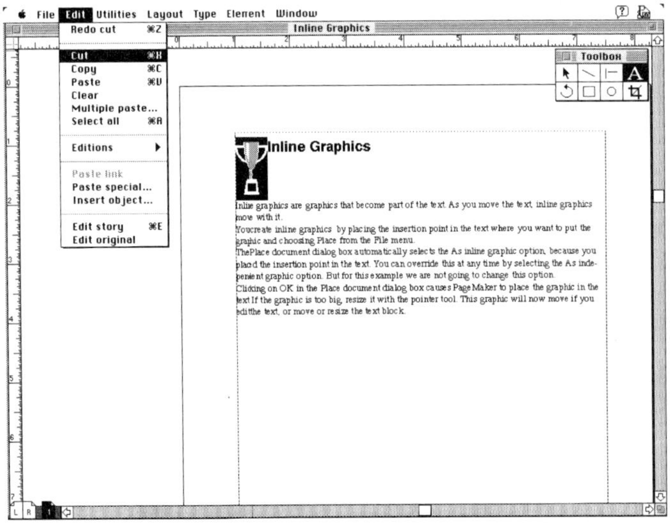

Figure 33. You can turn an inline graphic on your page into an independent graphic as follows: Select the graphic with the pointer tool, choose *Cut* from the **Edit** menu and then choose *Paste*.

The graphic reappears in the text in the same place. However, you can now select it with the pointer tool and move it independently of the text.

IMAGE CONTROL

Figure 34. You can alter the appearance of paint graphics and scanned images using the *Image control* command from the **Element** menu. The *Image control* command is available for black-and-white graphics only.

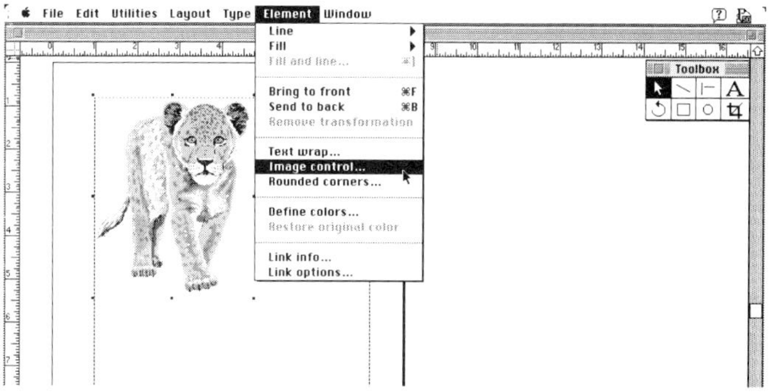

Figure 35. This is the *Image control* dialog box. You can change the lightness, contrast, screen patterns, angle and frequency of a selected graphic. If you change a setting here, press the Tab key to move to the next option; you can then click on the *Apply* button. Using the *Apply* button allows you to keep the *Image control* dialog box on screen while you experiment.

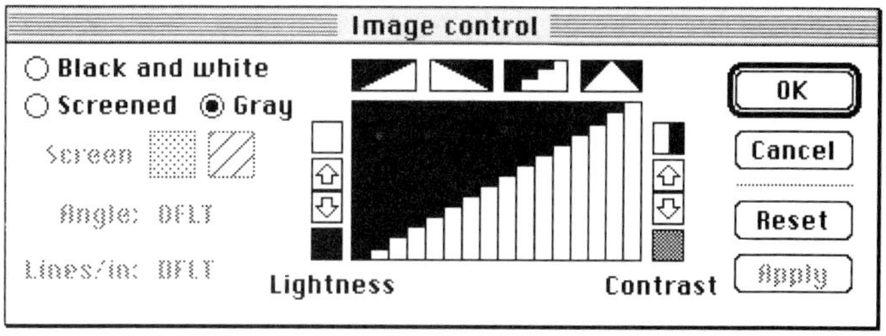

Figure 36. Here we have lightened the image by changing the *Contrast* using the scroll bar.

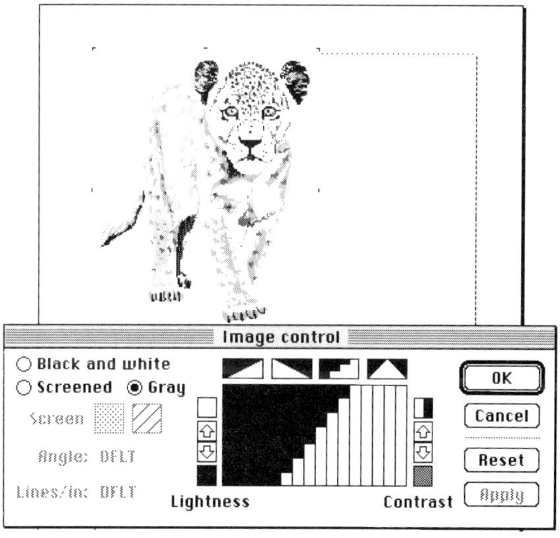

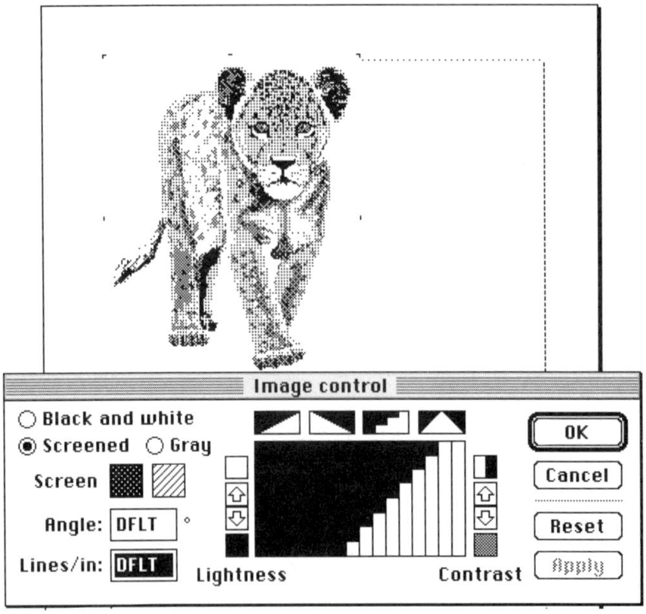

Figure 37. By altering the figures in both *Lightness* and *Contrast*, the image adjusts accordingly after you click on the *Apply* button.

Once you have adjusted the *Lightness* and *Contrast* of the image, you can alter the *Printing parameters* options. Here you have the option of changing the default line or dot angle and frequency settings for special effects.

MULTIPLE PASTE COMMAND

You can use the *Multiple paste* command if you want to paste multiple copies of an object from the clipboard onto your page. See Chapter 6, Figure 23 for more information.

IMPORTED GRAPHICS AND THE CONTROL PALETTE

You use the Control palette with imported graphics in the same way as you do with internal graphics—for moving, resizing, scaling, rotating, skewing and reflecting graphics (see **The Control Palette and Graphics** in Chapter 6). However, you can also use the Control palette to crop imported graphics. This is discussed below.

CROPPING

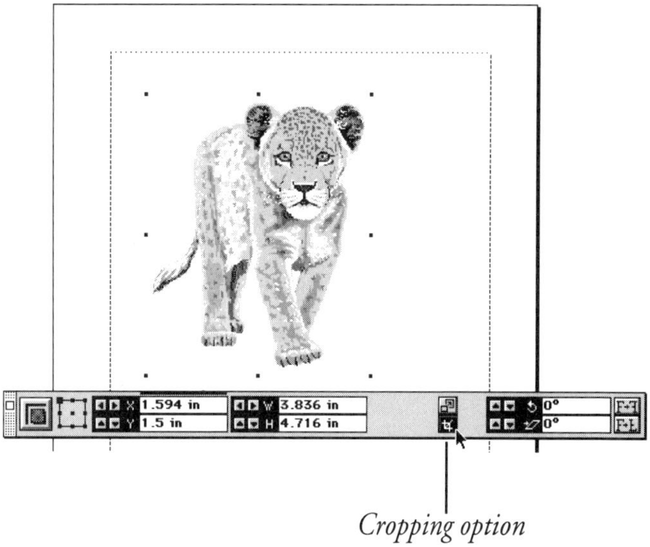

Figure 38. To crop a graphic using the Control palette, select the graphic, click on the *Cropping* option, and select a reference point on the Proxy.

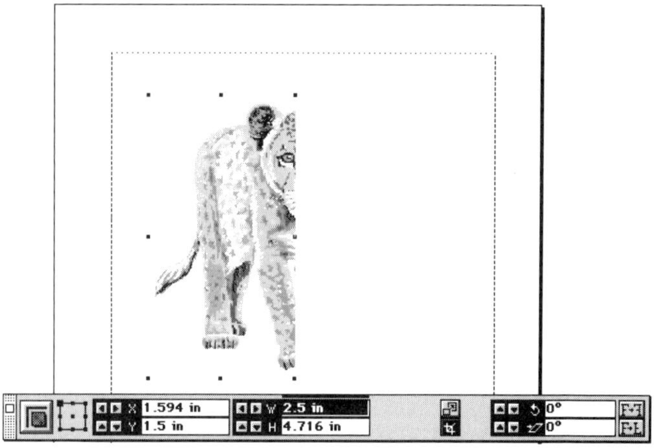

Figure 39. Change the values for *X* and *Y* or *H* and *W* and press the Return key or click on the *Apply* button to see the results. Here, we have cropped the right side of the graphic by selecting a reference point on the left side of the Proxy and decreasing the *W* value.

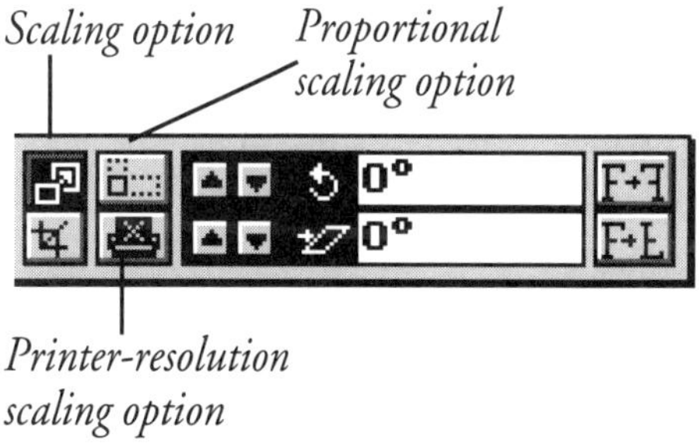

Figure 40. The other options available when you turn the *Cropping* option off are *Proportional scaling* and the *Printer-resolution scaling*. Use the latter option to resize monochrome bitmap images to an optimal size for your target printer.

WORKING WITH TEMPLATES

8

CREATING TEMPLATES

A PageMaker template is like any other normal publication, except that it has a specific application as a "dummy" document. A dummy document can contain formatting information for a standard publication, such as a monthly newsletter. When you open a template, you automatically open an untitled copy of the original document. This lets you add new information to a document without affecting the original template.

You can include text and graphics in a template, and PageMaker provides a number of features for simple and easy replacement of these objects with updated information.

Note: You can use the text and graphic replacement methods discussed in this chapter in any PageMaker publication.

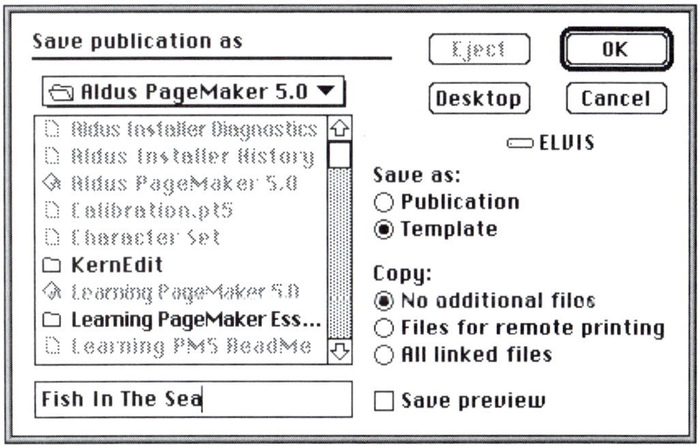

Figure 1. You create a template in the same way as any other PageMaker publication. Add text and graphics as required, adjust the layout as needed, and use master page items, imported graphics and other elements as you would for any document. The difference is when you save the file — the *Save* command from the **File** menu produces the *Save publication* dialog box. In the right half of this box, click on the *Template* radio button. Name the publication and select *OK* to create a template.

Opening Templates

(a)

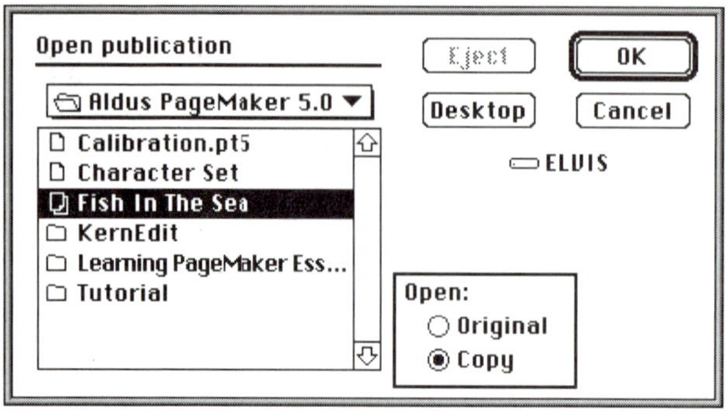

(b)

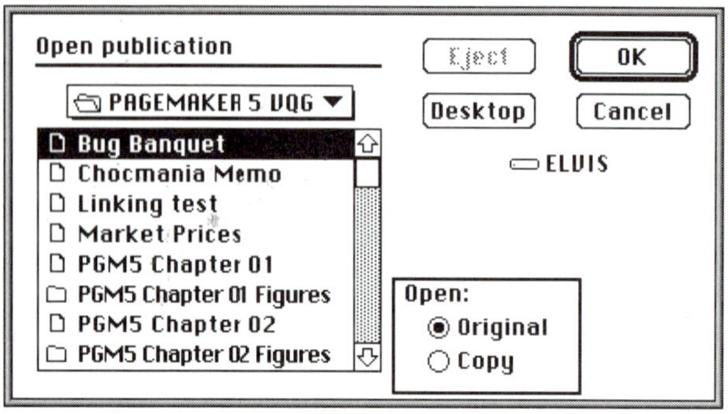

Figure 2. To open a template, use the *Open* command, as for any PageMaker publication. The dialog box automatically defaults to *Copy* when you select a template as shown in (a). You can select *Original* if you want to alter your original template. (See also the *Open template* addition in Chapter 9.)

Conversely, opening a normal publication automatically defaults to *Original* as shown in (b). You can also override this to open a copy of a publication.

The difference between opening a publication and a template is that a template automatically defaults to *Copy* when you are opening it.

Using Templates

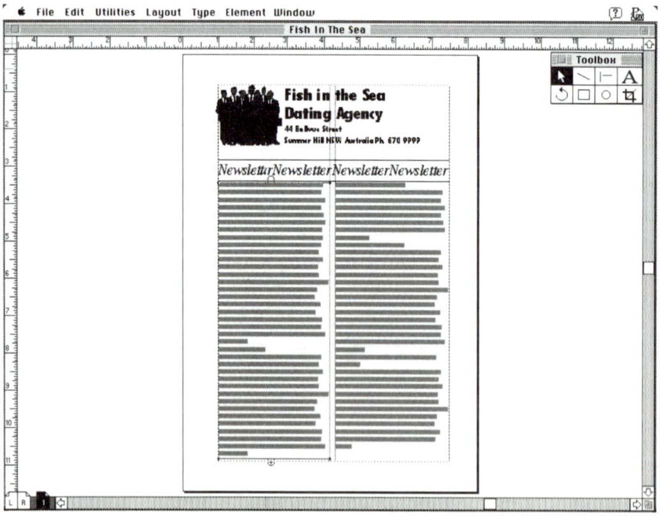

Figure 3. When you open a copy of a template to change it, you often need to replace the text with a file of your choice. Do this by selecting any part of the text file with the pointer tool (or placing the insertion point anywhere within a story), and choosing *Place* from the File menu.

If you want to replace only part of a text file, select that part with the text tool. In this figure, we have selected a block of text in column 1 with the pointer tool.

TEXT PLACEHOLDERS

Figure 4. The *Replacing entire story* in the *Place document* dialog box lets you replace the story selected in the template. If you have put the insertion point in the text, then you can select the *Inserting text* option. If you have selected a portion of text with the text tool, a new option, *Replacing selected text,* appears.

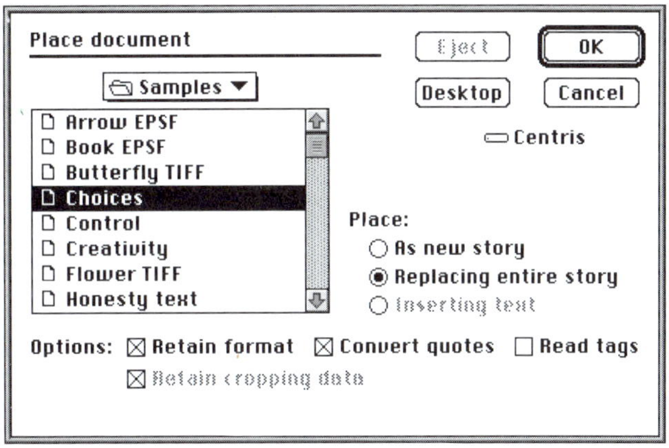

With these methods, you can quickly and easily replace outdated stories with new stories. The old and new text stories do not need to be of the same length.

The text contained within the original template is called a "text placeholder."

GRAPHIC PLACEHOLDERS

Figure 5. Replacing old graphics with new imported graphics is even simpler than replacing text. With the pointer tool, select the graphic you want to replace and choose *Place* from the **File** menu.

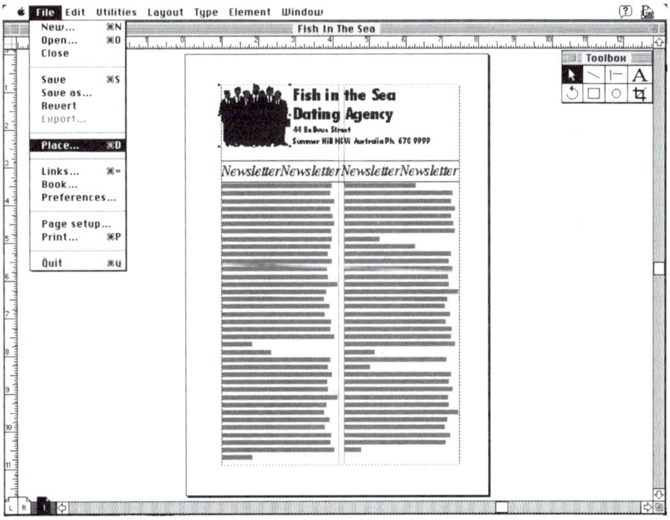

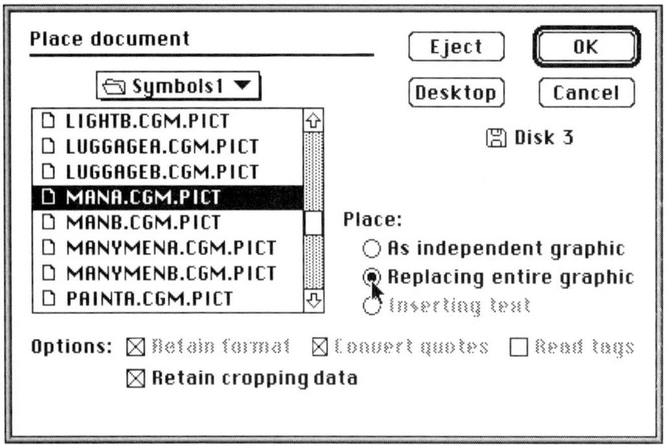

Figure 6. In the *Place document* dialog box you can choose either *Replacing entire graphic* selection or *As independent graphic.* Use the latter option to load graphics in the normal way. Use the former option to replace a selected graphic. Click on *OK* and PageMaker immediately loads the graphic into the selected graphic area on your page.

The graphic in the original template is called a graphic placeholder.

Figure 7. PageMaker keeps the same graphic size and parameters, including cropping and text wraparound attributes. You can change these if necessary.

Aldus Additions

9

What Are Aldus Additions?

PageMaker 5 comes with a number of additions which you can find in the *Aldus Additions* submenu in the **Utilities** menu. You can also get additions offered by independent developers as these become available. The additions give you extra features you can use to enhance and compile your publications.

Such features include balancing columns, adding bullets, adding drop capitals, displaying publication information and text continuation notices, and more.

Figure 1. The *Aldus Additions* submenu is in the **Utilities** menu. The additions in the submenu you see here are the ones that you install by default with PageMaker 5.0. Any extra additions you must install separately.

The following pages describe each of the additions in the submenu listed in this figure.

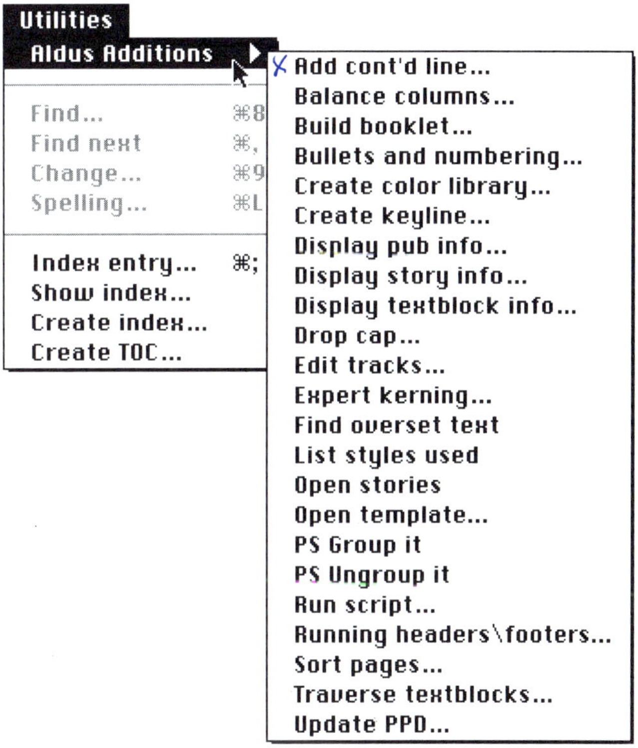

✱ Add Cont'd Line

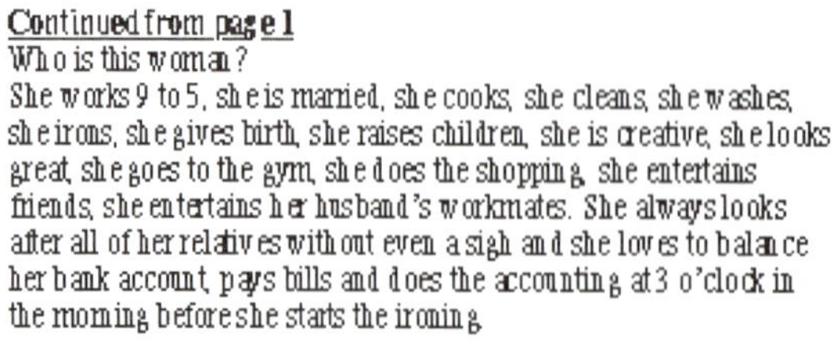

Figure 2. Use the *Add cont'd line* addition if you want a continuation notice at the top or the bottom of a text file that joins another one on another page.

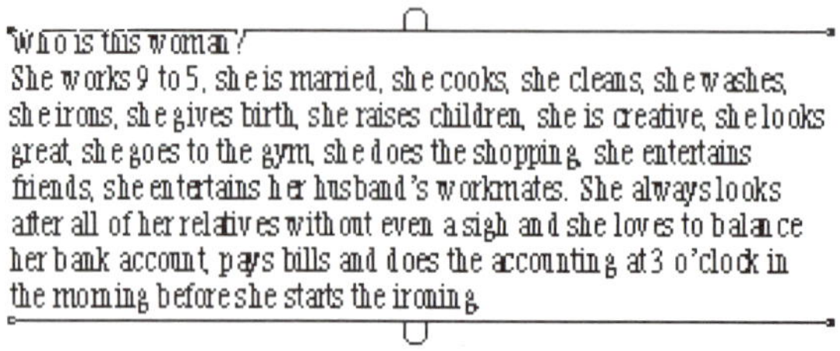

Figure 3. Select the text block with the pointer tool and select *Add cont'd line* from the *Aldus Additions* submenu.

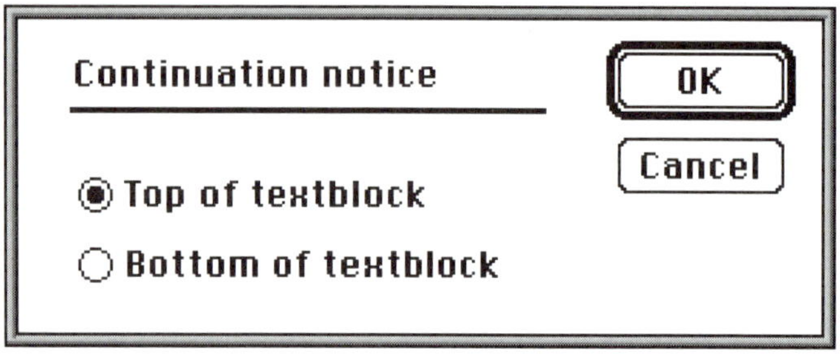

Figure 4. If the text appears on a page in front of the selected text block, choose the *Top of textblock* option from the *Continuation notice* dialog box. Choose the *Bottom of textblock* option if the text appears after the page you are on.

Balance Columns

Figure 5. Use the *Balance columns* addition to align multiple columns of a single threaded story. The page to the left is not balanced and the page to the right is.

Figure 6. To use this command, first select the columns you want to balance and select *Balance columns* from the *Aldus Additions* submenu. This opens the *Balance columns* dialog box shown in Figure 7.

Figure 7. The left *Alignment* option aligns columns from the top of the page downwards and the right *Alignment* option aligns columns from the bottom upwards.

The *Add leftover lines* options allow you to add any remaining uneven lines to the left column or to the right column.

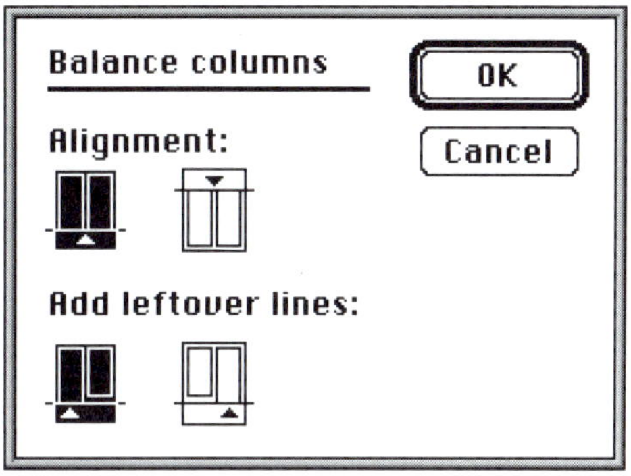

Build Booklet

Figure 8. With the *Build booklet* addition, you can create a copy of your current publication in booklet form. PageMaker rearranges the pages so that multiple pages print on a single sheet and if you then fold them, the pages assume the correct order.

If you were to print an eight-page, letter-sized brochure for example, you could print to a tabloid paper size and fold the pages in half. The correct page grouping required for this procedure is shown here.

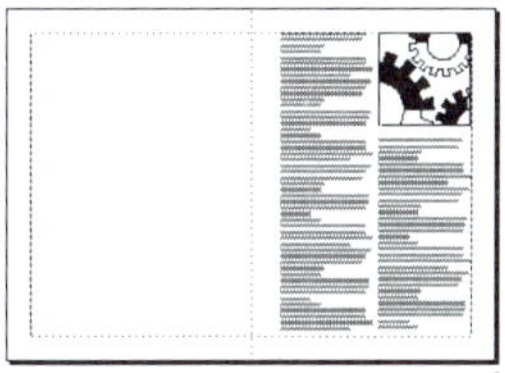

Pages 8 and 1

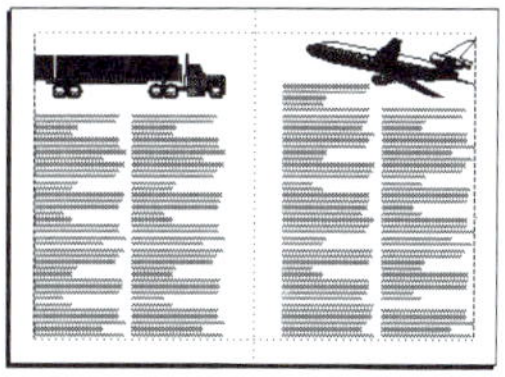

Pages 2 and 7

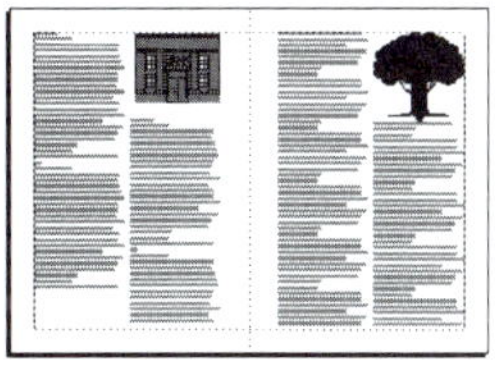

Pages 6 and 3

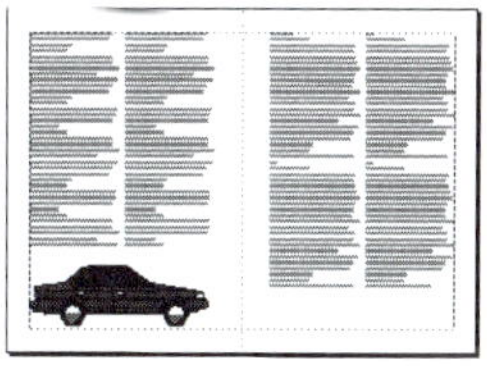

Pages 4 and 5

With the *Build booklet* addition you can do this automatically without having to think about the correct page imposition.

PREPARING YOUR PUBLICATION

To prepare your publication for building a booklet, you should have completed the following tasks:

- Check that you have at least two and a half times the size of the publication left on your hard disk.
- Check that you have completed the layout.
- Check that you have included your index and table of contents, if required.
- Check that the publication starts on an odd page.

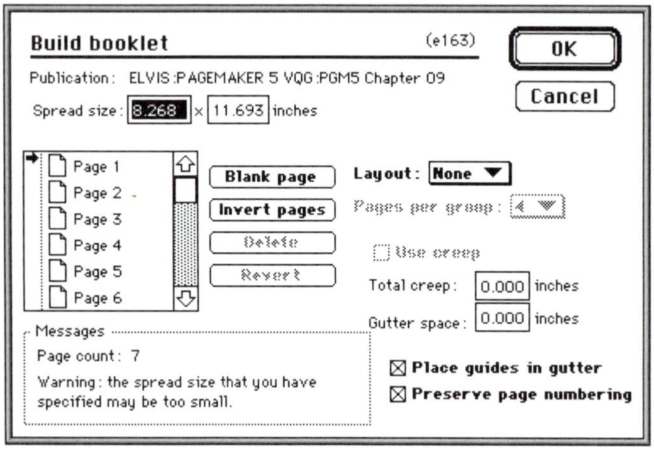

Figure 9. Once you have prepared your publication, you are ready to build a booklet. In the open publication, select *Build booklet* from the *Aldus Additions* submenu in the **Utilities** menu. This opens the *Build Booklet* dialog box.

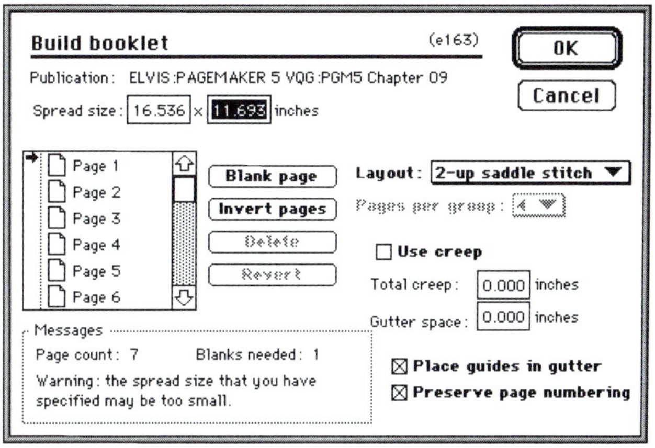

Figure 10. The *Spread size* boxes display the calculated size of the selected *Layout* option. You can adjust the size to provide room for crop marks or bleeds. A warning appears in the *Messages* section if the current spread size is not large enough to accommodate these options.

PageMaker displays any messages or warnings in the *Messages* section.

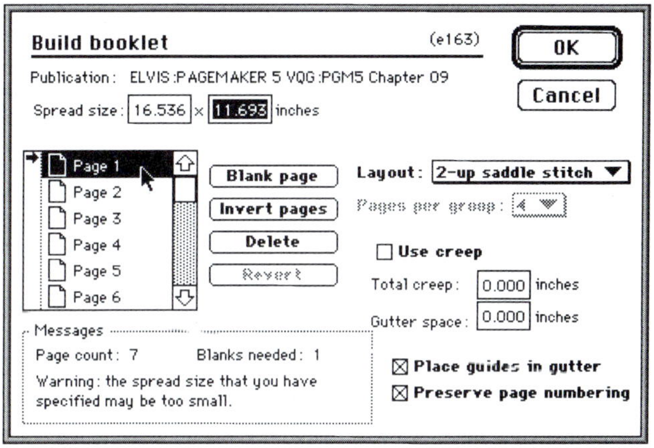

Figure 11. In the section we have labeled here, you can rearrange, add, and delete pages. To insert a blank page, move the arrow at the left of the list box between the relevant pages by clicking the mouse, then click on *Blank page.* To rearrange the order of the pages from first to last to last to first, click on *Invert pages.* Select a page and click on *Delete* to remove it. Click on *Revert* to undo any unwanted changes you have made.

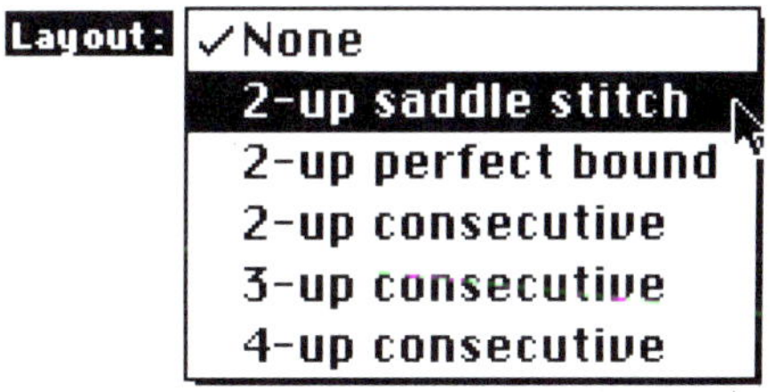

Figure 12. The *Layout* pop-up menu gives you six options to choose from:

- *None:* this option creates a new publication but does not automatically rearrange the pages or change the spread size.
- *2-up saddle stitch:* the default setting. Double-sided pages are printed, folded and fastened along the fold (see Figure 8 for an example).

- *2-up perfect bound:* this creates a series of folded booklets that are joined together to create a spine-bound book. You must specify the number of pages per group, PageMaker calculates the number of spreads needed to produce the publication, as well as the correct page imposition.
- *2-3-4-up consecutive:* use these options to create multi-page spreads. Each set of pages is combined side-by-side onto a single page. This allows you to create, for example two-, three-, or four-panel brochures with ease.

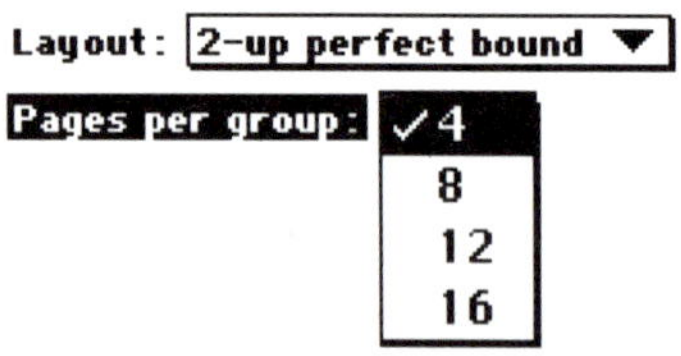

Figure 13. You can change the *Pages per group* option only when you have selected the *2-up perfect bound* option (see above). Select how many pages per group or booklet there will be for your perfect-bound book.

Figure 14. The *Use creep* option counteracts the problems you sometimes encounter when the folded sheets in a large booklet become offset due to the paper thickness. Turn the *Use creep* option on and in the *Total creep* text box insert a value that you estimate will offset the creep affecting your publication. PageMaker then adjusts the placement of the page elements to counter this problem.

Use the *Place guides in gutter* option if you want to position non-printing ruler guides in the gutters of the publication.

Figure 15. Turn the *Preserve page numbering* option on or off to turn the page numbering on or off, respectively. You must have page numbering in the master pages of your document for the numbering to work. PageMaker renumbers and places a number on any blank pages if you turn this option on.

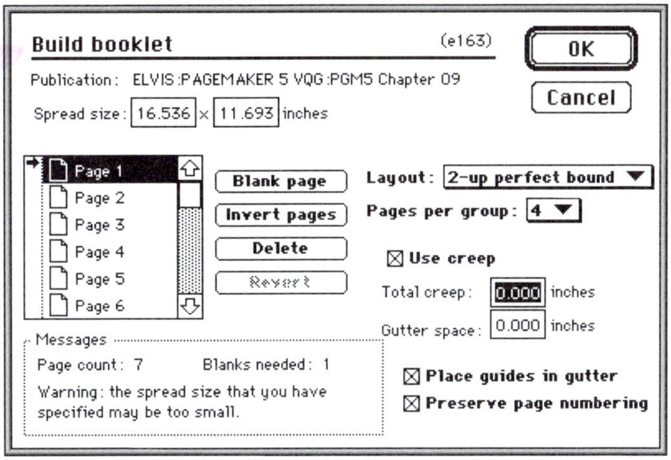

Type a value into the *Gutter space* text box to add space between pages. PageMaker automatically increases the *Spread size* values.

Once you have made all your changes in this dialog box, click on *OK*.

Figure 16. PageMaker creates a new untitled publication and closes the original file. The page size is equal to the dimensions displayed in the *Spread size* text boxes in the *Build Booklet* dialog box. The page numbering sequence changes according to the type of *Layout* you chose. After PageMaker has created the new publication, you can still manually edit the publication. The master pages are blank as PageMaker has copied all these elements onto the individual pages.

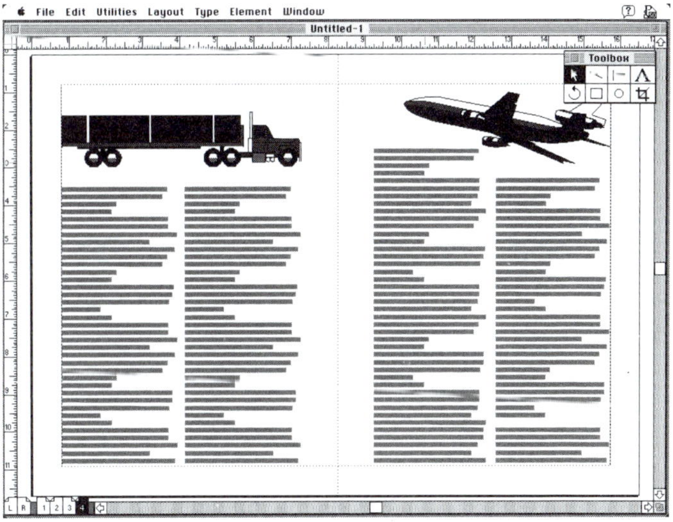

BULLETS AND NUMBERING

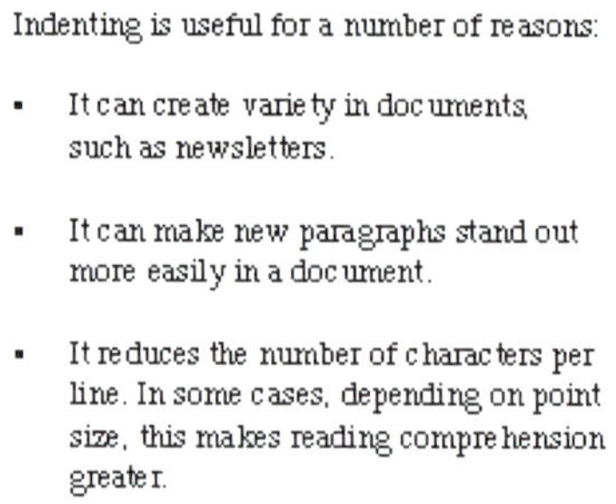

Figure 17. With the *Bullets and numbering* addition you can number paragraphs and add bullets or a specified character to any number of paragraphs in your publication.

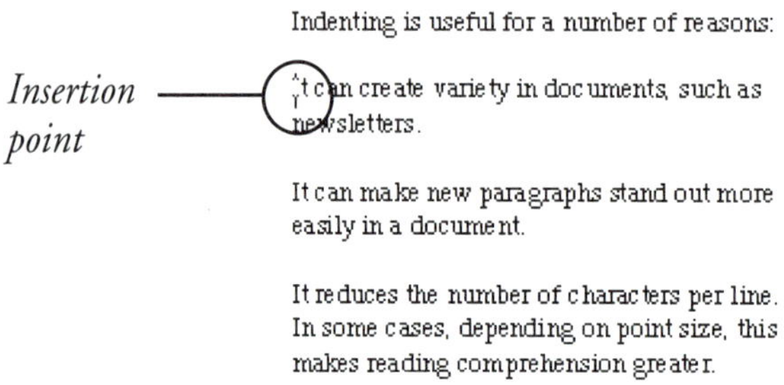

Figure 18. Before you select the *Bullets and numbering* addition, decide how many paragraphs you will be numbering and place the insertion point at the beginning of the first paragraph you want to mark.

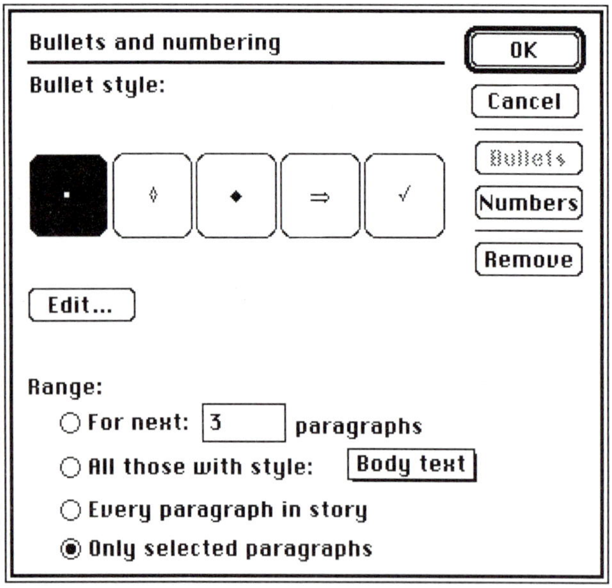

Figure 19. Select *Bullets and numbering* from the *Aldus Additions* submenu in the **Utilities** menu choose the *Bullet style* you want to use. The *Range* options in this dialog box are explained below:

- Enter the number of paragraphs to be marked in the *For next: x paragraphs* option;

or

- select the *All those with style* to number or mark only paragraphs to which you have applied a specific style;

or

- select *Every paragraph in story* to mark every paragraph in the story;

or

- select *Only selected paragraphs* if you only want to mark the paragraphs you have selected.

Figure 20. Click on the *Edit* button to change the bullet character you want to use. In the *Edit bullet* dialog box that appears, you can change the *Bullet character code* to a different ASCII character number, as well as the *Font* and the *Size* of the character. PageMaker displays your changed character in the *Example* box.

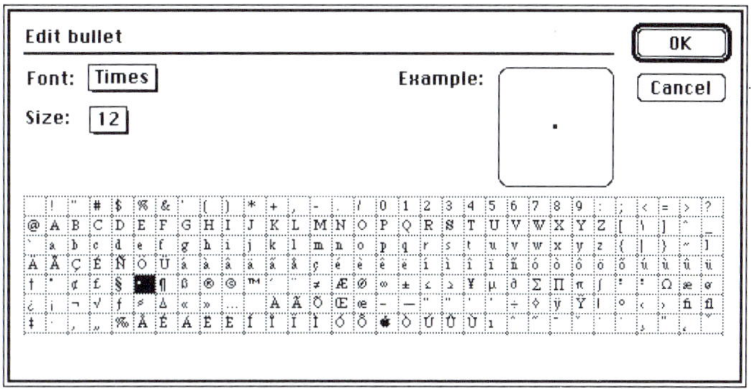

Figure 21. To number paragraphs in your story, click on the *Numbers* button to change to the options shown here. Choose a *Numbering style*, a *Separator* character, and the number you want to start at. The *Range* options are the same as they are for the *Bullets* option.

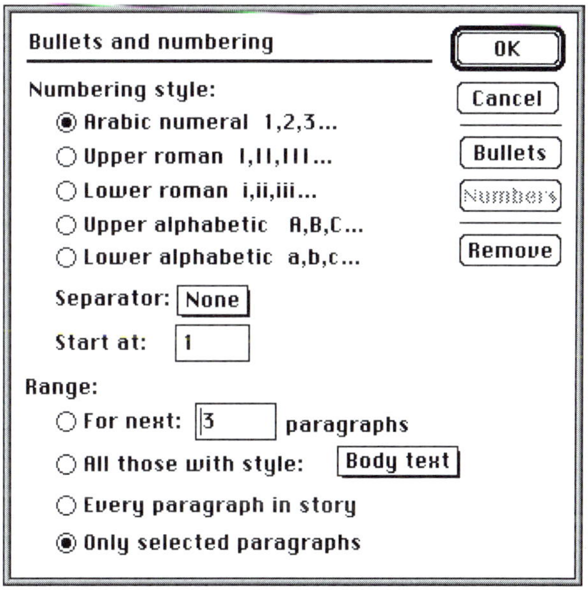

REMOVING BULLETS AND NUMBERING

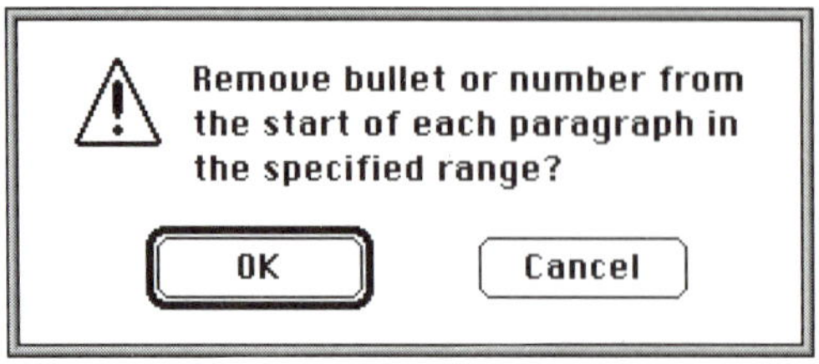

Figure 22. Click on the *Remove* button if you want to remove any bullets and numbering you have applied. You must have the insertion point in the text and specify a *Range* before doing this.

CREATE COLOR LIBRARY

Figure 23. The *Create color library* addition lets you name and save a group of colors in your color palette so that you can open this color library file at any time. To create your own color library, add the colors you need to the color palette by using the *Define colors* command (see Chapter 12 for more information).

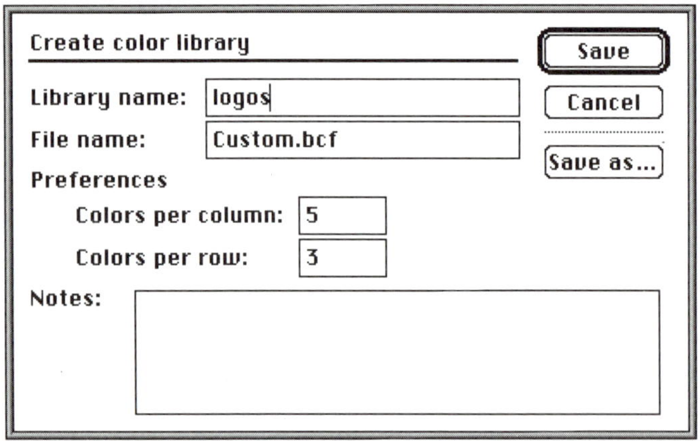

Figure 24. Next choose the *Create color library* addition to open the *Create color library* dialog box. Type in a name for the library, the number of colors per column and per row (maximum of 10 each way), and (optional) any comments about the library. Click on *Save* to save the library as a *bcf* file, or *Save as* to change its location.

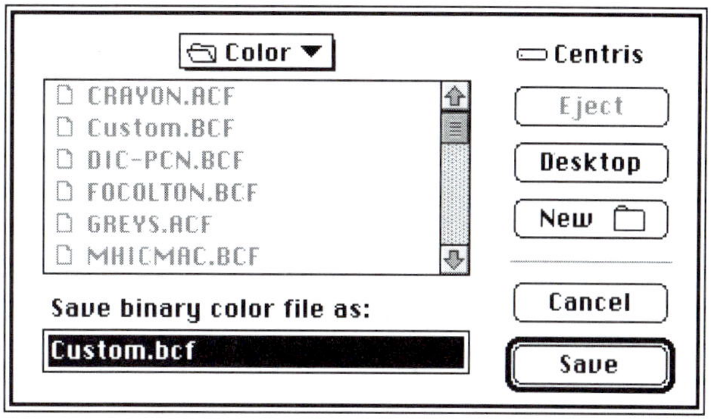

Figure 25. You must save all color files inside the *Color* folder. Once you click on *Save* in either dialog box, PageMaker saves the color library.

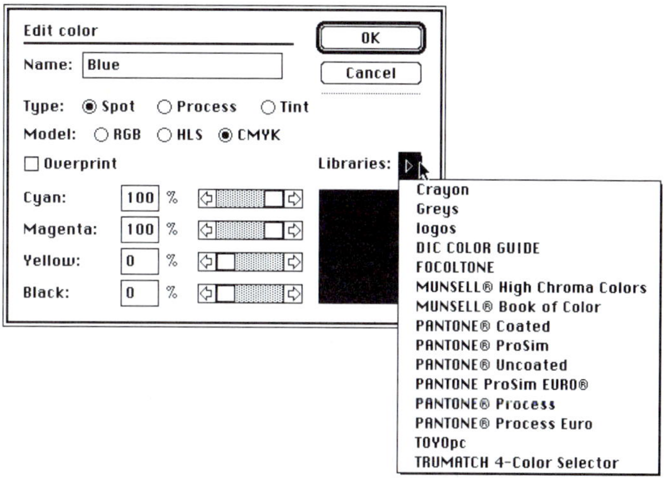

Figure 26. To access a color library in a different publication, click on the *New* button in the *Define colors* dialog box, select the library name from the list of libraries and click on *OK*.

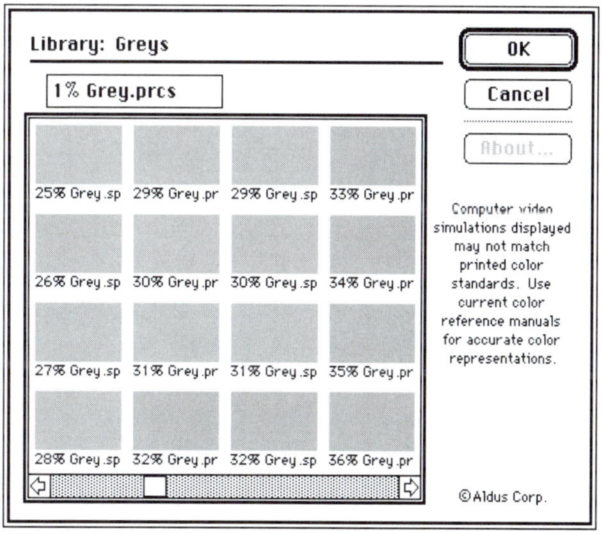

Figure 27. In the *Library* dialog box, drag-select the colors you want to add to the library palette and click on *OK* until you return to your document. When you display the Color palette, PageMaker adds the selected colors to the list.

Create Keyline

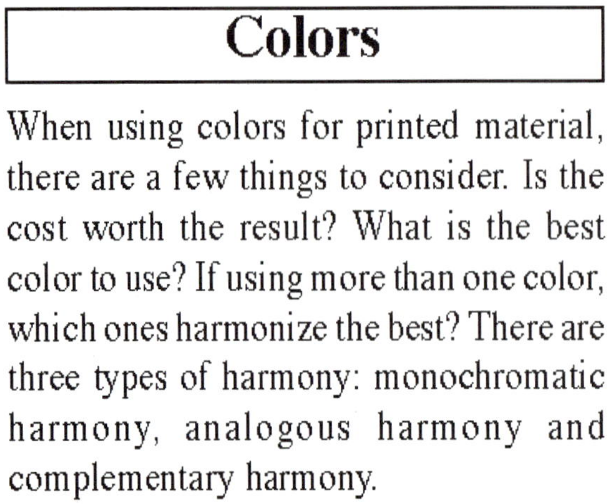
Colors

When using colors for printed material, there are a few things to consider. Is the cost worth the result? What is the best color to use? If using more than one color, which ones harmonize the best? There are three types of harmony: monochromatic harmony, analogous harmony and complementary harmony.

Figure 28. With the *Create keyline* addition, you can insert a box or a keyline around a selected object. A keyline proof is a bare-bones visual guide for the printer, indicating with boxes where text and graphics lie on the page and showing where to print different colors. You can choose to put the box either behind or in front of the selected object. You can define the distance the box is offset from the object and also set the fill and line attributes of the box. You can change the fill and line attributes even after you have inserted the box.

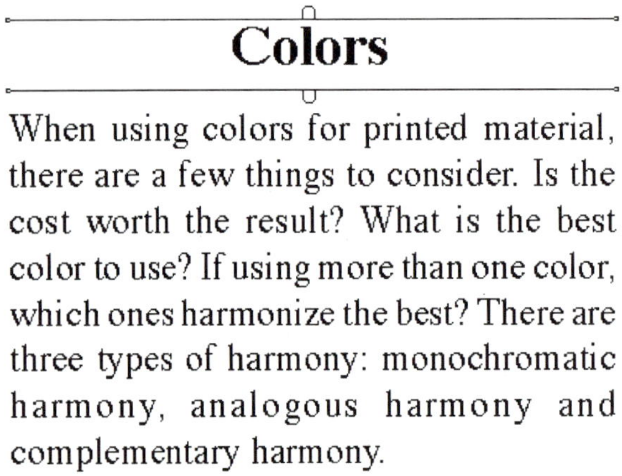
Colors

When using colors for printed material, there are a few things to consider. Is the cost worth the result? What is the best color to use? If using more than one color, which ones harmonize the best? There are three types of harmony: monochromatic harmony, analogous harmony and complementary harmony.

Figure 29. Select the object you want to box using the pointer tool and then select *Create keyline* from the *Aldus Additions* submenu. This opens the *Create keyline* dialog box.

Figure 30. Define the distance between the selected object and the box in points. Choose whether you would like the box to sit in front or behind the selected object. If you click on the *Attributes* button, you get the *Fill and line* dialog box where you can define the box's outline color and thickness, as well as its fill color. Turn the *Knock out under keyline* option on to define an overlap thickness (see Chapter 12 for more information on knockouts).

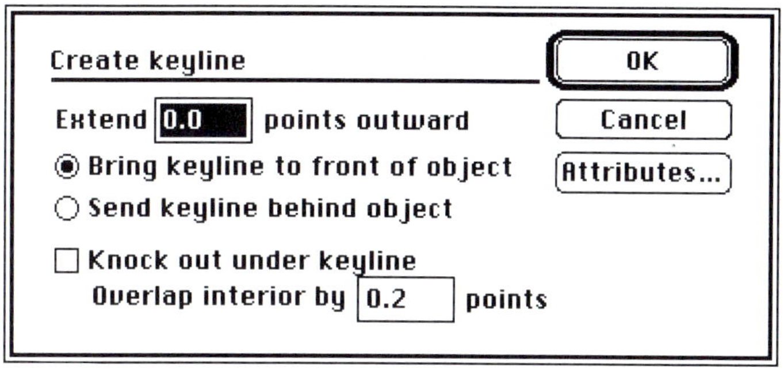

Display Pub Info

Figure 31. Use the *Display pub info* addition to display information about the currently opened file. PageMaker lets you save this as a text file.

You can choose to display fonts used and fonts available, links to graphics and text files, and the style names and their definitions. Do this by selecting or de-selecting the check boxes at the bottom of the dialog box.

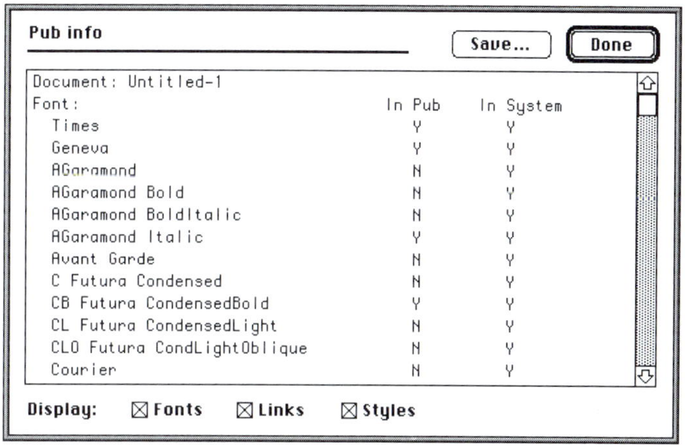

Figure 32. Click on the *Save* button to save the information as a text file. This opens the *Save As* dialog box. Type in a name or use the suggested name and then select *OK.* You can then load this into PageMaker and print it out.

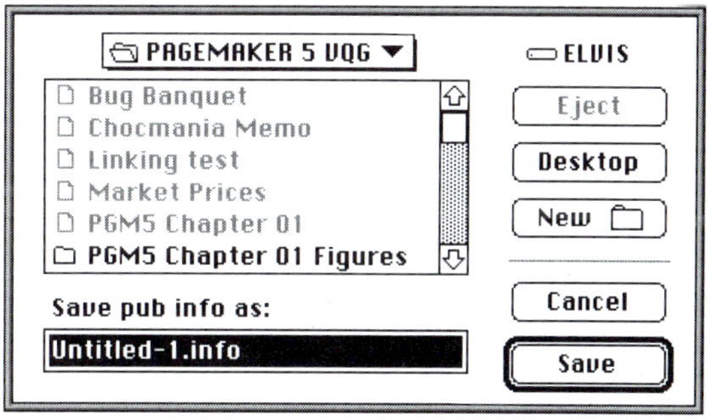

Display Story Info

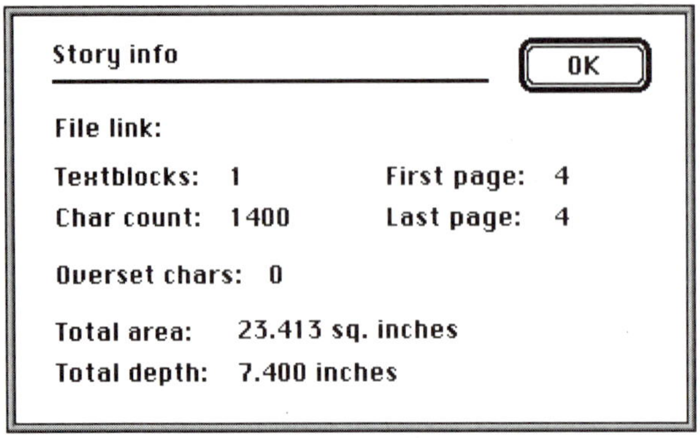

Figure 33. Use the *Display story info* addition to display information about the currently selected story. PageMaker opens the *Story info* dialog box, showing you the link to the file, the number of text blocks and characters, the page numbers on which you placed the story, any overset characters, and the total area and depth of the selected text file.

Display Textblock Info

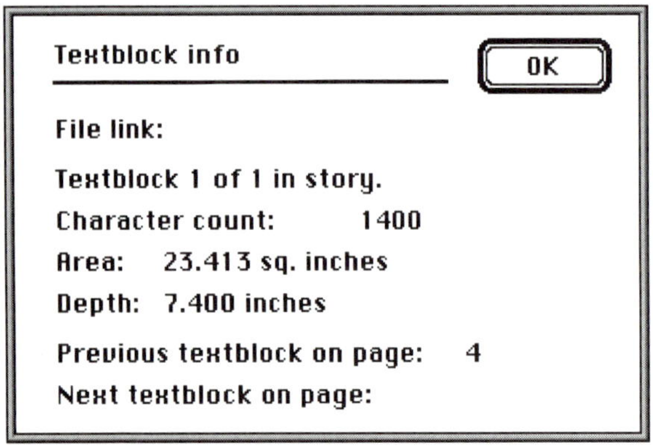

Figure 34. The *Display textblock info* addition gives much the same information as the *Display story info* addition, but only for the selected text block.

Drop Cap

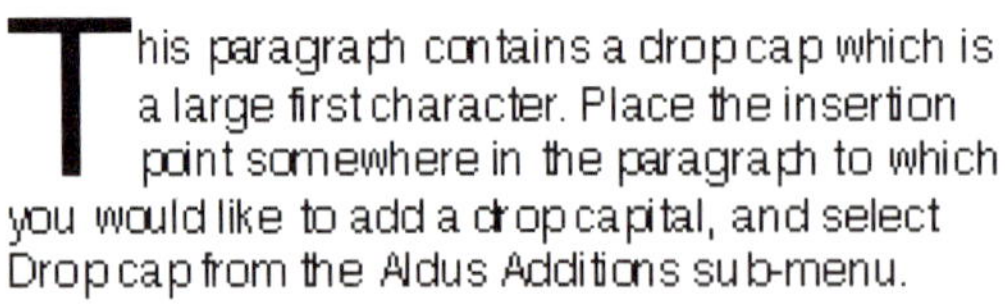

Figure 35. Use the *Drop cap* addition to create a large first letter of a paragraph, as shown here.

Figure 36. Place the insertion point somewhere in the paragraph you would like to add a drop capital to, and select *Drop cap* from the *Aldus Additions* submenu.

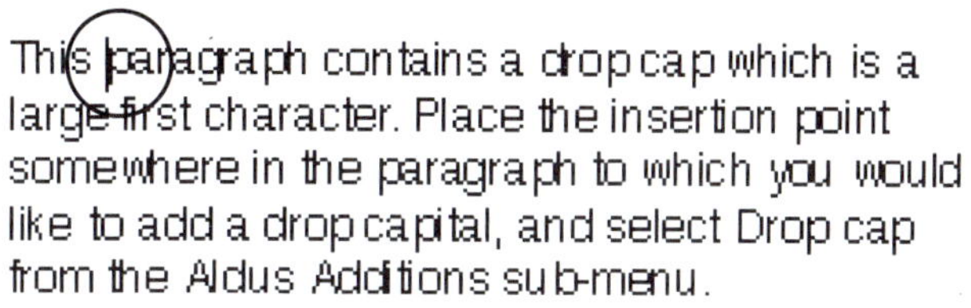

Figure 37. In the *Drop cap* dialog box, you can change the number of lines for the capital size and which paragraphs to use by using the *Prev* and *Next* buttons. You can preview the drop capital by clicking on the *Apply* button; you can remove a drop cap with the *Remove* button.

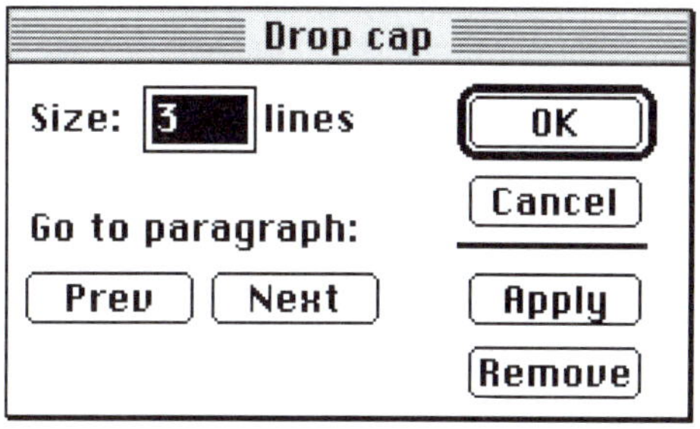

Edit Tracks

Figure 38. The *Edit Tracks* addition allows you to customize the tracking options you have in the *Track* command in the **Type** menu. These commands are *No track, Very loose, Loose, Normal, Tight,* and *Very tight.* (See the **Type** menu in Chapter 4 for more information on these commands.)

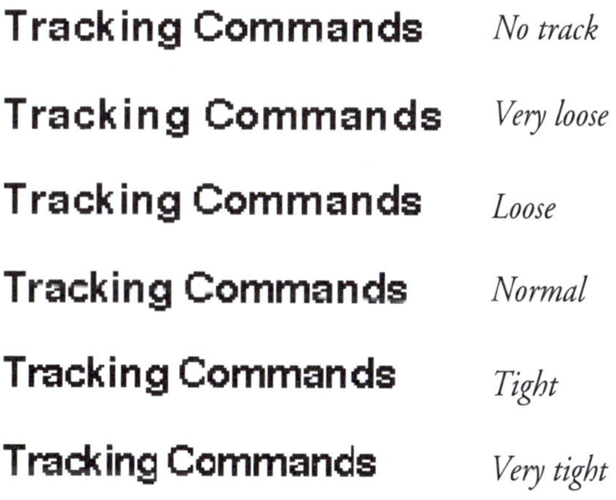

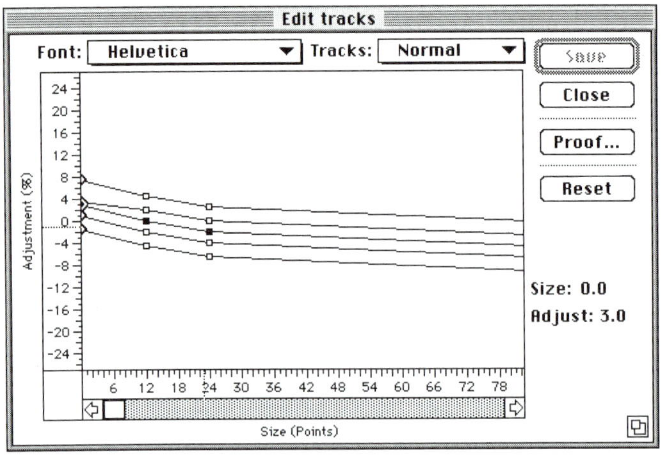

Figure 39. To edit one of these tracks, select the *Edit Tracks* addition and then select the font and track that you want to edit from their respective pop-up menus. Alternatively, you can click on a track line to select it. In this example, we are editing the font *Helvetica* and the track *Normal*.

Each line represents one track. *Very loose* is the top line and *Very tight* is the bottom one. The steepness of the line determines how much the letter spacing is tightened or loosened. A flat line, for example, keeps the spacing proportionally the same at all sizes.

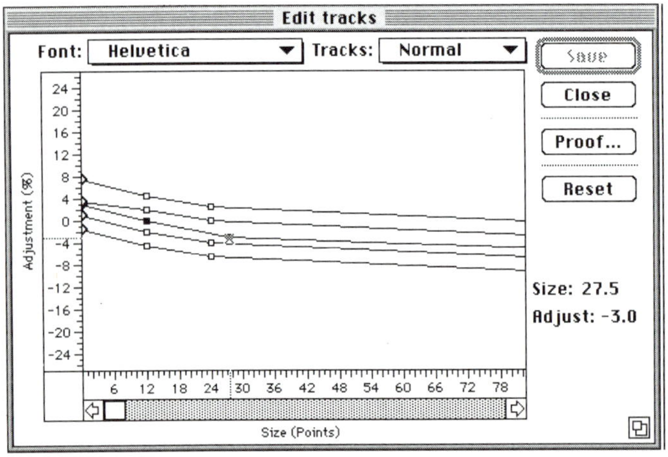

Figure 40. To adjust the tracking values, drag a handle to a new position. The values of the handle you have selected appear in the bottom-right of the dialog box as you move it. In this example, we are moving a handle of the *Normal* tracking line.

To add a track handle, hold down the Option key and click on a track line. To delete one, hold down the Option key and click on a handle you want to delete.

Figure 41. If you want to view a sample of the new tracking values you have created, click on the *Proof* button in the *Edit Tracks* dialog box. Select the tracks and the point sizes to include and whether you want the short or long text sample. You can change the display text in the text box by selecting it and typing in the text you want.

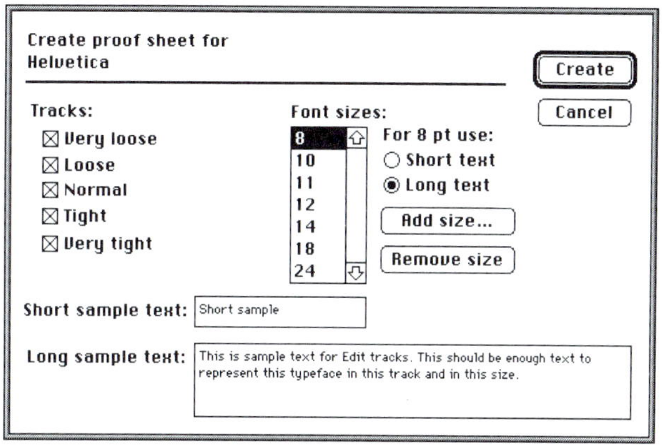

After you select *Create* in the *Create proof sheet* dialog box, PageMaker creates an untitled publication with the sample text, which shows you the changed tracking values.

Expert Kerning

Figure 42. The *Expert kerning* addition lets you finely adjust the letter-spacing between character pairs.

Note: You can use Expert kerning only on PostScript Type 1 fonts that are installed on your computer. We recommend that you use this addition only on small blocks of text, as it can be time consuming.

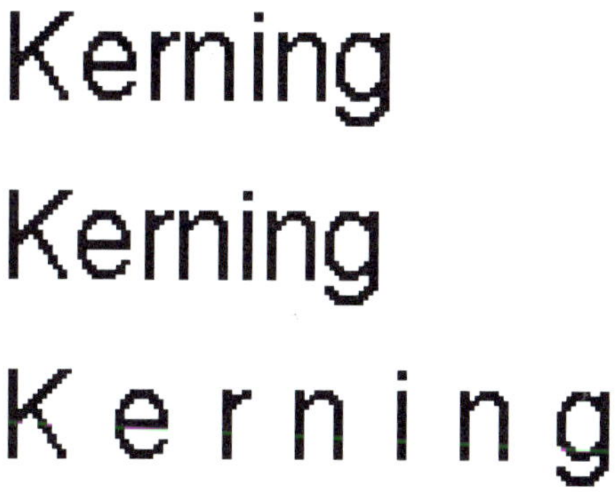

Kerning strength of 2 applied

Kerning strength of 0 applied

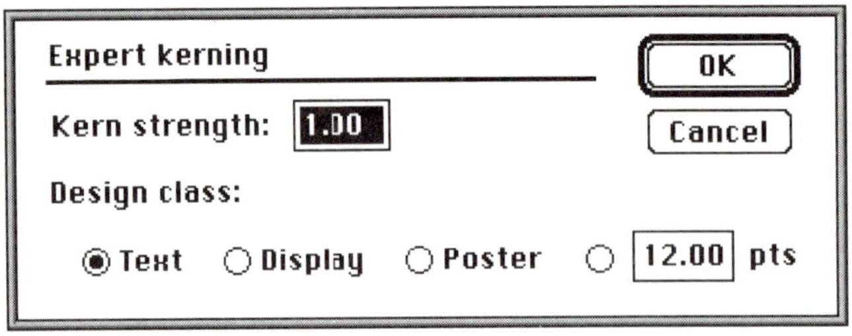

Figure 43. To kern your highlighted text, choose a kerning strength between 0.0 and 2.0 in the *Expert kerning* dialog box. The higher the value, the tighter the kerning. If you don't know the source of the master design of the font, click on the *Text* option in the *Design class* section.

Find Overset Text

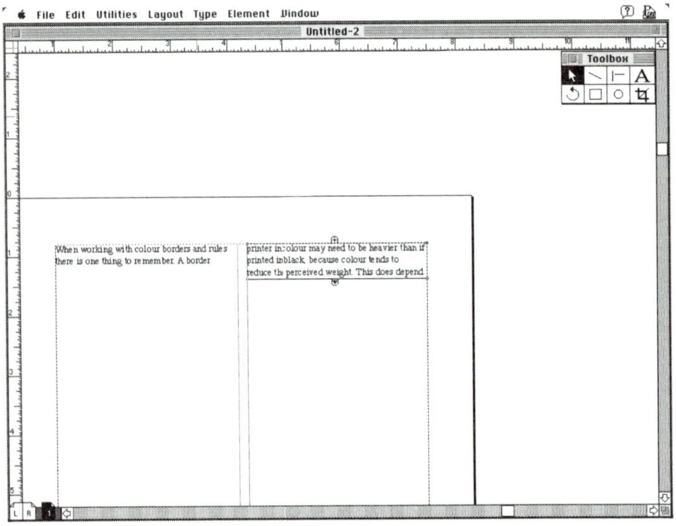

Figure 44. Use the *Find overset text* addition to find any stories which still have unplaced text. When you select this addition, PageMaker finds and selects any text blocks that contain unplaced text. You can then manually flow the text into the next available space.

If there is more than one story with unplaced text, select the command again until PageMaker has found all unplaced stories.

List Styles Used

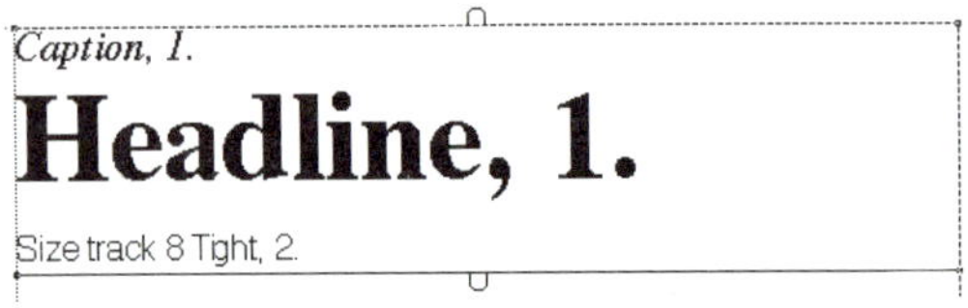

Figure 45. Use the *List styles used* addition to list all the styles you have used in selected story. You must select a text block of the story whose styles you want to view. PageMaker displays the styles you have used, followed by the number of paragraphs in that style.

Open Stories

Figure 46. Use the *Open stories* addition to open all the stories in the current publication in cascaded story windows. This allows you to view and edit all stories at once.

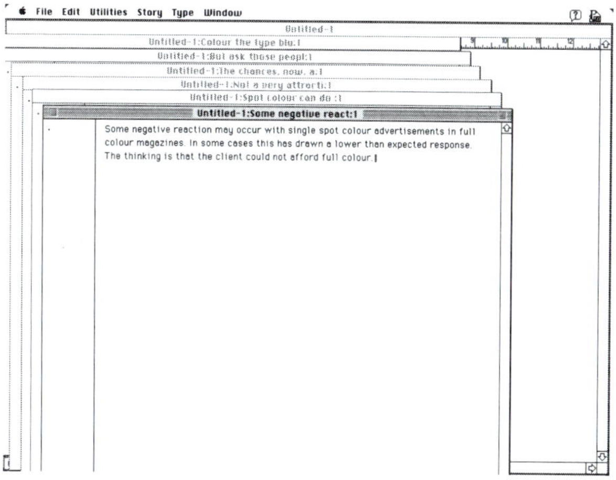

Open Template

Figure 47. The *Open template* addition lets you choose a document type from a number of predesigned templates for common publishing tasks. An untitled publication that contains preformatted components then opens. All you have to do is add your own text and graphics.

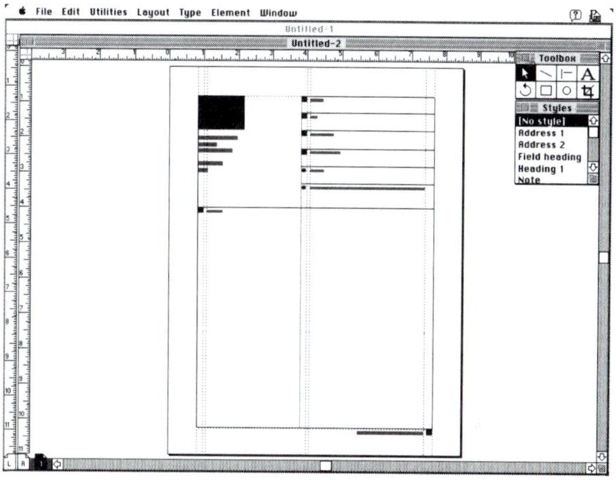

Figure 48. Select the document type from the *Templates* file list. As you do this, a thumbnail of the document appears in the *Preview* box. You also have the option of changing the *Language* and the *Page size*. In most cases, PageMaker opens an untitled publication after you click on *OK*.

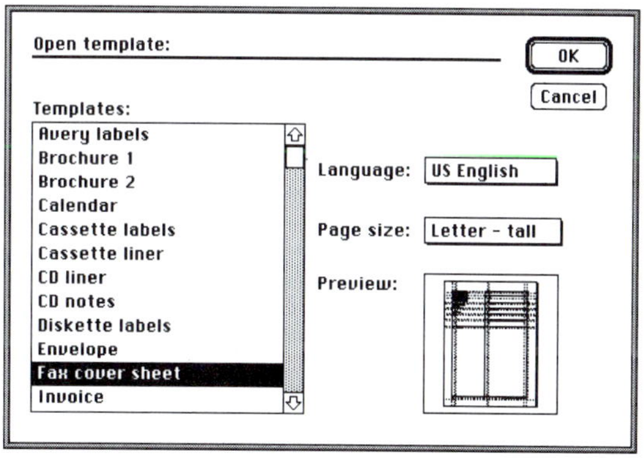

In some cases, PageMaker prompts you for more information before it opens the publication.

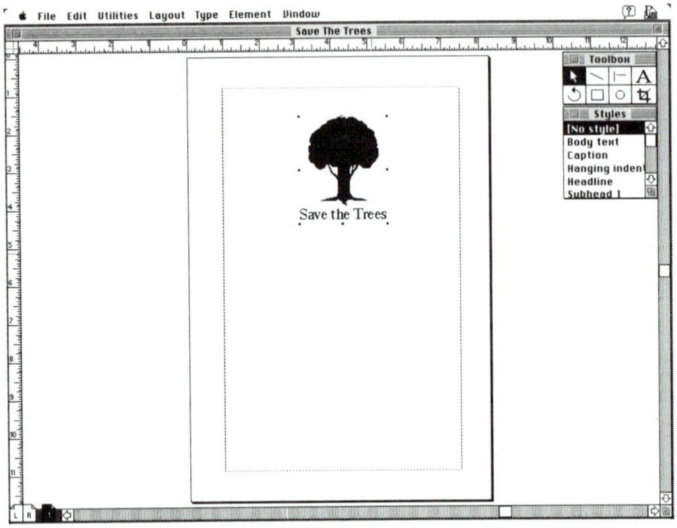

PS Group It

Figure 49. The *PS Group it* addition lets you combine separate objects so you can manipulate them as one object. When you group the objects, Page-Maker converts them to an Encapsulated PostScript (EPS) graphic which replaces the grouped objects.

You can resize, stretch, rotate, and crop grouped objects as well as adding grouped objects to other grouped objects.

Figure 50. To group objects, select the objects to be grouped with the pointer tool and select the *PS Group it* addition.

PS Ungroup It

If you want to ungroup any objects you have grouped together, use the *PS Ungroup it* addition to return them to individual objects again. Select the grouped object and then the *PS Ungroup it* addition; PageMaker converts the EPS graphic file back to its original format.

Note: If you have manipulated a group of objects and later ungrouped it, the individual objects remain in the same position but revert to their original attributes.

Running Headers/Footers

Figure 51. The *Running headers/footers* addition lets you create headers and footers based on the content of the text on the page. For example, if you are working on a glossary of terms, you can use this addition to add headers and footers that match the first or last term on the page.

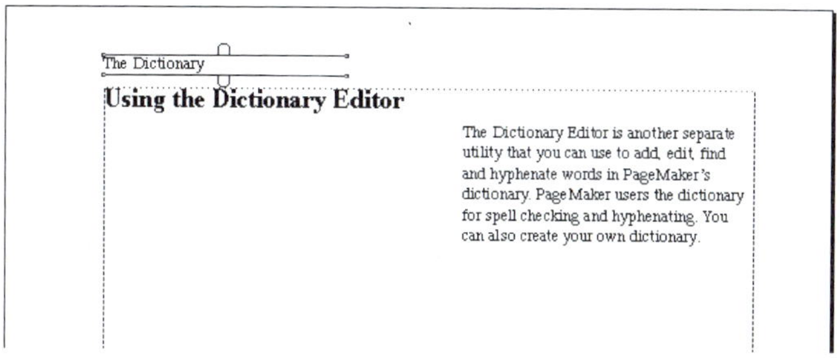

Figure 52. Select the text block on the page and then select the *Running headers/footers* addition. The *First instance* and *Last instance* options let you choose whether PageMaker includes specified text from the beginning or the end of the first or last paragraph (of the selected style).

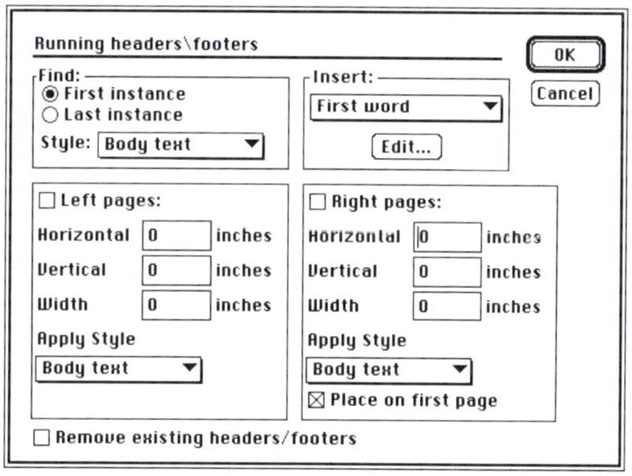

You can have PageMaker search for a specific style from the *Styles* submenu or you can select *None* so that PageMaker searches only for specific text. Next choose an option from the *Insert* pop-up menu (or click on *Edit* to customize a search pattern—see Figure 54).

Note: To define both headers and footers, you must use this addition twice and specify different Horizontal and Vertical positions.

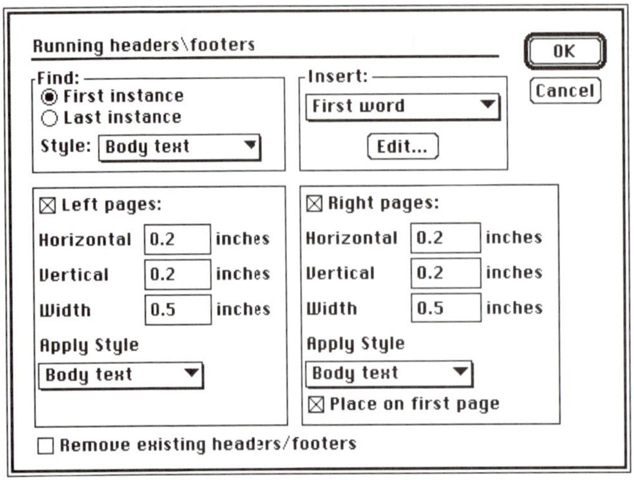

Figure 53. Turn the *Left pages* or the *Right pages* option on (or both). Enter the *Horizontal* or *Vertical* value where you want the headers or footers to be. This is measured from the zero point on the rulers. Also enter a *Width* value for the width of the header or footer text block and choose a style. You can also choose a style from the *Apply style* pop-up menu that PageMaker can apply to the headers and footers.

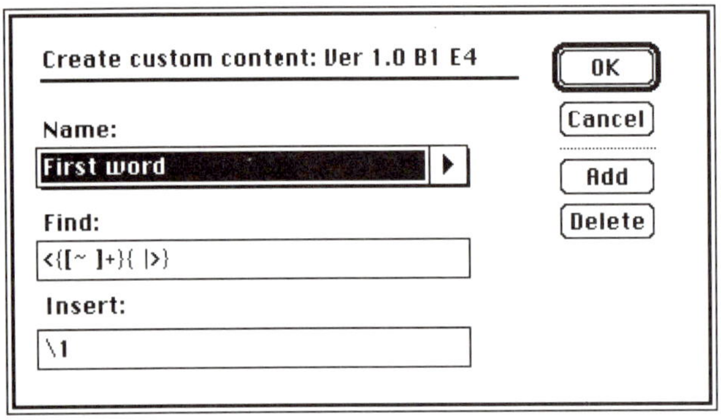

Figure 54. If you click on the *Edit* button, the *Create custom content* dialog box appears. You can type in specific text in the *Name* text box.

You can edit an existing search pattern or add a new pattern by clicking on the *Edit* button in the *Running headers/footers* dialog box.

DELETING HEADERS AND FOOTERS

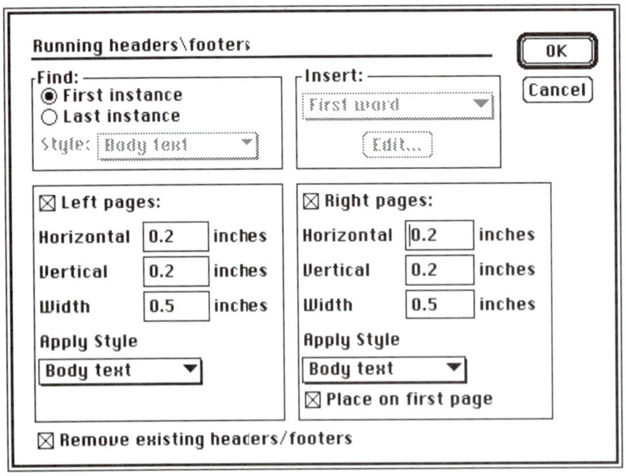

Figure 55. Select the first text block from where you started the headers or footers and choose the *Running headers/footers* addition. Click on the *Remove existing headers/footers* command and select *OK*. PageMaker removes all headers and footers.

Run Script

The *Run script* addition lets you select a script for PageMaker to execute. A script is a set of instructions, written in PageMaker's script language, that performs steps for which you would normally use the mouse or the keyboard.

Scripts are similar to macros you often use in word processors to automate time-consuming and often-performed tasks. There are two ways you can run a script. You can run a script created in PageMaker or you can run a script created in another program and saved as a text-only file.

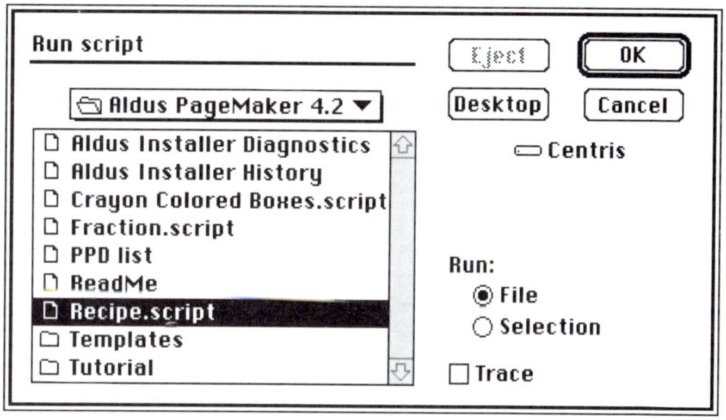

Figure 56. To run a script you have created in PageMaker (use the *PageMaker 5.0 Script Language Guide* for information on how to write your own script), select the script text in the publication with the pointer tool and then select the *Run script* addition. You can also run a part of the script that you have selected with the text tool. In the *Run script* dialog box click on the *Run selection* button.

If you select the *Trace* option before you run a script, a window opens and you can scroll through the selected text to review each step or you can stop PageMaker carrying out the script as it is running.

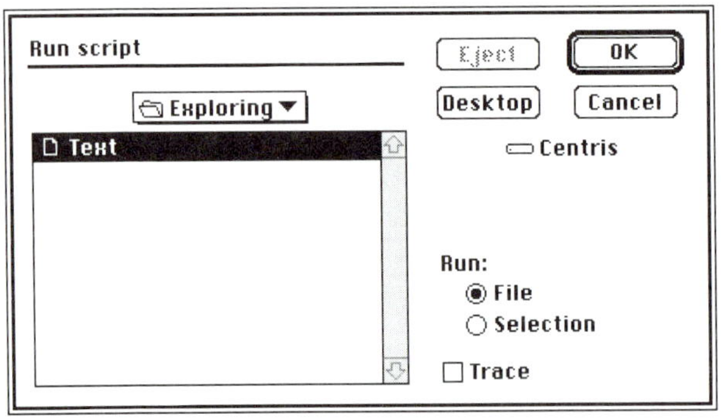

Figure 57. To run a script that has been saved as a text-only file, you can place the text in your publication and use the first method described. You could also find the text file within the *Run script* dialog box and click on *OK*.

Sort Pages

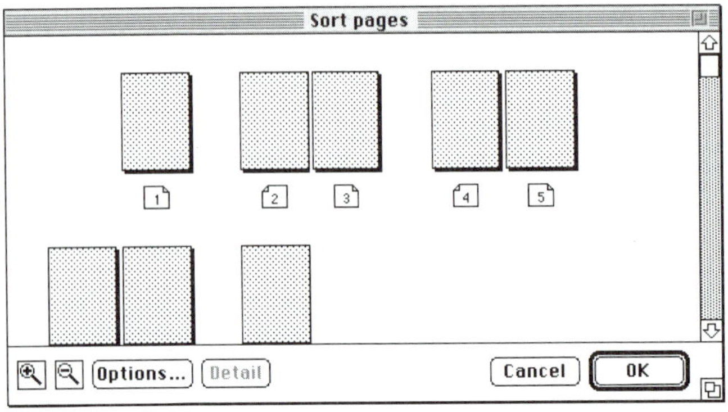

Figure 58. The *Sort pages* addition lets you arrange pages in your current publication by moving thumbnail representations of your pages into the order you would like. If you are re-arranging a double-sided document, you may need to manually adjust text and graphics to accommodate for a left page becoming a right page.

PageMaker does not change the way text is threaded in a number of text blocks if you sort pages in this way.

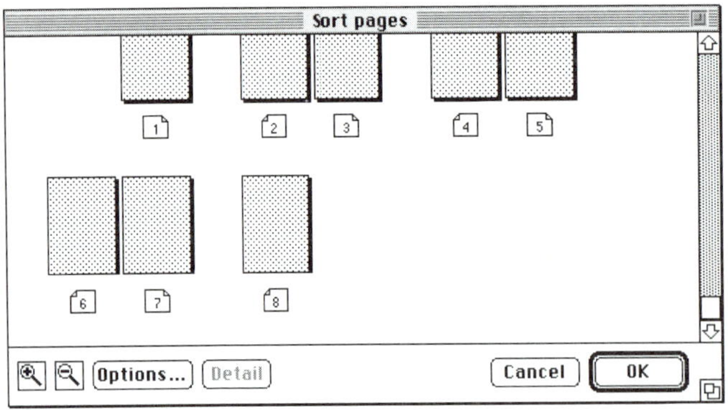

Figure 59. Select the page or pages you want to move (use the Shift key to select multiple pages, use the Command key to select one page of two facing pages), drag the pages to the left or the right of the page where you want to move them and release the mouse. Here we have moved pages 2 and 3 to where 6 and 7 were. When you release the mouse, PageMaker dims the icons below the original page and places new icons to the left of them, indicating that you have put a new page there.

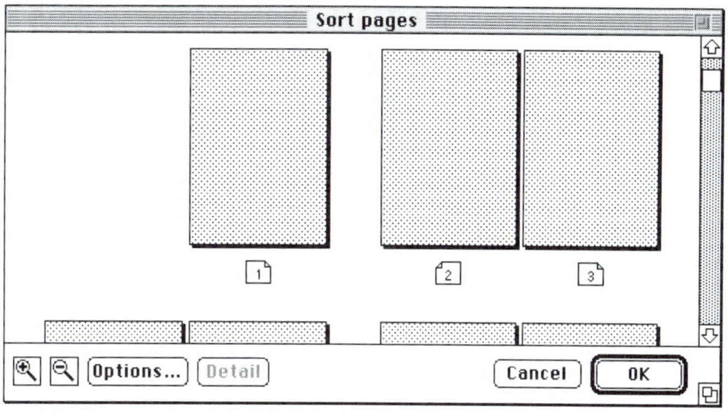

Figure 60. Click on the *magnifying* icon to enlarge the thumbnails. You can enlarge them to three levels. Click on the *reduction* icon the same number of times you clicked on the magnifying icon to bring the thumbnails back to the original size.

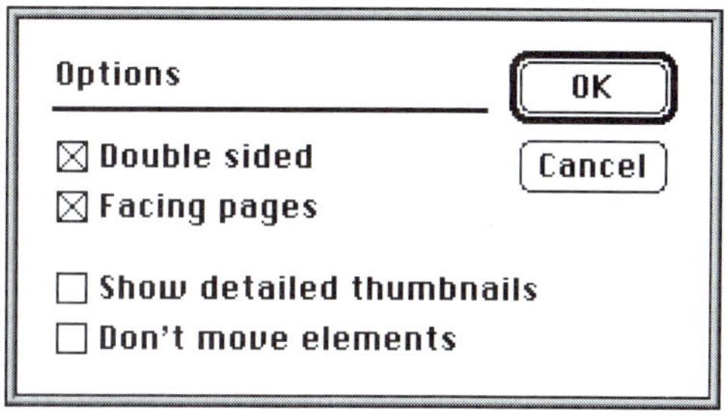

Figure 61. Click on the *Options* button in the *Sort pages* dialog box to open the *Options* dialog box. Here you can change a double-sided document to a single-sided document and vice versa.

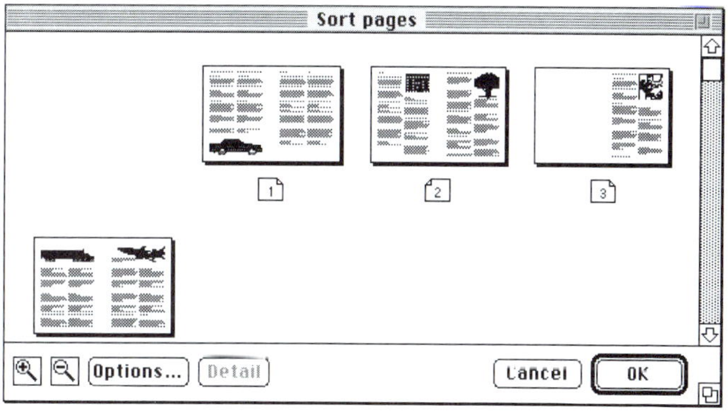

Figure 62. Select the *Show detailed thumbnails* option to view the elements of the pages more clearly. Select the *Do not move elements* option if you do not want PageMaker to adjust elements relative to the inside and outside margins of a double-sided publication.

Once you have made all the necessary changes, select the *OK* button in the relevant dialog boxes and PageMaker automatically sorts the pages of your publication into the new order.

Traverse Textblocks

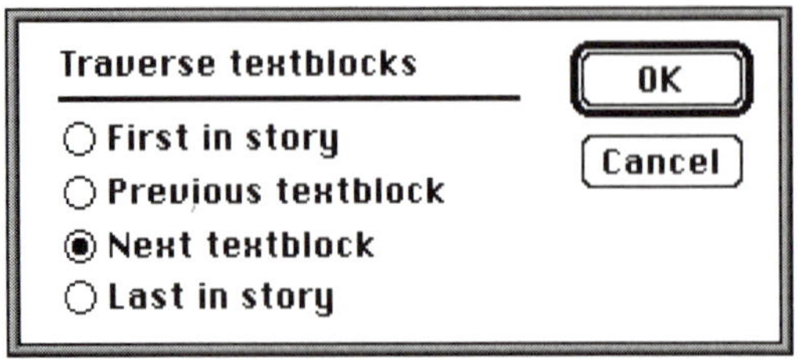

Figure 63. Select the *Traverse textblocks* addition to find the first, previous, next, or last text block of the selected text block in a story. This addition is handy if you are working with a large publication with a number of different stories, and you need to find a specific part of a threaded text file.

Update PPD

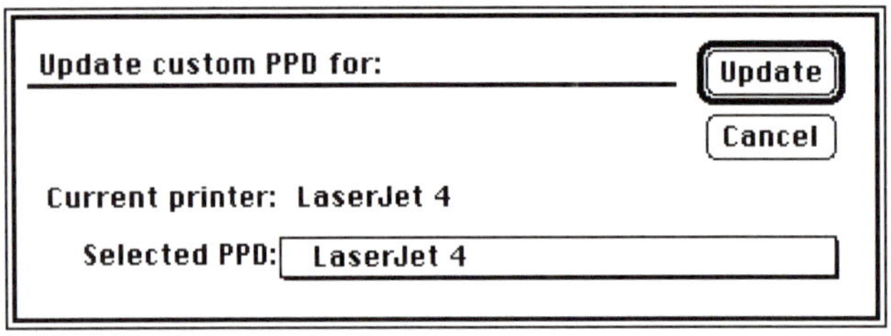

Figure 64. The *Update PPD* command in the *Aldus Additions* submenu of the **Utilities** menu lets you update your PostScript printer descriptions (PPDs). When this dialog box appears, you can select a PPD from the *Selected PPD* pop-up menu. You then click on the *Update* button.

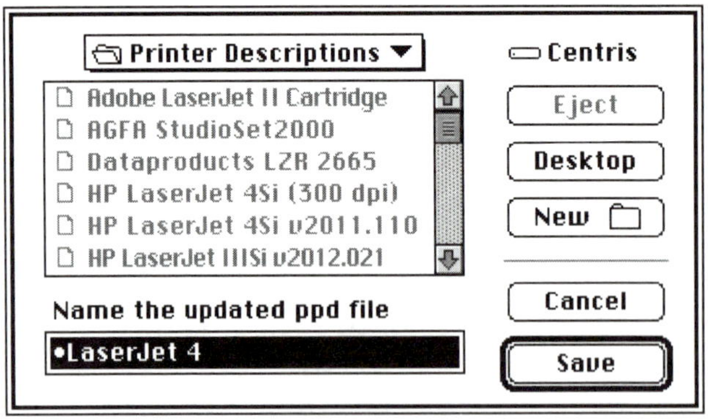

Figure 65. When this dialog box appears, you can save the changed printer description under a different name. Click on *Save* to save the printer description.

PageMaker Defaults

10

Application and Publication Defaults

PageMaker is shipped with preset options for many of its settings. These may differ between US, International English, and other foreign language versions. PageMaker includes two kinds of defaults: *application* and *publication*. *Application* defaults are wide-ranging and apply to every new publication that you open. You can set them up before you enter a new or existing publication. *Publication* defaults apply to the currently open publication only.

APPLICATION DEFAULTS

If you want to have the same settings for every new PageMaker file, use *application* defaults. For example, the number of columns by default is one. If you want to change this to three columns, you alter this before you open a new PageMaker file. You can select all menus (but not all commands) in PageMaker before you open or start a new document (see Figure 1).

Figure 1. To change any *application* defaults, open PageMaker by double-clicking on the PageMaker icon (or choose *Close* from the **File** menu if you have a PageMaker publication open). You will then be at the PageMaker 5 window. Normally, at this level, you select *New* for a new publication or *Open* to open a previously saved publication.

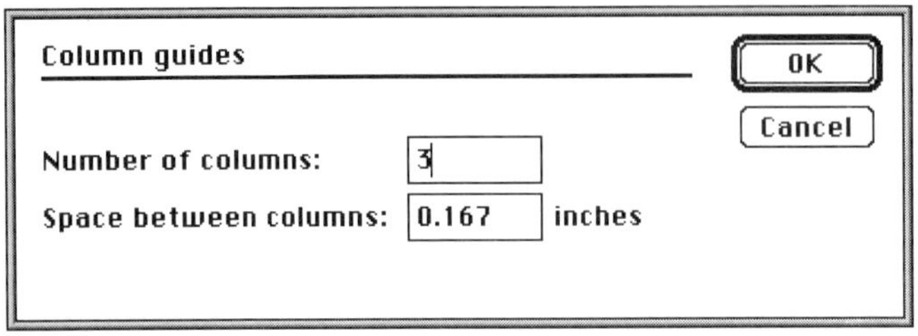

Figure 2. Before selecting *New* or *Open*, you can change any default setting, which then applies to all new publications until you change it again in the PageMaker 5 window. Here we have changed the *Column guides* option to 3.

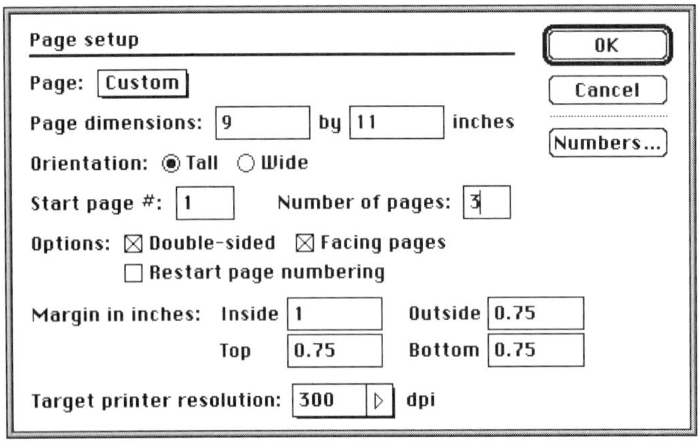

Figure 3. We have set the page size to *Custom,* the orientation to *Tall* and the number of pages at 3 through the *Page setup* command in the **File** menu. All new documents you create now open with these parameters as standard.

To determine which options you can set and change at the PageMaker window, check each menu in turn. You can select and alter all commands in black (except of course *New, Open* and *Quit*).

Figure 4. You cannot select the commands that appear in gray at first. All but one of the commands in the **Edit** menu is grayed out. Such commands are not associated with default settings, as you apply them when you are using a publication.

PUBLICATION DEFAULTS

Publication defaults are different from *application* defaults in that you set them up inside an open publication; they apply to that publication only. (You can use publication defaults to override application defaults.) For example, you may want to change the default text option for typing text within a single publication. Normally this is set by default at 12 point Times.

Figure 5. In this example, the next time we draw a graphic, it will have a line thickness of 4 points.

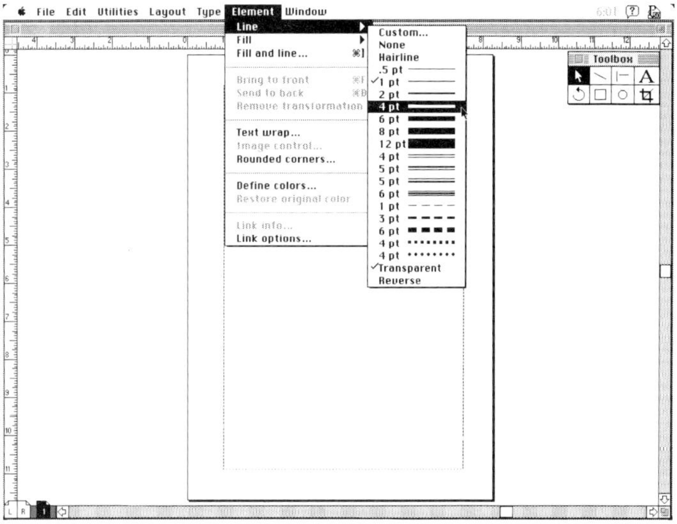

Figure 6. From inside a publication, we are adjusting the default text type to 12 point Palatino. Again, you can adjust any default setting in this way. When you do this, ensure that you have selected the pointer tool and you have no text or graphics selected on the page.

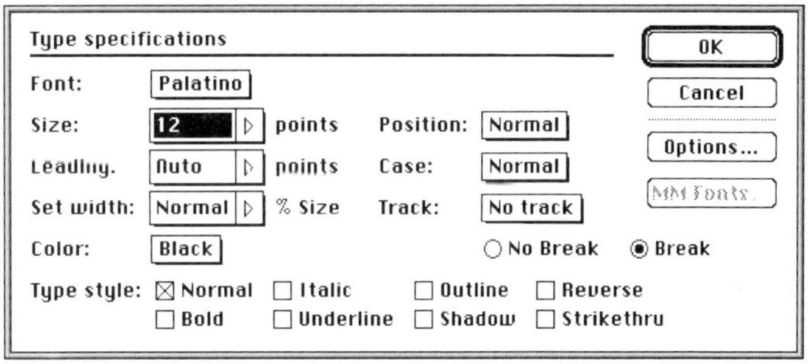

Using Styles 11

What is a Style?

A style is a set of formatting attributes that you apply to text. When you use styles, you save time by applying many formatting changes to indicated text simultaneously. You name the style and then specify its attributes. The style name then appears both in the *Style* submenu in the **Type** menu and the Style palette. This creates consistency within the publication and between publications, as you can copy styles from one publication to another.

Figure 1. PageMaker provides a number of default styles, containing text and paragraph attribute descriptions that you can apply to text. To access these styles, choose *Style palette* from the **Window** menu.

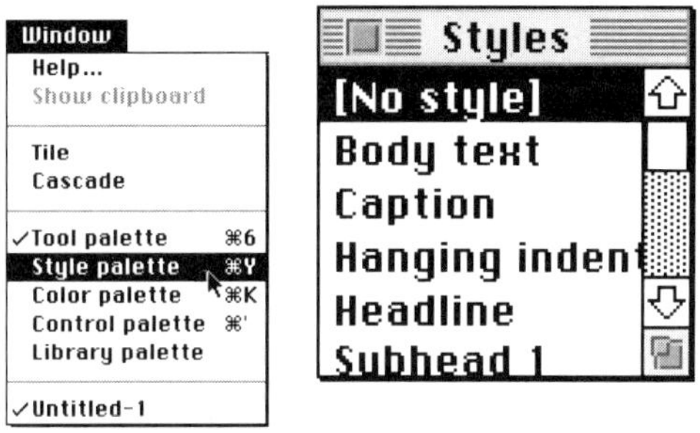

APPLYING STYLES

Figure 2. The result of applying a style to text means that you apply all the text and paragraph attribute descriptions contained in the style to the text. In this figure we have placed the insertion point in the top paragraph (the heading). If we click on the *Headline* style in the Style palette, we apply this style to the whole paragraph. Figure 3 shows the immediate result.

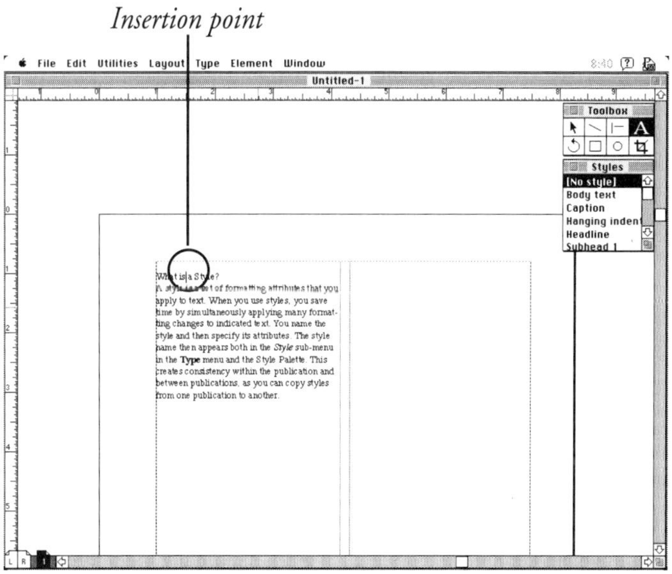

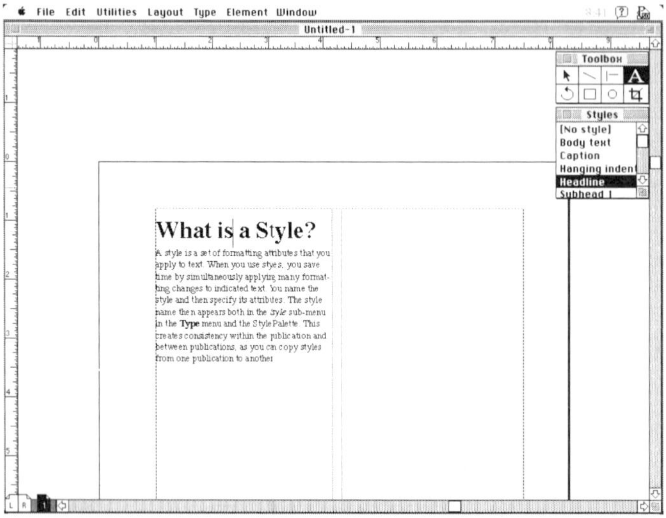

Figure 3. The paragraph now takes on the text attributes defined under the *Headline* style.

Note: You need only place the insertion point in the paragraph you want to apply the style to—you do not have to highlight it.

CREATING STYLES

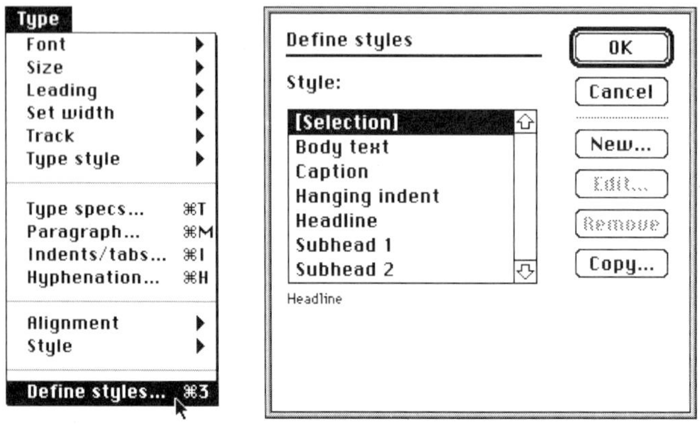

Figure 4. You create new styles by selecting *Define styles* from the **Type** menu, or by pressing the Command key and clicking on a style name in the Style palette. This opens the *Define styles* dialog box. The *Style* list contains all the current style names.

If you click on a style name in the list, its specifications appear at the bottom of the dialog box. Click on the *New* button to create a new style. The *Edit style* dialog box (Figure 5) appears.

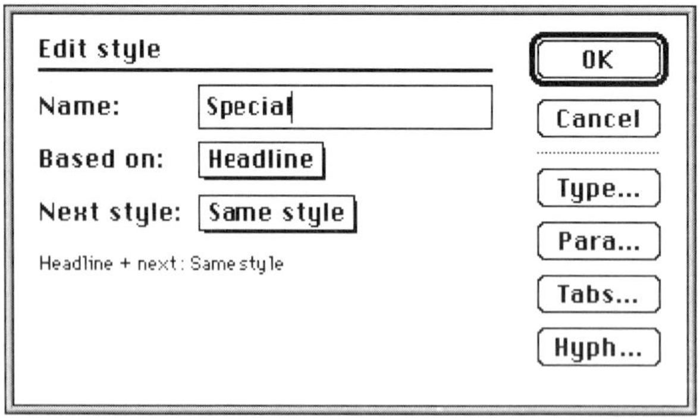

Figure 5. Type the name of the new style in the *Name* text box. We have typed in the word *Special.* The four buttons to the right, *Type, Para, Tabs,* and *Hyph,* let you set a variety of text and paragraph specifications for any new style. Click on the button you require. See Figures 6 through 9 for more details.

Figure 6. You get the *Type specifications* dialog box by clicking on the *Type* button in the *Edit style* dialog box. Choose the attributes you need and click on *OK*. You are then returned to the *Edit Style* dialog box. See Chapter 4 for more information on the *Type specifications* dialog box.

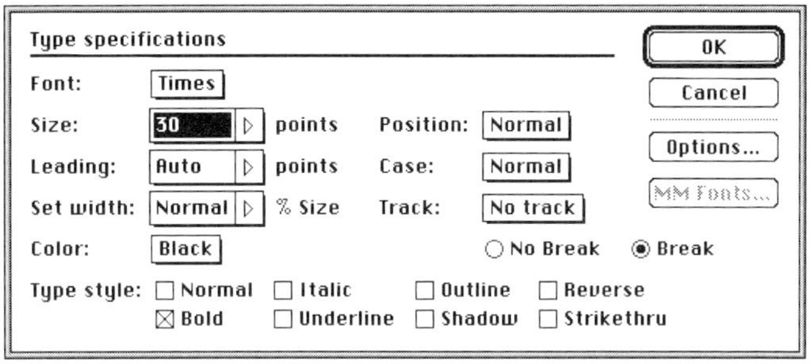

Figure 7. You get the *Paragraph specifications* dialog box by clicking on the *Para* button in the *Edit style* dialog box. Clicking on *OK* after you make any changes returns you to the *Edit style* dialog box. The options available in the *Paragraph specifications* dialog box are explained in Chapter 4.

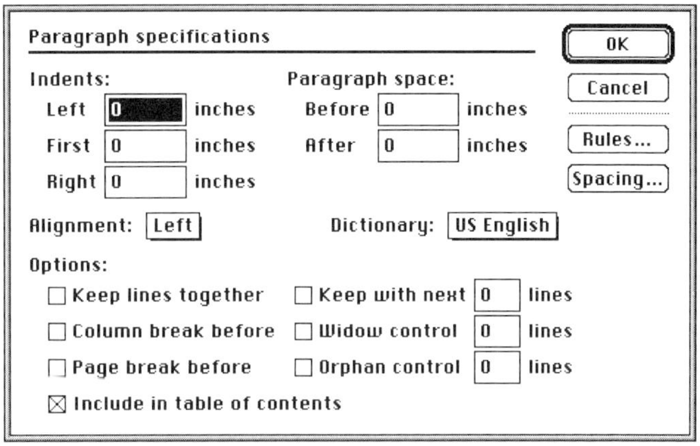

Figure 8. You can change tabs and indents in the *Indents/tabs* dialog box, which you get by clicking on the *Tabs* button in the *Edit style* dialog box. Once you have made changes, clicking on *OK* returns you to the *Edit style* dialog box. The *Indents/tabs* dialog box is explained in Chapter 4.

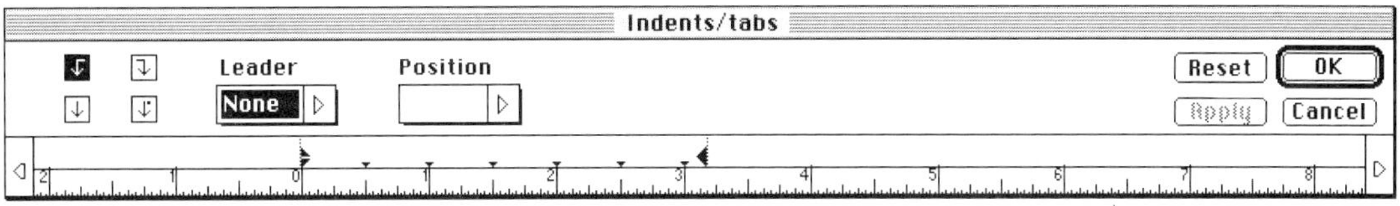

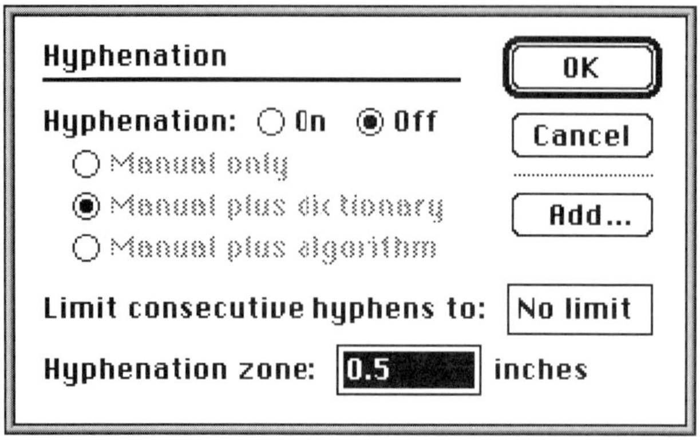

Figure 9. You open the *Hyphenation* dialog box by clicking on the *Hyph* button in the *Edit style* dialog box. Once you have made changes, clicking on *OK* returns you to *Edit style* dialog box. The *Hyphenation* dialog box is discussed in Chapter 4.

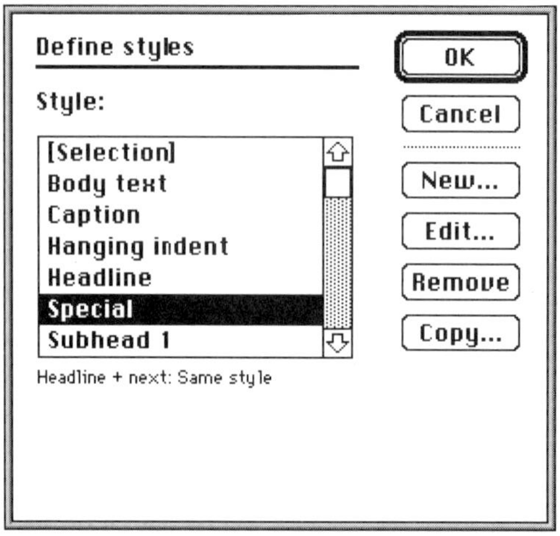

Figure 10. This is the way the *Define styles* dialog box appears after the changes shown in Figures 6 through 9. PageMaker includes and highlights the style *Special* in the list. PageMaker displays the attributes we gave to the *Special* style below the list box.

EDITING STYLES

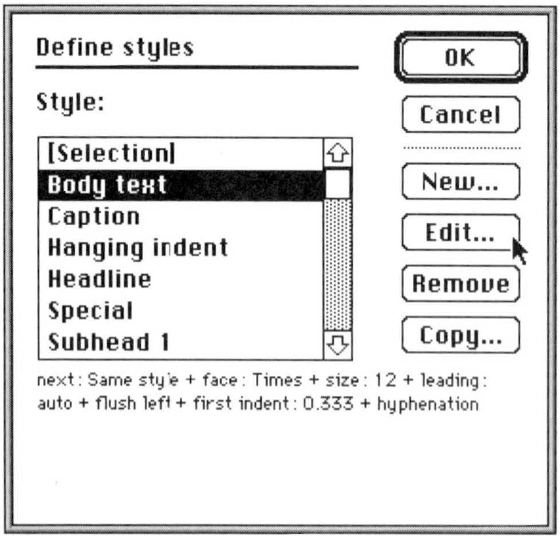

Figure 11. To edit a style, open the *Define styles* dialog box, highlight the style you need to edit, and click on the *Edit* button as shown here.

Figure 12. The *Edit style* dialog box opens, since we selected *Body text* in Figure 11, the dialog box automatically displays this style. You can now edit the options described in Figures 6 through 9.

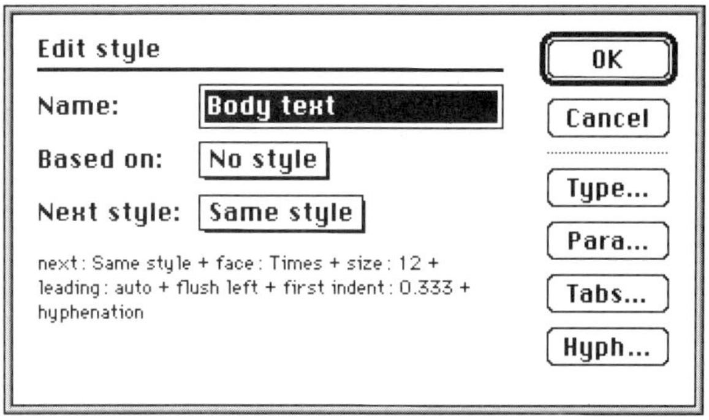

Figure 13. If you change the attributes of selected text (without using the *Define styles* command) to which you have applied a style, PageMaker adds a "+" next to the style name in the Style palette.

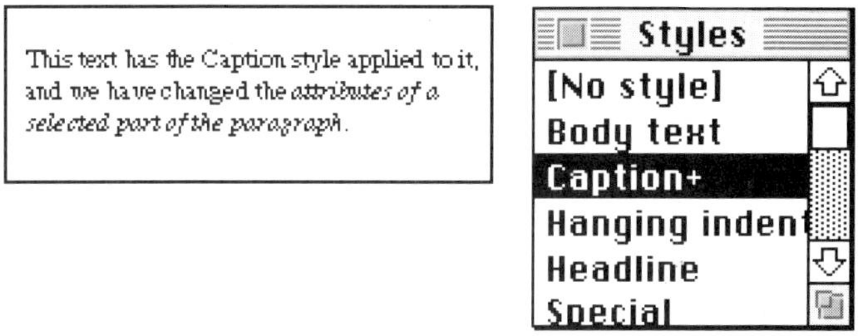

Removing a Style

Figure 14. To remove a style, select the style name in the *Define styles* dialog box (in our case *Special*) and click on *Remove.*

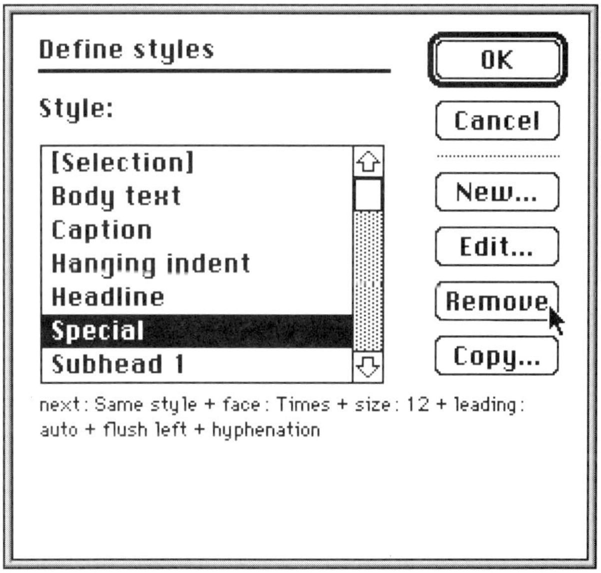

BASED ON

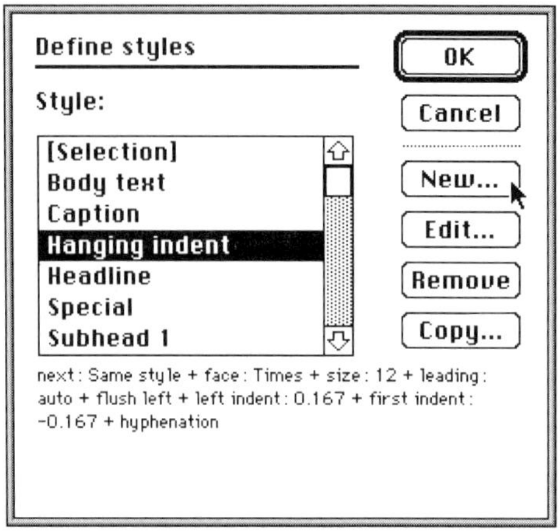

Figure 15. To add a new style that is based upon an existing style, select the style name you want to base the new style on (in our case *Hanging indent*) and then click on *New* in the *Define styles* dialog box.

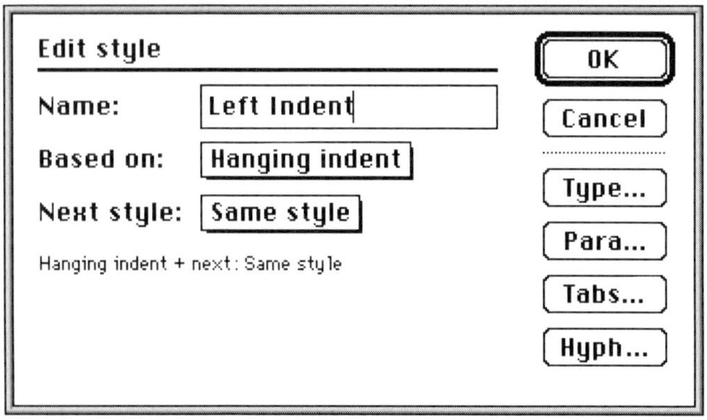

Figure 16. The *Edit style* dialog box appears with the name *Hanging indent* in the *Based on* box. The new style name you are defining (say *Left indent*) starts off with the same attributes as *Hanging indent.* Make any necessary changes to *Left indent* using the same approach outlined in Figures 6 through 9. You could also select a different style from the *Based on* pop-up menu once you are in this dialog box.

NEXT STYLE

Figure 17. The *Next style* pop-up menu in the *Edit styles* dialog box contains the list of current styles available in the publication. If you select a style from the pop-up menu, this style is the default style for the next paragraph following a paragraph in the style that you are creating.

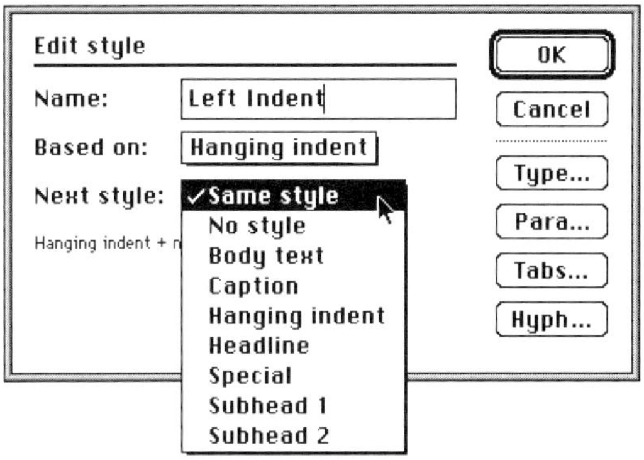

COPYING STYLES

Figure 18. You can copy styles from other PageMaker publications. This feature imports a list of styles and adds them onto the current styles list from another publication.

Click on the *Copy* button from the *Define styles* dialog box to open the *Copy styles* dialog box.

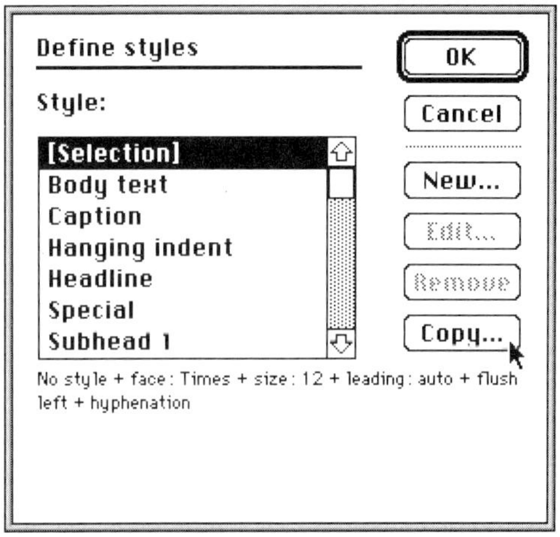

Figure 19. Find and select the publication you need from this dialog box and select *OK*. Any styles with matching names are replaced with the new style if you select *Yes* in the alert box that appears.

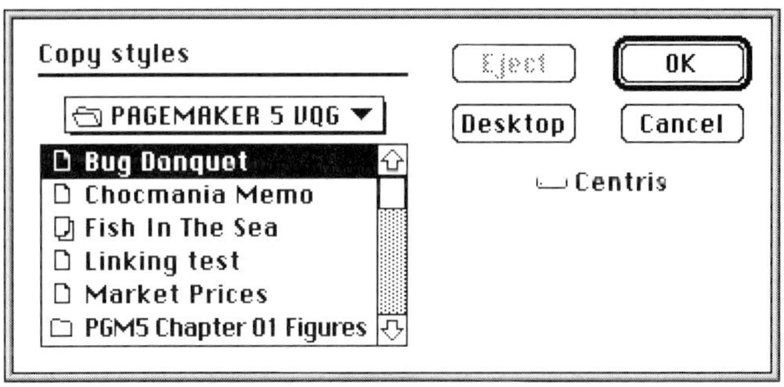

IMPORTING STYLES

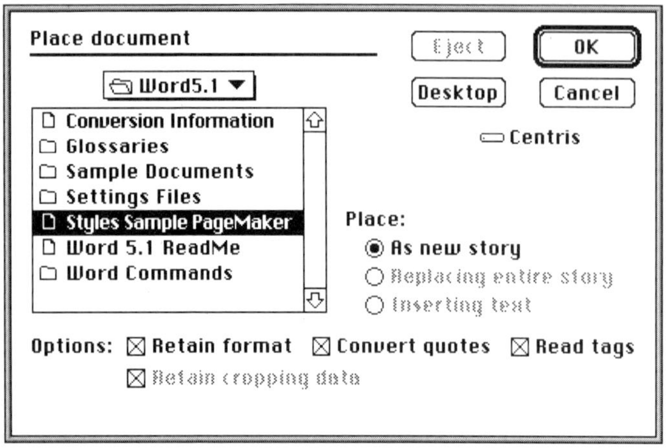

Figure 20. You can import style names from word processing documents by including style names in angle brackets (<>) at the beginning of each paragraph in your word processor file. These will come across into your PageMaker document with the named style automatically applied to that paragraph if you choose the *Read tags* option when you place the document. Some word processing packages such as Word automatically bring their own styles into PageMaker when you import them.

Figure 21. You see an asterisk "*" in the style palette next to any style names that you have imported with word processing text files.

THE CONTROL PALETTE AND STYLES

You can use the Control palette both to apply existing styles to a selected paragraph and to create new styles based on the formatting of selected text.

Figure 22. Activate the Control palette and click on the *Paragraph view* button.

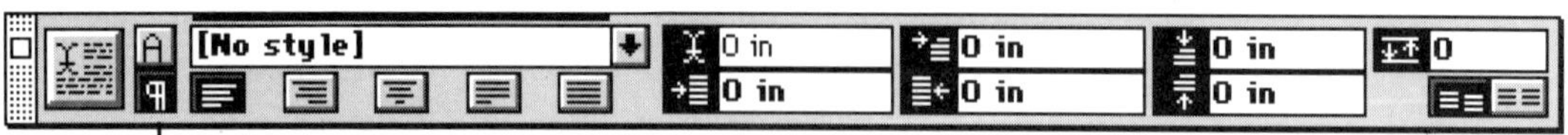

Paragraph view button

APPLYING STYLES USING THE CONTROL PALETTE

Figure 23. It is easy to apply styles by using the Control palette. Put the insertion point into a paragraph (as we have done here) or select a number of paragraphs. The current style (if any) is displayed in the *Paragraph style* window in the Control palette—in this case *Headline.*

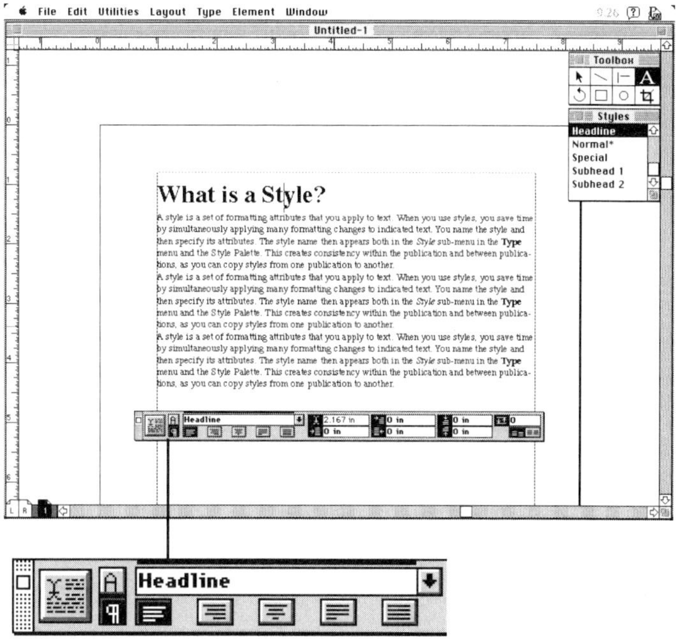

Figure 24. Hold the mouse button down when the cursor is on the down arrow to open the pop-up menu of styles. Select the style you want and release the mouse.

Alternatively, you can type the first few letters of the style name into the text box and press Return.

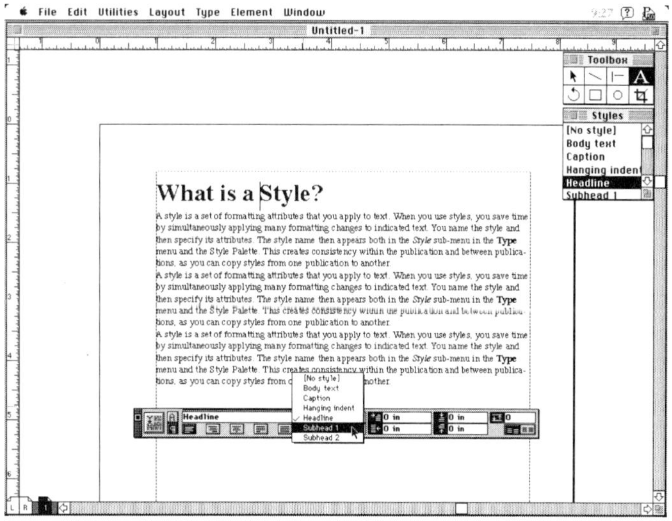

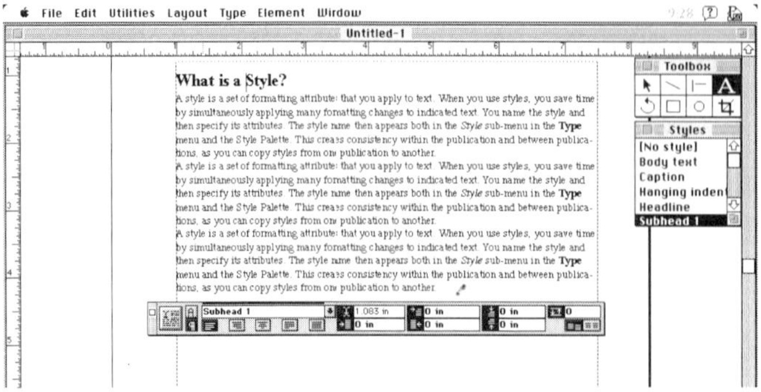

Figure 25. The results display immediately.

CREATING STYLES USING THE CONTROL PALETTE

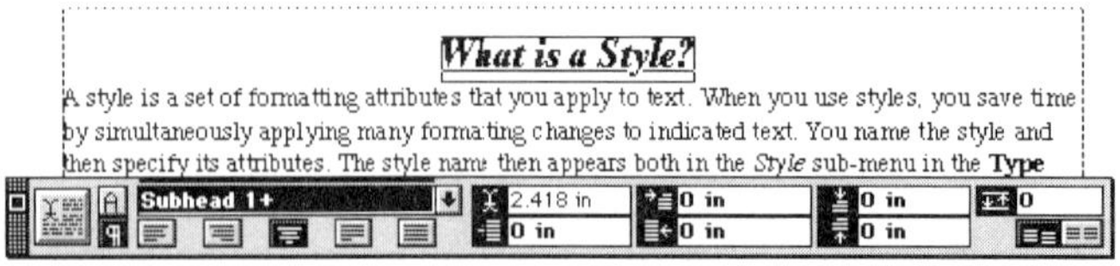

Figure 26. Format a paragraph of text with the attributes you want to include in the new style. Select the paragraph with the text tool and select the current style name in the *Paragraph style* window.

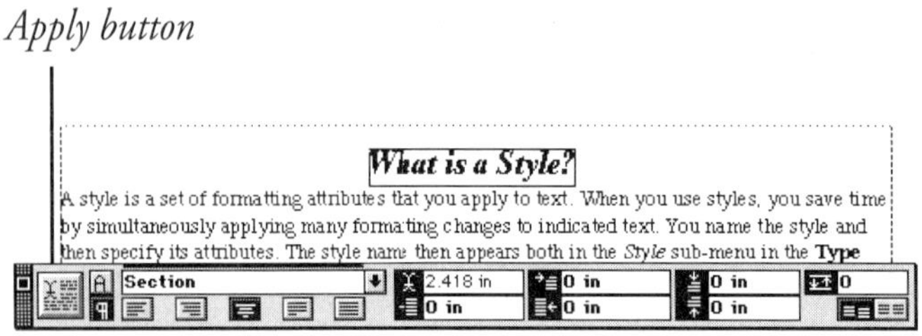

Figure 27. Type a new, unused name over the top of the old one and click on the Apply button.

Figure 28. PageMaker alerts you that you are about to create a new style, which you do by clicking on *OK*. The new style name, in this case *Section*, appears in the list of styles.

You can edit any styles you create in the *Define styles* dialog box, as described in Figures 11 and 12.

Using Color 12

Spot and Process Colors

If you are working with color it is necessary to understand the difference between spot and process colors. In PageMaker, you can define both spot and process colors and apply them to objects and text.

SPOT COLORS

Figure 1. Spot colors are printed by using premixed inks. There are hundreds of different spot colors from which to choose. When you send a file to a bureau for color separations of spot colors, the printer must make a separation for each color you have used—so 10 colors equals 10 separations.

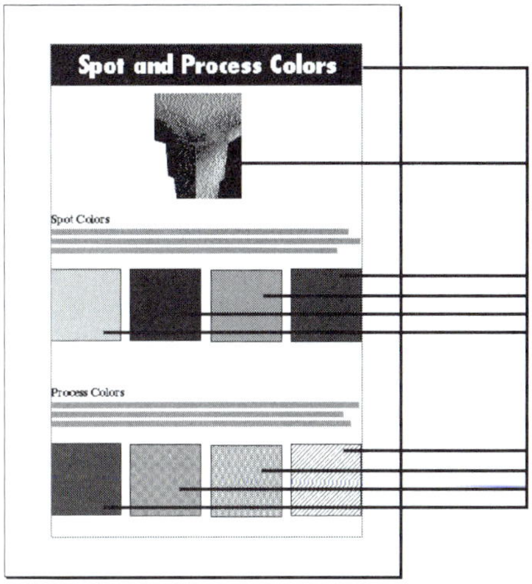

The printer must make a separation for each different spot color used

PROCESS COLORS

Figure 2. Process colors are made up of varying combinations of four basic colors—cyan (C), magenta (M), yellow (Y), and black (K). When you send a file to a bureau for color separations of process colors, one separation for each of the four process colors is made, regardless of how many colors you have used in your publication.

The printer needs to make only four color separations

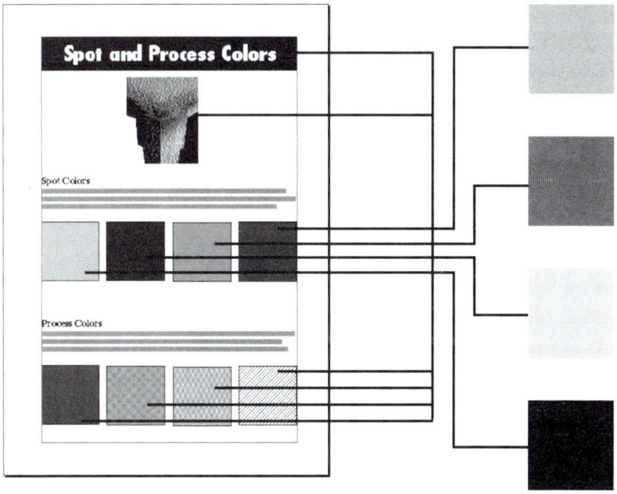

Use spot colors when you are using less than four colors in your publication, or when you need precise color matching of inks (for example fluorescent or metallic). Use process colors when you are using four or more colors, or you have imported scanned color photographs.

You can use both spot and process colors if you need precise color matching as well as a variety of colors. You might need this, for example, in a brochure that includes color photographs (four color process) and a corporate logo in a specific spot color.

APPLYING COLOR TO TEXT AND GRAPHICS

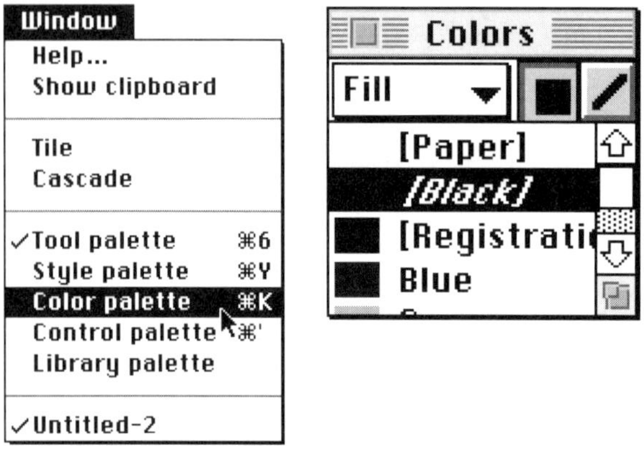

Figure 3. You can apply color to text and graphics—including monochrome bitmaps. (You must select text with the text tool before applying color to it.) Display the Color palette by selecting *Color palette* in the **Window** menu.

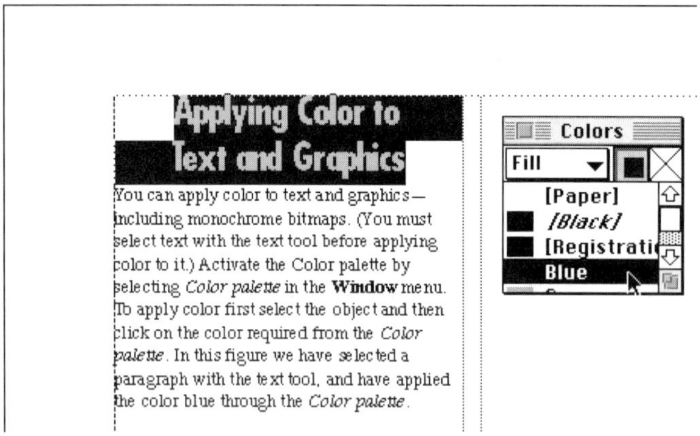

Figure 4. To apply color, first select the object and then click on the color you want from the Color palette. In this figure, we selected a paragraph with the text tool, and made it blue with the Color palette.

Figure 5. To apply color to an object, select the object and click on a color from the Color palette. PageMaker displays the results immediately.

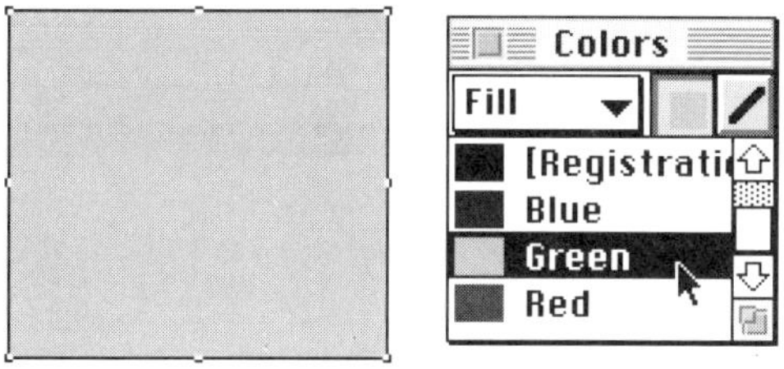

Figure 6. To change the percentage of the fill, you can apply one of the percentage options in the *Fill* submenu from the **Element** menu.

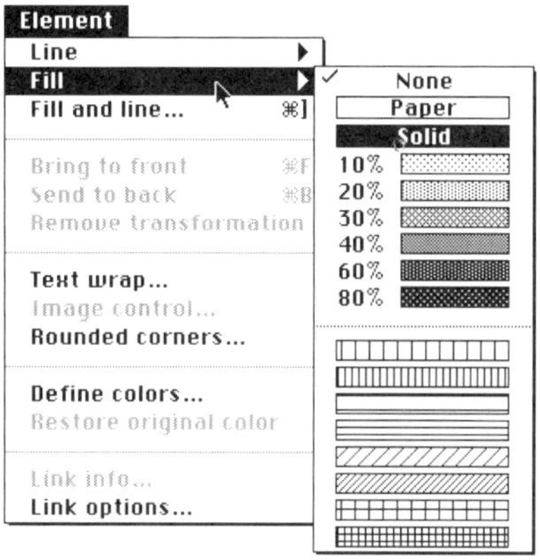

Figure 7. To apply the color to both the fill and outline, click on the down arrow in the *Color palette* and choose *Both* (a). To color the *Line* and *Fill* options individually, click on the down arrow and select the *Fill* and *Line* options alternately. Alternatively, to switch between the *Line* and *Fill* options, click on the Line or Fill icon in the Color palette (b).

Note: You cannot change the outline color of text.

(a)

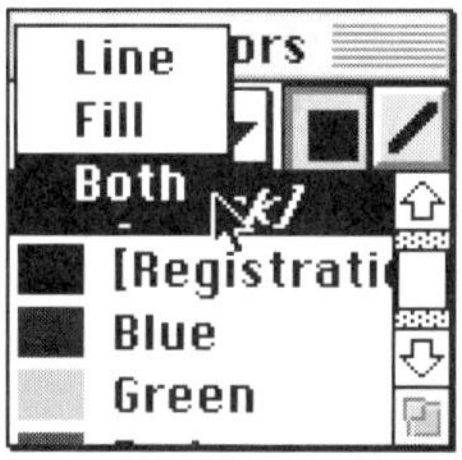

(b)

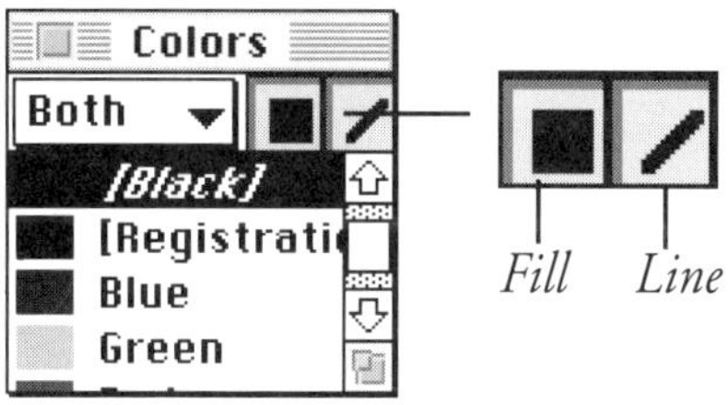

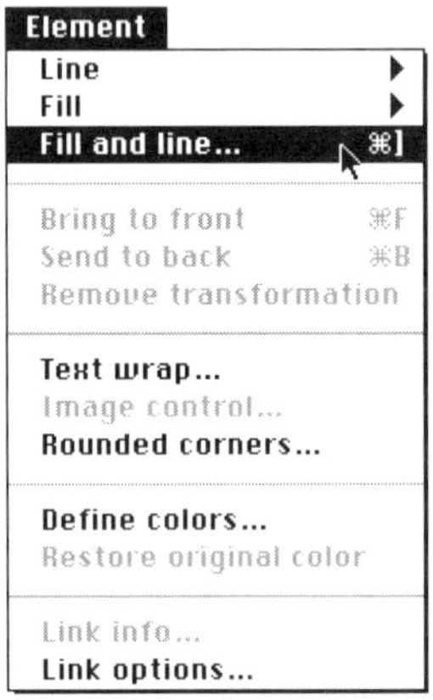

Figure 8. An alternative way to apply color to an object is to select *Fill and line* from the **Element** menu.

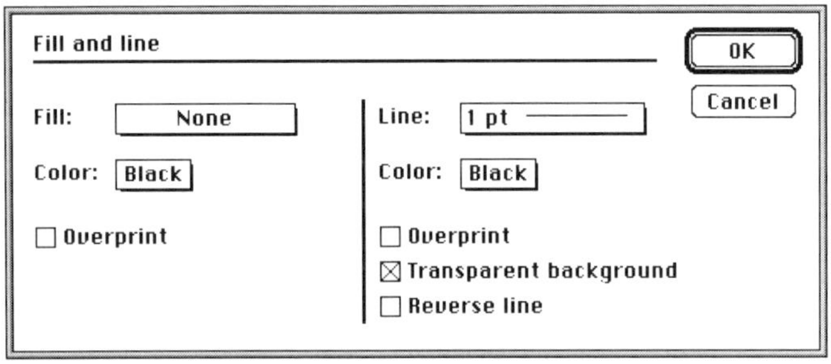

Figure 9. In the *Fill and line* dialog box, you can change both options at the same time.

OVERPRINT OPTION

Overprint concept

Knockout concept

Figure 10. The default setting for colors in PageMaker is *Knockout.* You can override this with the *Overprint* option in the *Fill and line* dialog box. The *Knockout* option means that when you have two overlapping objects both filled with color, the top object prints but the bottom object does not print where the two objects overlap (this is visible in color separations). When you select the *Overprint* option for a color, this color prints on top of any other color it overlaps, creating a third color that you may not possibly want.

Creating Colors

PageMaker supports Pantone and other color libraries as well as giving you the option of defining your own colors. You can also choose predefined colors from 10 commercial color libraries. (For more information on commercial color libraries see the *Aldus PageMaker 5 Commercial Printing Guide* or talk to your printer.)

Figure 11. You create new colors by selecting *Define colors* from the **Element** menu. This opens the *Define colors* dialog box. The list shows the various colors that are currently defined; these include the default colors provided with PageMaker. To create a new color, click on the *New* button. This opens the *Edit color* dialog box.

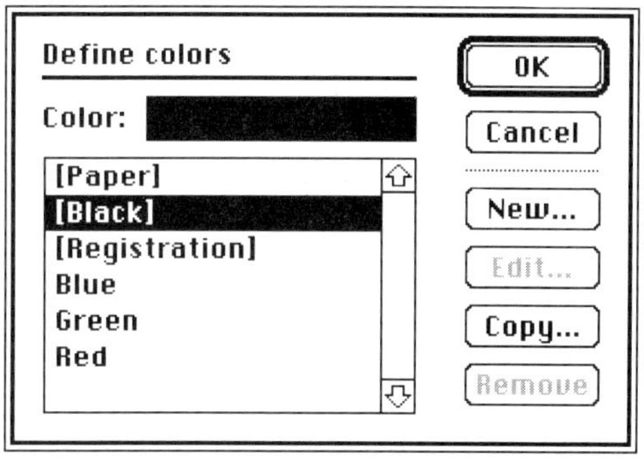

Alternatively, to open this dialog box, use the Command key and click on a color in the Color palette.

Figure 12. In the *Edit color* dialog box, type the name of the color you are creating in the *Name* text box. Then choose the *Type* of color you want to create: *Spot*, *Process* or *Tint*, and then choose the *Model* type: *RGB*, *HLS* or *CMYK*. You can adjust the color percentages or degrees using any of the *Model* options; the top-half of the color rectangle constantly changes to reflect the new color.

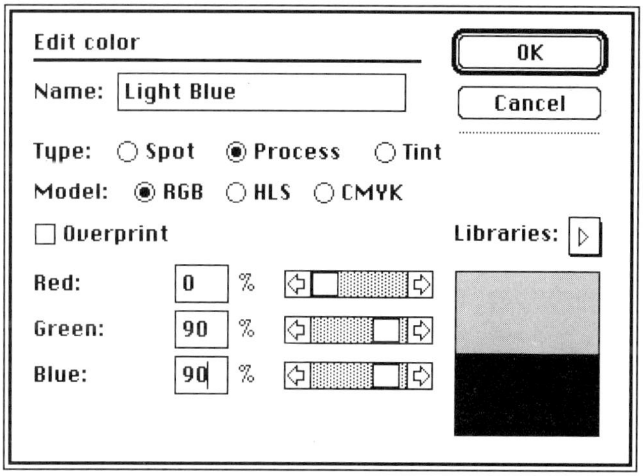

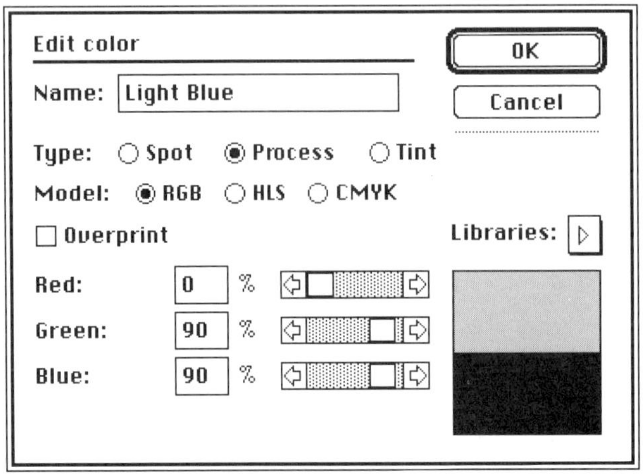

Figure 13. The RGB model lets you define a color by varying the percentages of red, green, and blue.

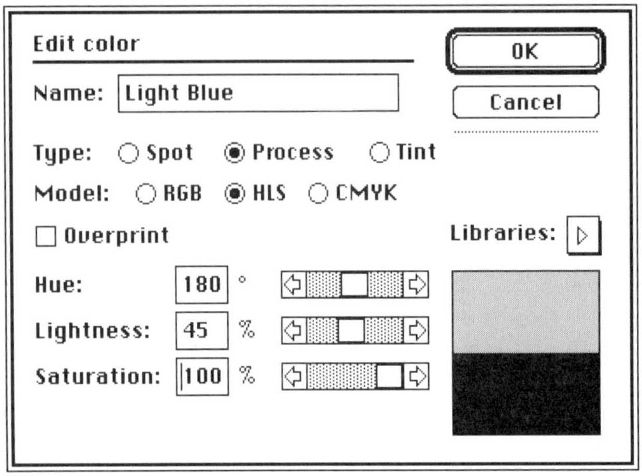

Figure 14. The HLS model is similar to RGB but you define the hue in degrees from 0 to 360.

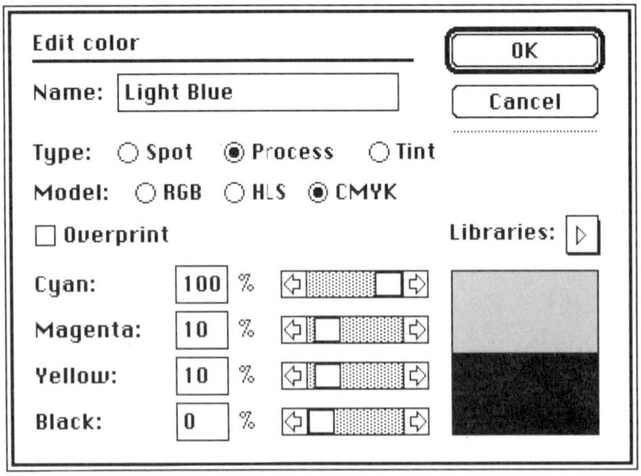

Figure 15. To define a color using the CMYK model, adjust the percentages of cyan, magenta, yellow and black.

The CMYK model is the most common model used for printing.

Figure 16. Regardless of which *Type* you select (*Spot*, *Process*, or *Tint*), you can choose any library (spot or process) from the *Libraries* pop-up menu. Each library listed is a commercial color-matching system. You may not have all these color libraries installed. You should use the appropriate color reference manuals, which you can get from printers if you want accurate results.

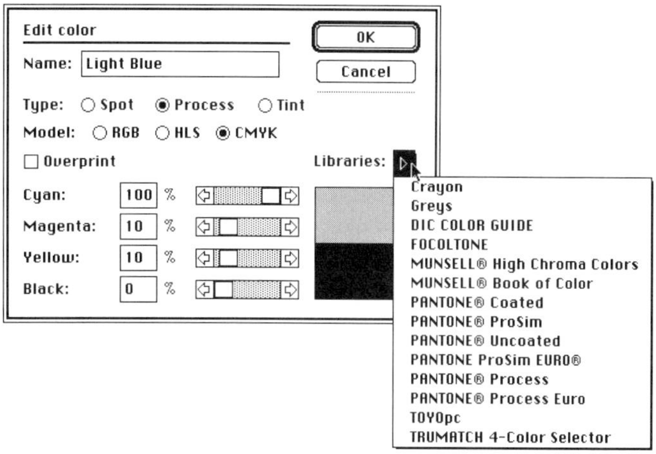

Figure 17. This table shows what type of color each library contains.

Color Matching System	Type of Color	Color Matching System	Type of Color
Crayon	Process	Pantone ProSim	Spot
DIC Color Guide	Spot	Pantone Uncoated	Spot
Focoltone	Process	Pantone ProSim Euro	Spot
Greys	Spot & Process	Pantone Process	Process
Munsell High Chroma Colors	Process	Pantone Process Euro	Process
Munsell Book of Color	Process	TOYOpc	Spot
Pantone Coated	Spot	Trumatch 4-Color Selector	Process

Figure 18. If you choose the *PANTONE Coated* option from the list, for example, this opens the *Library* dialog box shown here. The other libraries appear with a similar dialog box. You choose Pantone colors by scrolling to the one you need and clicking on it with the mouse. Alternatively, if you know the color, enter the name or its number directly into the *PANTONE* text box at the top of the dialog box and click on *OK*.

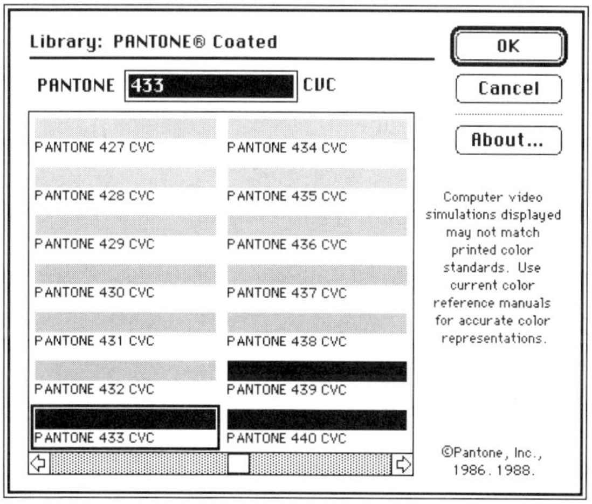

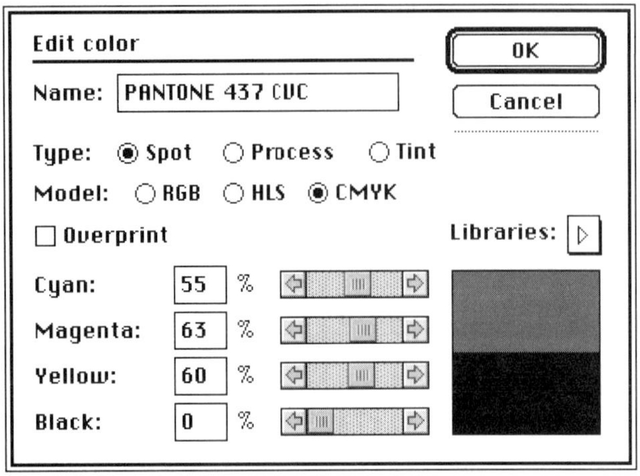

Figure 19. If you leave the *Name* text box blank in the *Edit color* dialog box, then you make a selection from the *Libraries* pop-up menu, PageMaker automatically inserts the name of the selected color in the *Name* text box. You should keep this name otherwise the printer cannot match your colors easily. This is the point of color matching systems; in effect, it is a standard language of color.

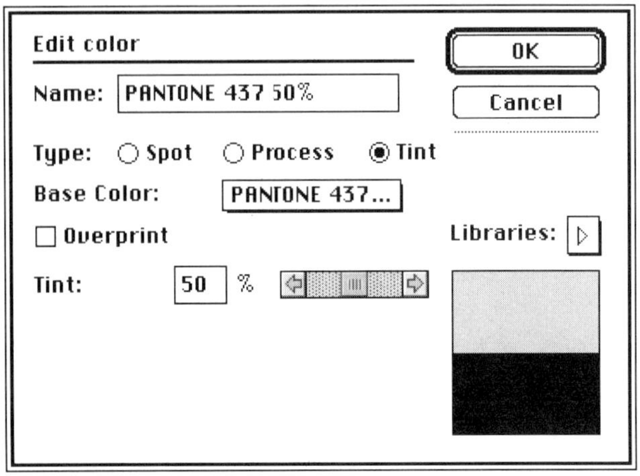

Figure 20. To create a tint, which is a lighter version of a spot color, click on the *Tint* option and select the spot color from the *Base Color* pop-up menu. Choose a percentage of that color from the *Tint* option, and then type in a new name in the *Name* text box.

Tints are a useful way to create more colors without adding separations. A tint prints on the same separation as the color it comes from.

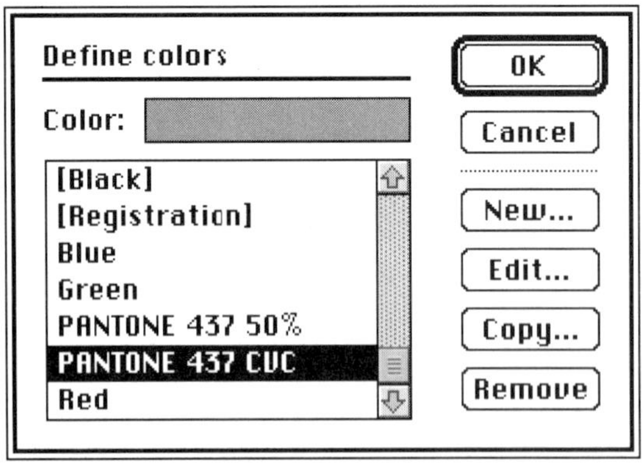

Figure 21. After defining a color by using any of the above methods, click on *OK* in the *Edit color* dialog box to return to the *Define colors* dialog box again. This figure shows the Pantone spot colors we chose in Figures 19 and 20, now appearing in the *Color* list. PageMaker displays these colors in the Color palette.

Editing Colors

Figure 22. You edit colors the same way you create them. The *Edit color* dialog box lets you change any color at any time.

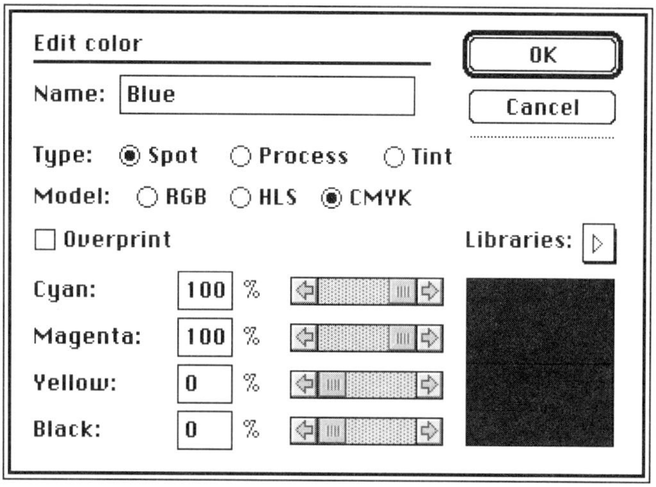

To edit a color, select the color you want to edit from the list in the *Define colors* dialog box and click on the *Edit* button. You cannot edit the default colors of *Black* and *Registration.*

Alternatively, to open the *Edit color* dialog box, use the Command key and click on the color you want to edit in the Color palette. (See the *Create color library* addition in Chapter 9 for information on creating your own color library.)

Removing and Copying Colors

Figure 23. To remove a color, select it and click on the *Remove* button in the *Define colors* dialog box.

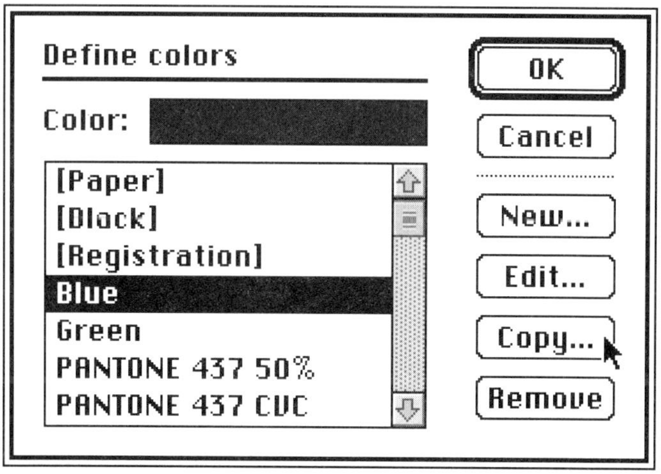

To copy colors from other PageMaker publications, click on the *Copy* button to open the *Copy colors* dialog box.

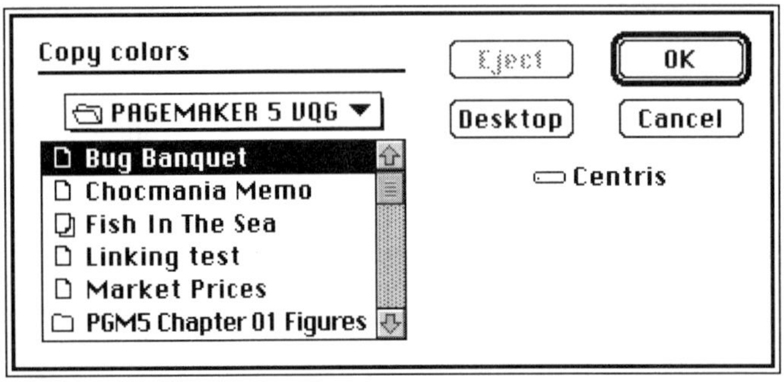

Figure 24. This is the *Copy colors* dialog box. In the file list, select the file you want to copy the colors from and click on *OK*.

PRINTING 13

PRINT DIALOG BOX

You can print a publication whenever you want to, whether it is finished or not. You can print the whole document or just a couple of pages. You can scale the size of these pages, add crop marks, and print full color separations. The *Print* command in the **File** menu makes a hard copy of the current PageMaker publication.

Figure 1. You select your printer from the *Chooser* dialog box. Select *Chooser* from the **Apple** menu to open the Chooser. Select your printer, then click on the Close box to return you to your PageMaker document.

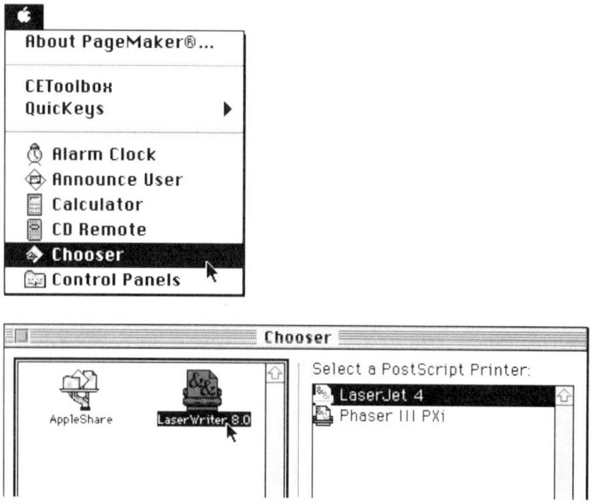

Figure 2. Any time you want to print your publication select *Print* from the **File** menu.

Note: The Print dialog box options in this chapter are for a PostScript printer driver only. Non-PostScript printer drivers have different options.

PRINTING OPTIONS

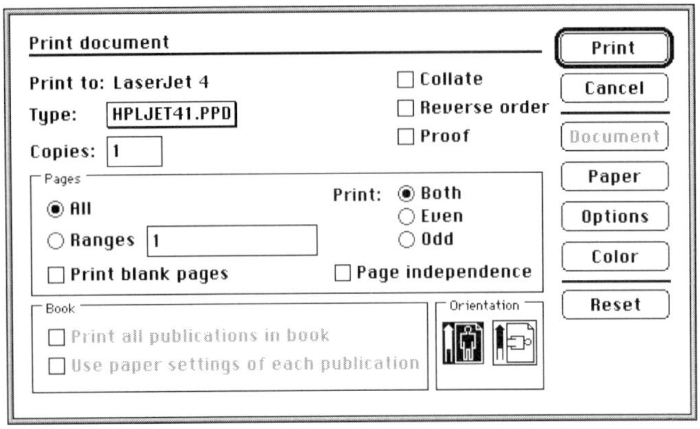

Figure 3. When you select the *Print* command, this opens the *Print document* dialog box. This dialog box contains the PostScript options. If you do not have a PostScript printer some these options will not be available to you.

The *Print to* option displays the name of the target printer that you have chosen (see Figure 1). If it does not, use the pop-up menu to make your selection.

The *Type* option lets you select the specific printer model. The pop-up menu contains the PPD (PostScript printer description) names for the printers that you installed. Selecting the correct PPD file from this menu lets you print more successfully. It is supplied by the printer manufacturer and holds specific information about the printer.

The *Copies* option lets you specify how many copies of your publication you want printed. You can enter any figure between 1 and 32,000 in this text box which, by default, is set to 1.

Use the *Collate* option to print multiple copies of a publication that contains more than one page. If your document contains many complex graphics, collating automatically can be a very slow process.

When you select the *Reverse order* option, your pages print in the opposite order to how your printer normally prints them, either first to last or last to first.

Use the *Proof* option to print all graphics as rectangles only. This speeds up printing considerably.

The *Pages* options let you select all or some of your document to print. To print the whole publication, click on the *All* option. To print part of the publication, click on the *Ranges* option (e.g. 1–6) or you can print several ranges (e.g. 2, 5–6, 8–13). The *Both* option is the default setting to print both odd and even pages, or you can choose to print *Even* or *Odd* pages only—useful for double-sided printing.

To print on both sides of the page, using a single-sided printer, print the even pages by selecting the *Even* choice, then, put the even pages back into the printer, and print the odd pages.

The *Print blank pages* option lets you print any pages that are blank. If you check *Page independence,* PageMaker downloads all the font information with each page rather than once for the whole publication. Unless you specifically need the font information for each page, such as if you use page imposition software that requires it, you should leave this option unchecked.

The *Book* options let you control printing of publications belonging to a book list (see Chapter 14). To print all the publications in the current book list, select *Print all publications in book.* To print each publication in the book list using its own printer settings, select *Use paper settings of each publication.* This lets you print documents, for example, of different page sizes, or to different paper trays. The options not affected by this setting are the orientation, the number of copies, the *Collate* option and the page range.

Note: *If your current book list is empty, you cannot access the two options in the Book section.*

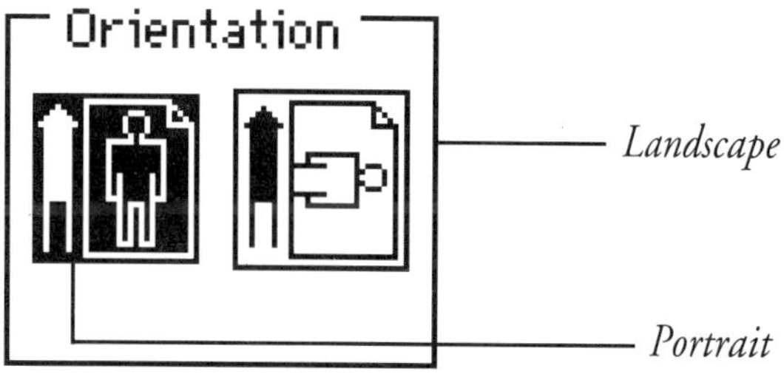

Figure 4. In the *Orientation* section of the *Print document* dialog box, you can select either *Portrait* (vertical) or *Landscape* (horizontal).

PAPER

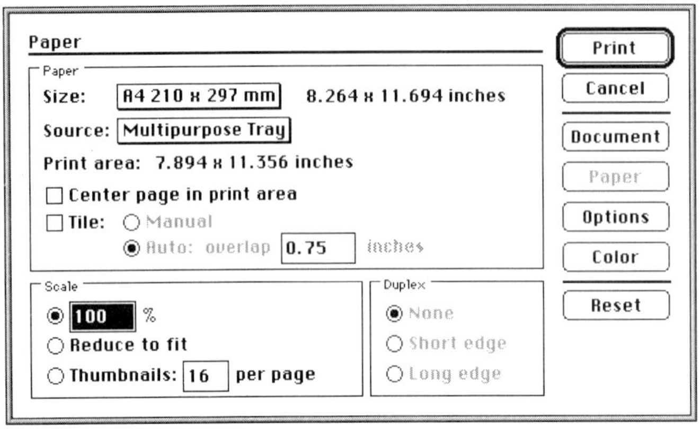

Figure 5. Click on the *Paper* button in the *Print document* dialog box to access your printer's settings. Here, you can change the paper size, the paper source and you can center your document on the page.

Note: Because different printers have different capabilities, the options available here may vary depending on your printer.

The *Tile* option lets you print page sizes that are larger than the paper in the printer. You split each page into segments (called tiles) that fit onto the printer's page. You set how much of the image or page to overlap in the *Auto overlap* box. Selecting *Manual* for this option lets you set each tile by dragging the zero point to the start of each new tile.

The *%* option in the *Scale* section lets you scale the size of your page between 6 and 1600%, in increments as small as 0.1%. If you need to reduce or enlarge the pages of your document to better fit the paper in your printer, enter a percentage in the *%* text box. If you are printing an enlarged version of your page, you may need to use the *Tile* option.

The *Reduce to fit* option automatically scales the size of your page down to fit on your printer's page size.

Use the *Thumbnails* option to print a miniature version of your publication. You can print up to 100 miniature pages of a publication on the one page. The default setting is 16 thumbnails per page.

If your printer can print on both sides of the page, you can use the *Duplex* options to control how it does this. Choose *None* to print your document single-sided. If you are printing portrait, the *Short edge* option prints both sides so that they read correctly when you bind them along the short edge of the paper. The *Long edge* option prints both sides so that they read correctly when you bind them along the long edge of the paper.

OPTIONS

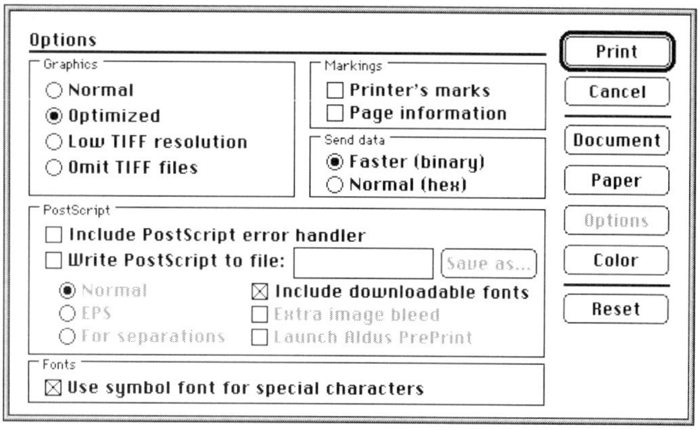

Figure 6. When you click on the *Options* button at the right of the dialog box, these settings become available to you.

In the *Graphics* section, you can choose *Normal* to print a normal copy of your document's graphics or *Optimized* to omit data that your printer can't use (which speeds up printing).

If you have TIFF files in your document, you can print them at a lower resolution by choosing the *Low TIFF resolution* option or you can choose not to print them at all by selecting the *Omit TIFF files* option. You can use these options to speed up printing considerably.

If you select the *Printer's marks* option, PageMaker adds crop marks, registration marks, color-control bars and density bars to the page. However, if you are printing, for example, a letter-sized page on letter-size paper, these marks do not appear.

The *Page information* option prints the file name, the current date, and the colors used in the lower-left corner of each page.

Choose the *Faster (binary)* option in the *Send Data* section to send the data for bitmap (TIFF or paint-type graphics) to your printer faster. The *Normal (hex)* option sends bitmap graphics in hexadecimal format.

If you want to print your PageMaker document to a file but not to a printer, use the PostScript options in the *Options* dialog box (Figure 6). You may want to print your document to a file because the printer you are using is in a different location, or you are sending it to a service bureau for printing.

To print the file to disk, first select the *Write PostScript to file* option in the *PostScript* section. Key in the name of the print file in the edit box next to the *Write PostScript to file* option. Click on the *Save As* button to open a dialog box so you can select a drive and folder to save the print file in.

If you choose the *Normal* option, the file is given a ***ps*** extension by default. Choose the *EPS* option to create an encapsulated PostScript file for any page in your document. PageMaker gives each EPS file a default name, made up of the first six characters of the filename plus the page number and an ***eps*** extension. You can place these EPS images into PageMaker.

Choose the *For separations* option if you plan to have the print file separated by an outside separation program more advanced than PageMaker. The file in this case will have an ***sep*** extension.

The *Include downloadable fonts* option includes any fonts in the document that you need to download to your printer before printing.

The *Extra image bleed* option is useful when sending pages to post-processing programs, as it extends the bleed for TIFF images to 1 inch.

Choose the *Launch Aldus Preprint* option when you want to save your document as a separation file. When you click on *Save,* Aldus Preprint automatically opens.

The *Fonts* section lets you specify if you want to use the Symbol font for special characters, such as the copyright ©, registered trademark ®, and degree symbols °. Leave unchecked if you know the fonts in your document include these characters, otherwise you may get some unexpected characters.

POSTSCRIPT ERRORS

When you check the *Include PostScript error handler* option, your printer prints a message on a page if an error occurs while printing. This message identifies the PostScript command that caused the error.

PRINTING COLOR

Figure 7. When you click on the *Color* button you get the options shown here.

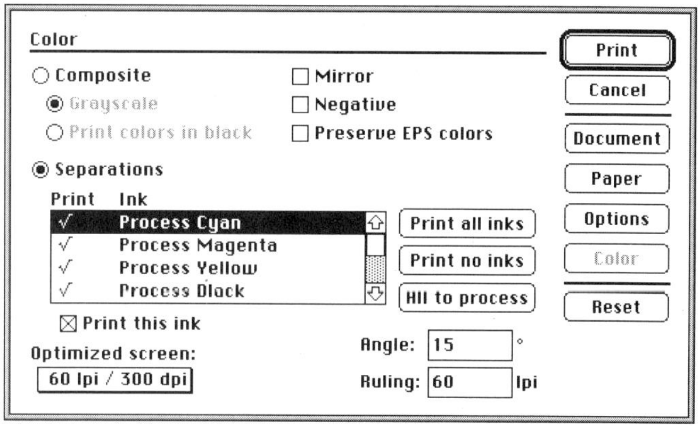

Select the *Composite* option to print your color document to a color or black and white printer. The *Grayscale* option prints a color version of a document to a color printer, or a grayscale version to a non-color printer. When you print a grayscale version, PageMaker simulates the intensity of the color in shades of gray.

The *Print colors in black* option prints your publication in percentages of black, which you need to do for separations. The *Mirror* option mirrors your document when you print it, and the *Negative* option prints your document as a negative; both these options are used for outputting your files to film from an imagesetter. The *Preserve EPS colors* prints the colors saved with the EPS graphics in your files, rather than any colors you have applied in PageMaker.

Select the *Separations* option to print spot and process color separations. If you want to print only specific colors as separations, click on the color you need in the *Print ink* list and click on the *Print this ink* option. You can also double-click on the color. The colors that you select or that PageMaker has pre-selected have a tick to the left of the ink name.

Use the *Print all inks* button if you want to print a color separation for every color in the *Print Ink* list. After you click on this button, PageMaker places a tick to the left of every color name. Click on the *Print no inks* button to specify that you do not want to print separations. You can then select a specific color and click on *Print this ink.*

Click on the *All to process* button to temporarily convert all spot colors to process for printing. PageMaker converts spot colors to the closest possible process color it can, which may not exactly match the original color.

Use the *Optimized screen* pop-up menu to specify the screen ruling to use for your composite publication or color separations. The menu displays the screen ruling and resolution combinations listed in the printer's PPD file. Each printer comes with a PPD file that contains certain information about the printer. The option you select here is reflected in the *Angle* and *Ruling* text boxes.

You can also enter a custom screen angle and screen ruling for your publication, but default angles and rulings defined for each specific printer give the best results. You need to get more information from your bureau on the best options to choose.

When you have selected all the required print options, click on the *Print* button to send your publication to print.

MULTIPLE PUBLICATION FEATURES

14

BOOK COMMAND

PageMaker's *Book* command lets you link together multiple PageMaker publications to form one large document. With this command, you compile a list of the names of all publications that form part of a total document. You can link many chapters together to form a complete book.

Figure 1. By using the *Book* command, you can create a list of PageMaker publications that become part of a book list. These may be, for example, all the separate chapters of a book.

Once you have created a book list, you can include all the publications when you generate a table of contents and index (see Chapters 15 and 16 for more information on these features). You can also print these multiple publications without having to open each publication individually.

Creating a Book List

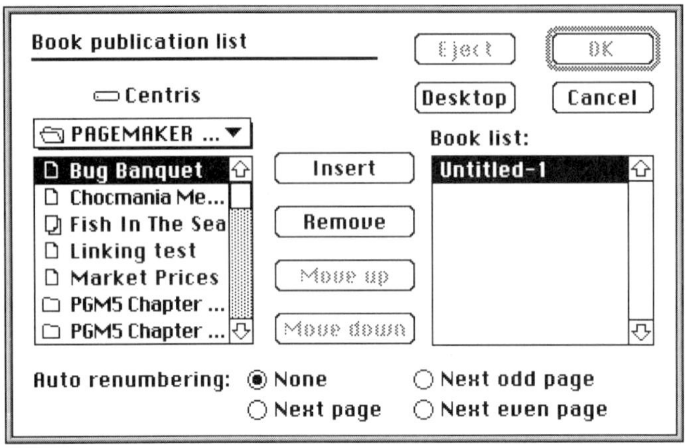

Figure 2. The *Book publication list* dialog box appears after you select the *Book* command (Figure 1). The *Book list* box, on the right of this dialog box, is where PageMaker adds the names of the different publications you specify for the book list. The file list lets you search through your PageMaker publications on disk to find the documents you want to add.

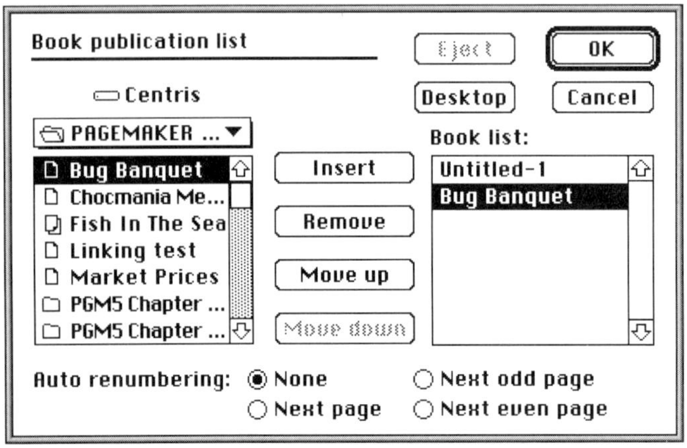

Figure 3. You add to the book list by clicking on a specific publication listed on the left and then clicking on the *Insert* button. This puts the publication in the book list. Repeat this to add all the publications you need. You can also double-click on the name of the publication to add it.

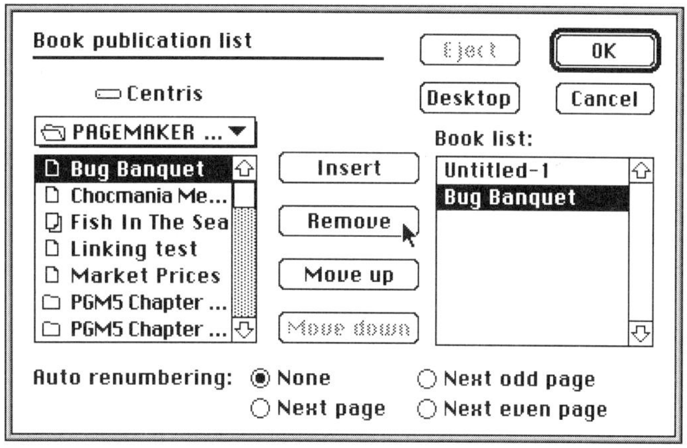

Figure 4. You can easily remove documents from the book list by clicking first on the name you want to delete and then on the *Remove* button. This automatically deletes the publication from the list.

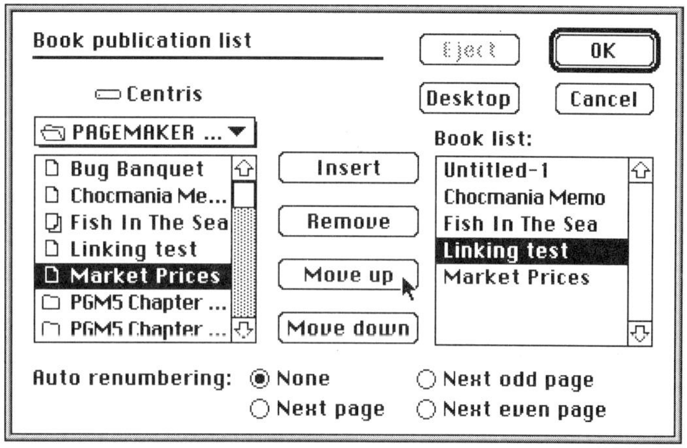

Figure 5. It is important that the publications in the book list are in the correct order, as this is the order that the book list prints in and also determines page numbering (if you are using the *Auto renumbering* option). You can change this order by using the *Move up* and *Move down* buttons. Highlight the publications you want to movc and click on the *Move up* or *Move down* buttons as required.

PRINTING A BOOK LIST

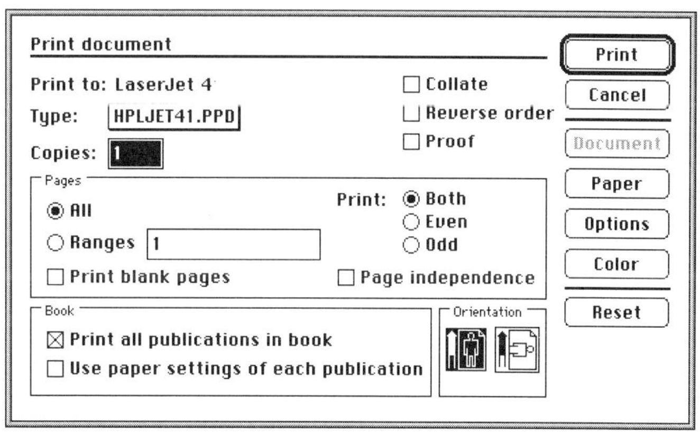

Figure 6. The *Print document* dialog box lets you print a single publication or the entire book list. To print the entire list, click in the *Print all publications in book* option in this dialog box.

You can copy the book list to every publication in the list by holding down the Command key and choosing *Book* from the **File** menu in the file where you created the book list. If you later modify the list in any one of the publications, you must re-copy them by following this same procedure.

COPYING AND PASTING BETWEEN PUBLICATIONS

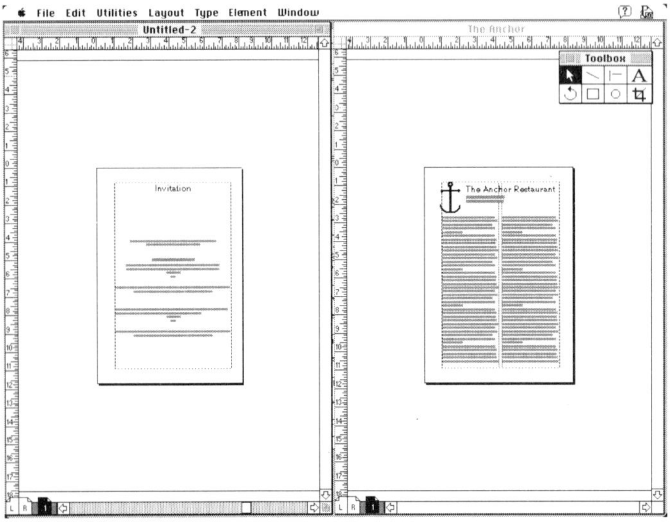

Figure 7. You can copy information between multiple open documents by dragging selected text and graphics from one open window to another. In this figure, we have opened two publications.

We are going to copy the graphic from the publication window on the right to the one on the left.

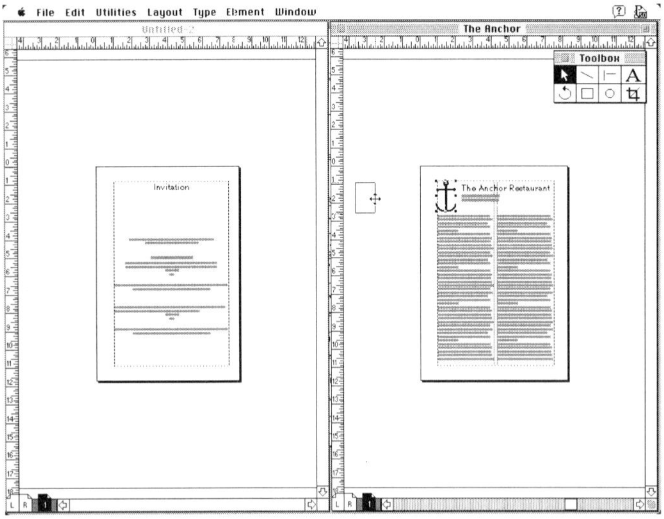

Figure 8. Select the item you want to copy to the other publication (it can include both text and graphics) and drag it from one publication window into another.

Figure 9. You can see the result here. When you drag an object from one publication to another, PageMaker makes a copy of the object in the other open publication.

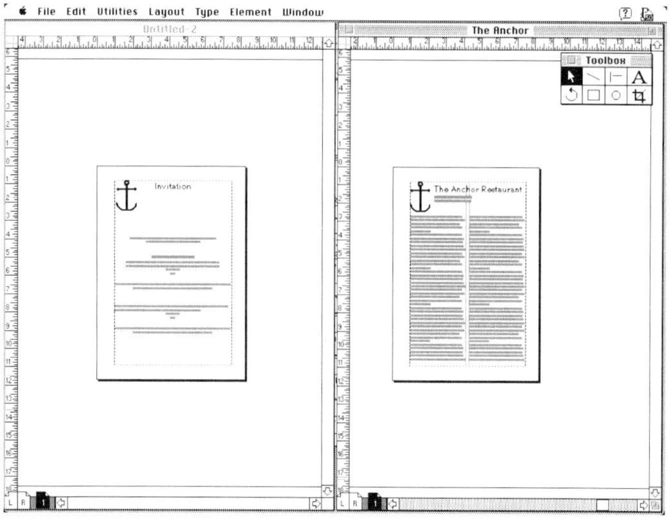

Creating a Table of Contents 15

Table of Contents

PageMaker can generate a table of contents for a single publication or a series of publications contained in a book list. PageMaker searches for specific styles to create the table of contents.

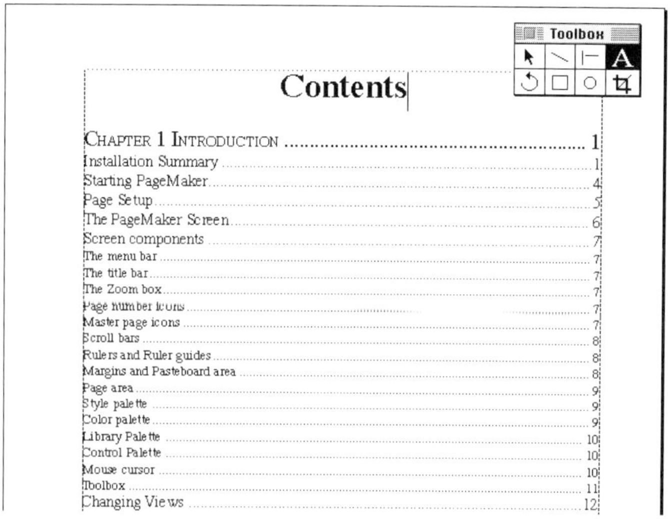

Figure 1. PageMaker generates a table of contents based on how you set up the different paragraph styles. If you define the styles to be included in the table of contents, PageMaker searches only for these paragraphs when it generates its contents.

You specify which styles to include in a table of contents in the *Paragraph specifications* dialog box (Figure 2). In these styles, you must select the *Include in table of contents* option before PageMaker can generate the list.

You can also select individual paragraphs (as opposed to applying a style) and add the *Include in table of contents* option.

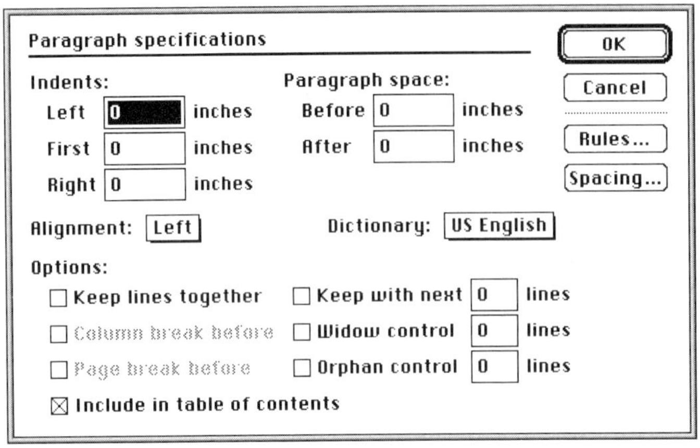

Figure 2. At the bottom of the *Paragraph specifications* dialog box is the *Include in table of contents* option. If you check this option when you create a style, all the paragraphs that have this style form part of the table of contents.

You can create many different styles within a publication with this option (see Chapter 11 for more information).

Creating Contents

If you are creating a table of contents for more than one publication, it is a good idea to first create a new publication and then create your book list before generating your table of contents (see Chapter 14).

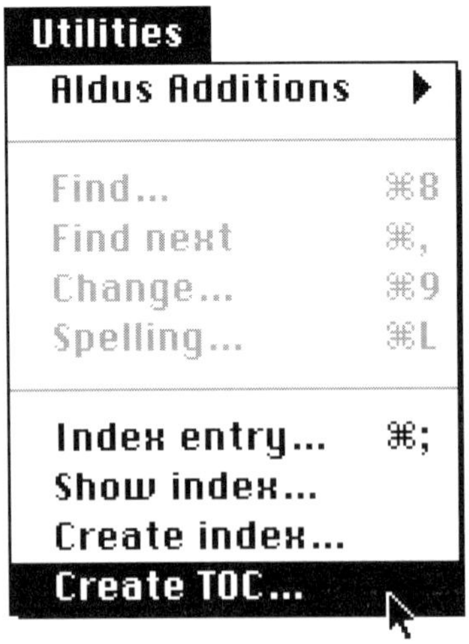

Figure 3. To create the table of contents, you first choose *Create TOC* in the **Utilities** menu.

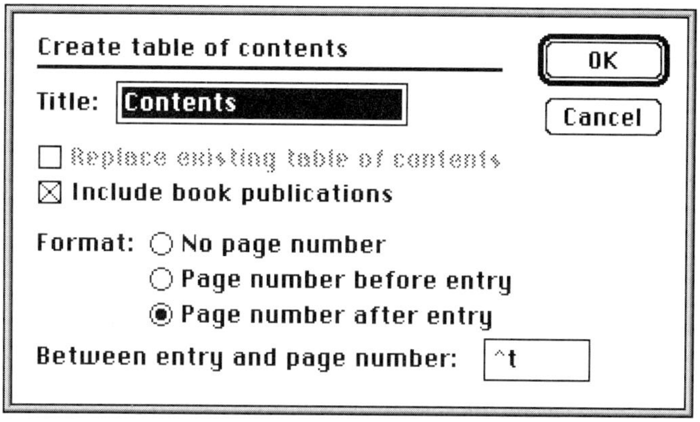

Figure 4. This is the *Create table of contents* dialog box. The word *Contents* appears by default in the *Title* text box. This is the word that appears at the top of the contents. You can delete this and replace it with a title of your own, up to 30 characters long.

You can select the *Replace existing table of contents* option only if you have generated a previous table of contents. If you have, this option is automatically checked. You can uncheck it if you want to compare old and new versions.

You can select the *Include book publications* option only if you have included the publication in a book list. If you have, this option is automatically checked. You can uncheck it if you want to see the contents for that publication only.

In the *Format* section, you can choose whether your table of contents includes page numbers and if so where they appear: *Page number before entry* or *Page number after entry.* The bottom line, *Between entry and page number,* lets you specify what is between a contents heading and the various page numbers. The default format code is '^t' for a tab with dot leaders. (You can use other codes which you will find listed in Appendix A of the *PageMaker User Manual.*)

Clicking on *OK* in the *Create table of contents* dialog box generates the table of contents. This may take some time, depending on the number of publications you include. You can then place this as you do any text file in PageMaker.

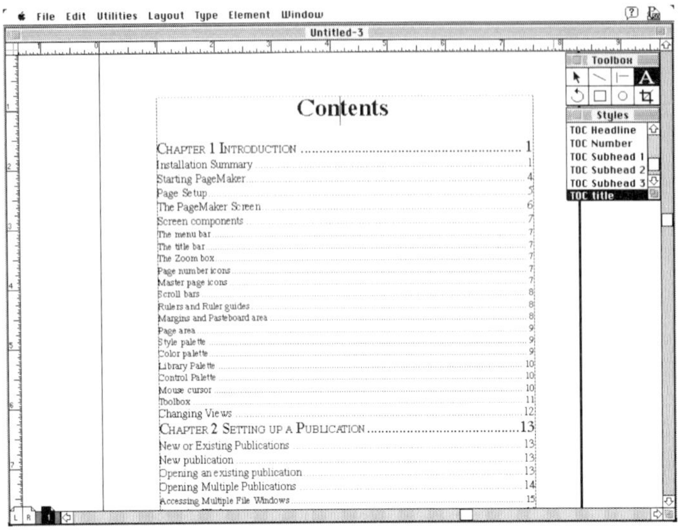

Figure 5. When you generate the contents, PageMaker automatically creates TOC styles based on the styles of the original paragraph but with "TOC" in front of them. TOC styles use the font Times by default.

You can edit these TOC styles in the same way as you edit other paragraph styles.

CREATING AN INDEX 16

INDEXES

PageMaker lets you generate an index for your publication automatically. Your index can be a simple one based on keywords or a more detailed multi-level index that spans several publications. Index entries contain two elements: a topic and a page reference. In some cases the page reference may be a page range or a cross-reference to another index entry.

CREATING INDEX ENTRIES

Figure 1. When you create an index entry, PageMaker adds an index marker to your text. These are visible only in the Story editor, although you can create index entries both in Layout view and Story editor.

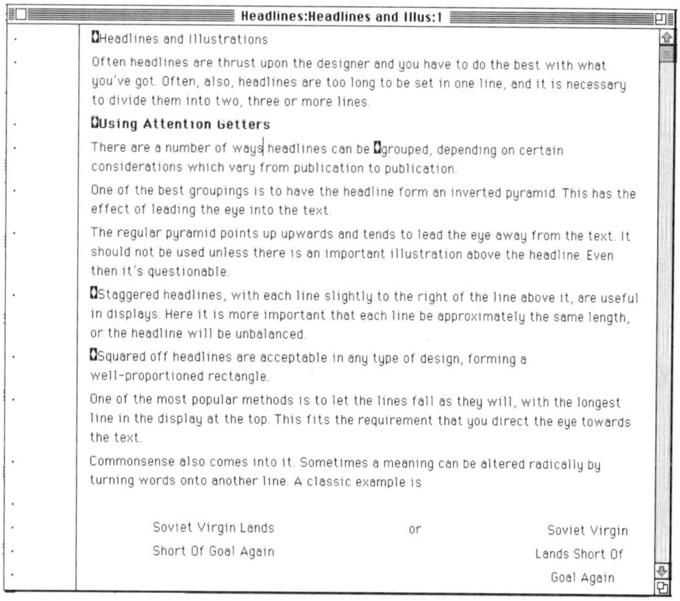

To create an individual index entry, either

(a) insert the text near where you want to reference a word or topic; or alternatively,

(b) select the text you want to index.

Figure 2. Use the *Index entry* command in the **Utilities** menu to create the reference.

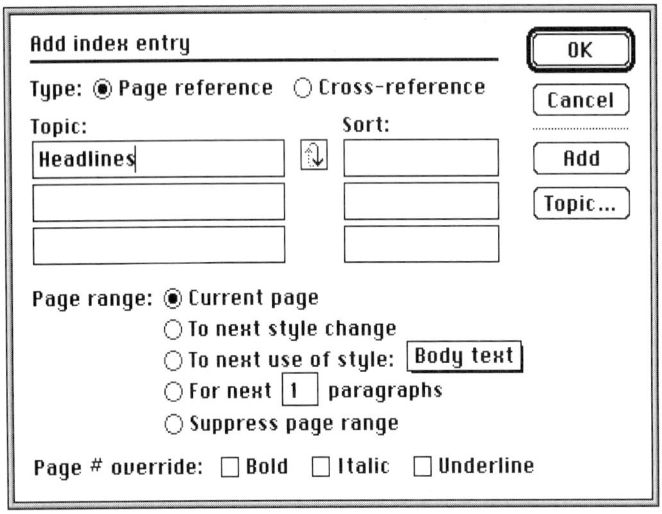

Figure 3. If you have selected text, then this text appears in the level 1 *Topic* text box (in this case *Headlines*). If you merely placed the insertion point, the *Topic* levels will have no text in them. Use this latter method when you wish to insert a different word or phrase in the index than what appears in your text. You are then free to type in your own index word into the level 1 *Topic* text box. There are three different *Topic* levels available.

You can enter up to three levels of topics. Click on the *Topic* button to see what other topics you have already defined.

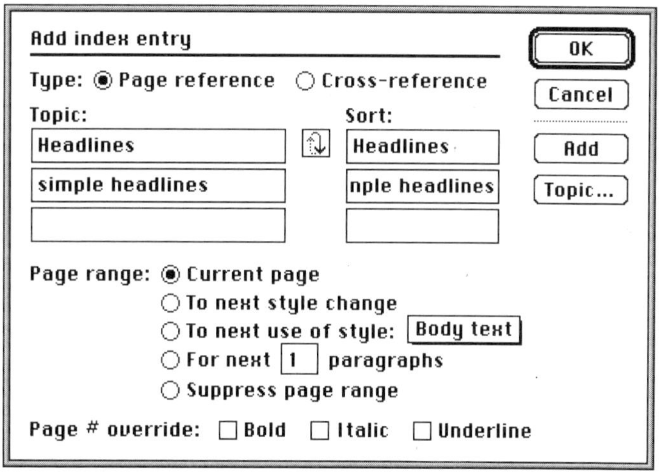

Figure 4. We now have entered both primary and secondary index entries. We have also entered additional information in the *Sort* text boxes, indicating to PageMaker how we want it to sort the *Topic* index entries. If you leave the *Sort* text box blank, you may not get the alphabetic sequence you want when dealing with items such as numbers.

The *Page range* options let you decide how many pages you want to reference for each index entry.

The *Page # override* option gives you control over the type style of page numbers and cross-referencing for additional emphasis.

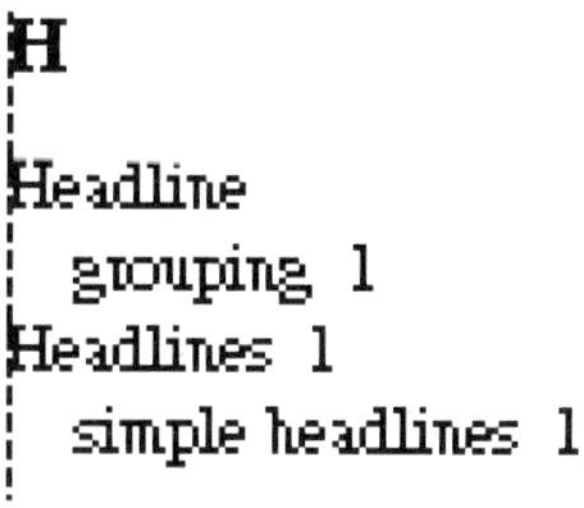

Figure 5. The index entry options in Figure 4 produce entries in the index like this example.

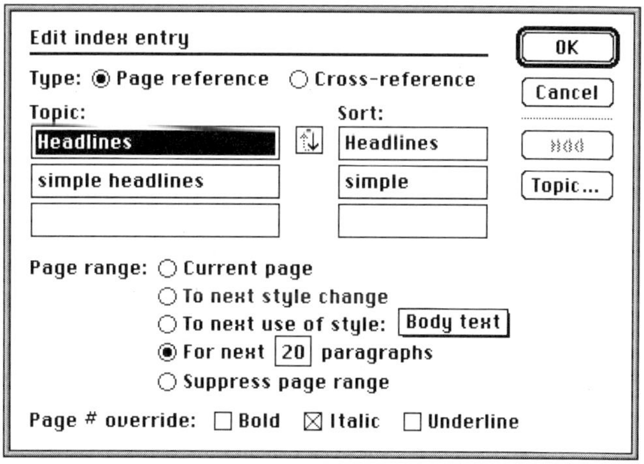

Figure 6. This is same index entry as in Figure 4, but we have selected different *Page range* and *Page # override* options. See Figure 7 for the result.

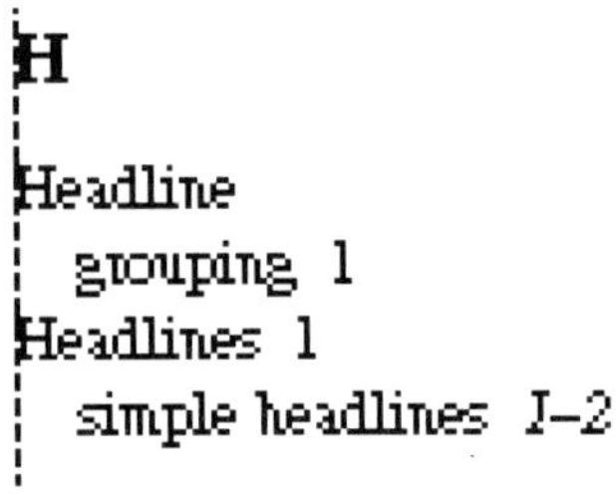

Figure 7. The index entry options in Figure 6 produce entries like this.

MULTIPLE INDEX ENTRIES

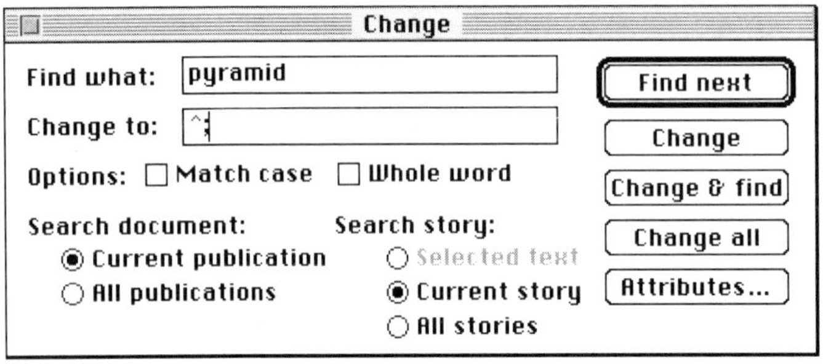

Figure 8. If you want to create multiple index entries of a particular word or phrase that occurs throughout your publication, select *Change* from the **Utilities** menu. (You can select this only when you are in Story editor.) In the *Change* dialog box, enter the text you need to index in the *Find what* edit box and insert '^;' (caret+semicolon) in the *Change to* text box. This is the symbol for an index entry marker.

Then click on the *Change all* button and PageMaker marks every occurrence of the text with an index entry marker.

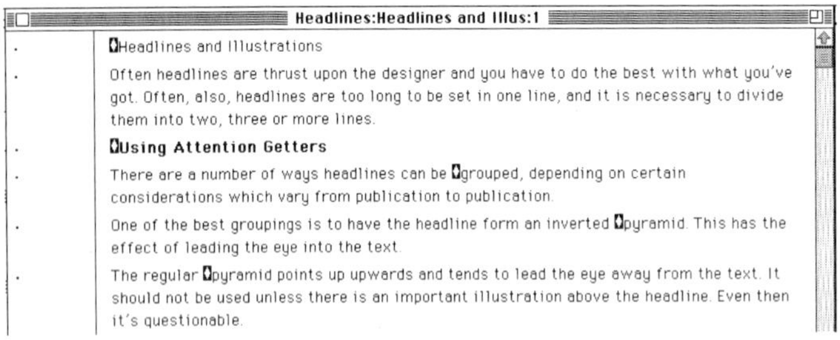

Figure 9. PageMaker has marked every occurrence of the word "pyramid" with an index entry marker.

Topic and Cross-Referencing

Figure 10. Use the *Topic* button from the *Add index entry* dialog box to select a topic that you have already created elsewhere in your document. First, put the insertion point near the word and select the *Index entry* command. Next, open the *Select topic* dialog box by clicking on the *Topic* button in the *Add index entry* dialog box. Finally, use the *Topic section* to find the letter that begins the word you are searching for.

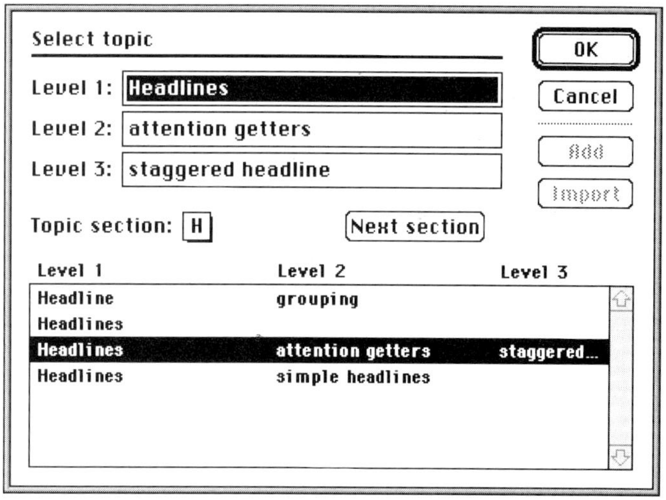

This dialog box lets you select an index entry you have already included. This simplifies your work and reduces the possibility of misspelling subsequent entries of an existing index topic.

Figure 11. To cross-reference another index entry, first enter the word you want to cross-reference in the *Add index entry* dialog box. Choose the *Cross-reference* option at the top of the dialog box and then the *X-ref* button.

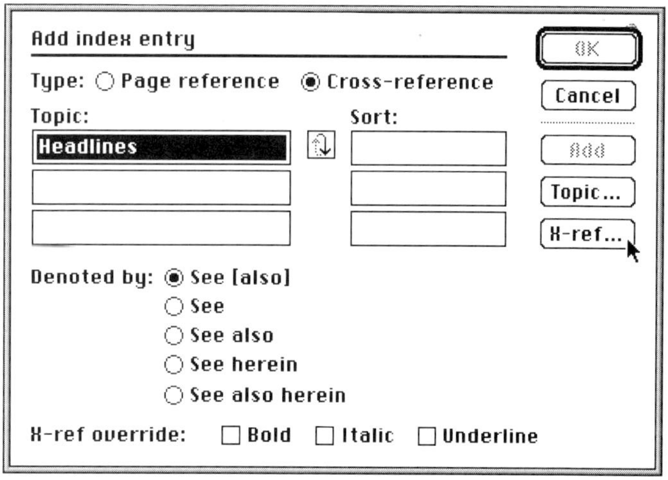

In this example, we entered *Headlines* so we can cross-reference it to another entry, called *grouping* (e.g. Headlines. *See* grouping).

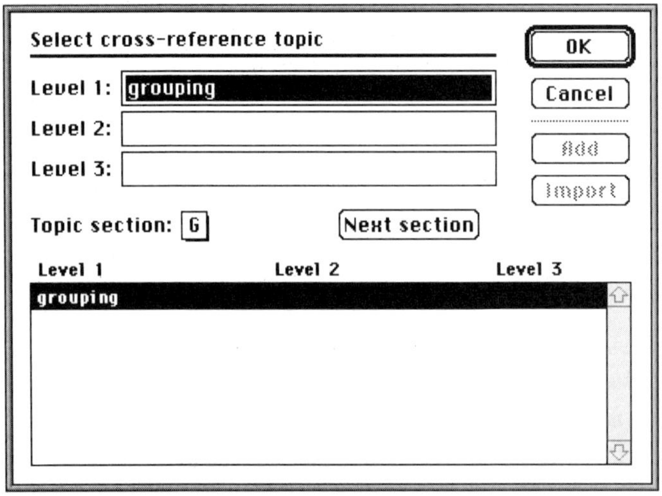

Figure 12. The *X-ref* button brings up the *Select cross-reference topic* dialog box. In this box, find the *grouping* entry by selecting the *G* alongside *Topic section,* or click on *Next section* until *grouping* appears. Select *grouping* and click on *OK.* This brings you back to the *Add index entry* dialog box. Click on *OK* once more to finish the operation.

Show Index Command

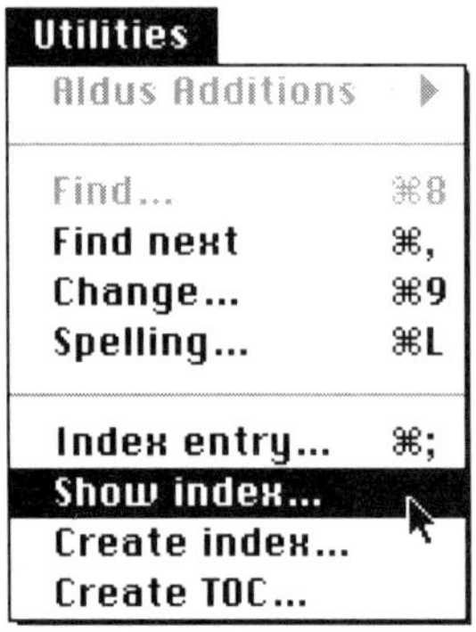

Figure 13. To review all index entries before generating the index, choose *Show index* from the **Utilities** menu.

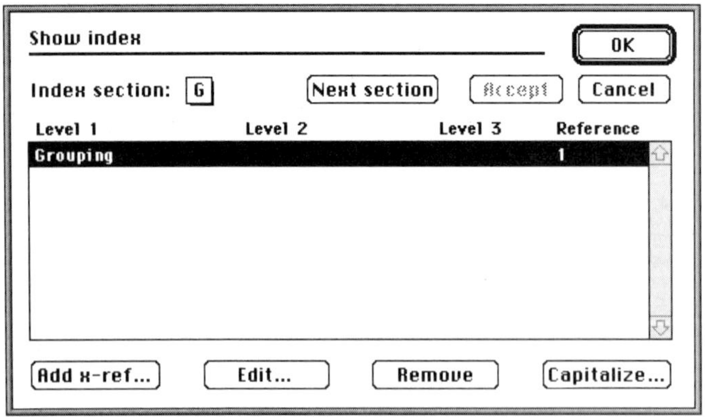

Figure 14. The *Show index* dialog box lets you add cross-references and edit or remove index entries. For example, if you want to cross-reference *Grouping* by adding the following: "Grouping. *See also* Headlines" you would first find the *Grouping* entry as shown in this figure. Then click on the *Add x-ref* button.

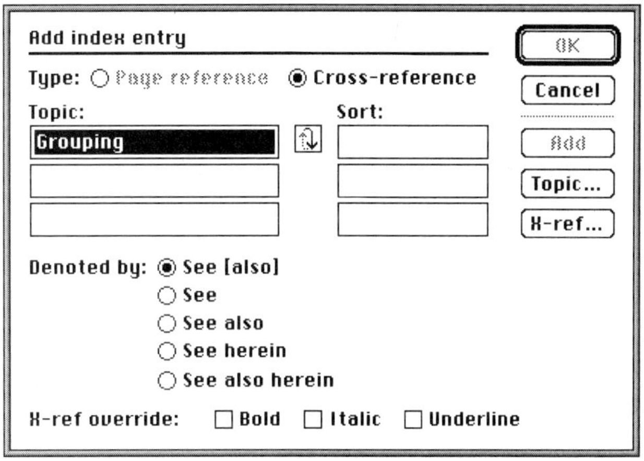

Figure 15. PageMaker displays the *Add index entry* dialog box with the *Cross-reference* radio button selected. Choose one of the options to the right of *Denoted by* and then click on the *X-ref* button.

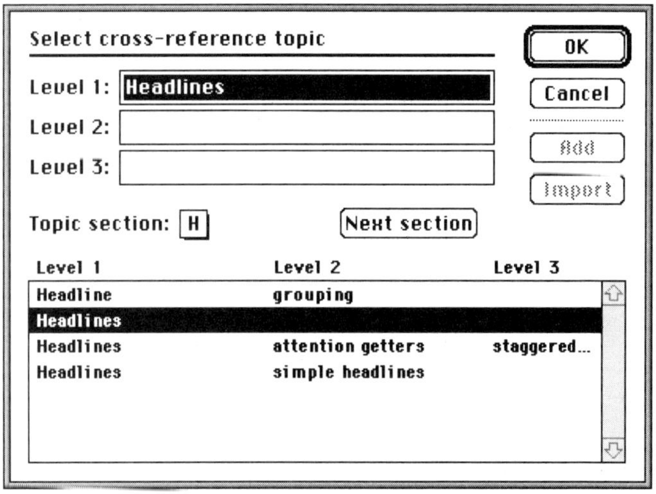

Figure 16. Search for the topic you need to cross-reference (in our example "Headlines") by using the *Topic section* pop-up menu. Select the topic you want to cross reference ("Headlines") and click on *OK* in the two dialog boxes to return to the *Show index* dialog box.

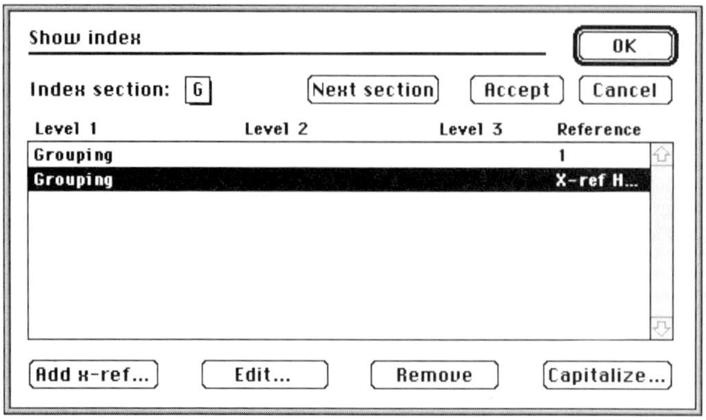

Figure 17. This dialog box now displays *Grouping*, which has been cross-referenced to *Headlines*. Click on *OK* once you have finished reviewing your index entries.

Creating the Index

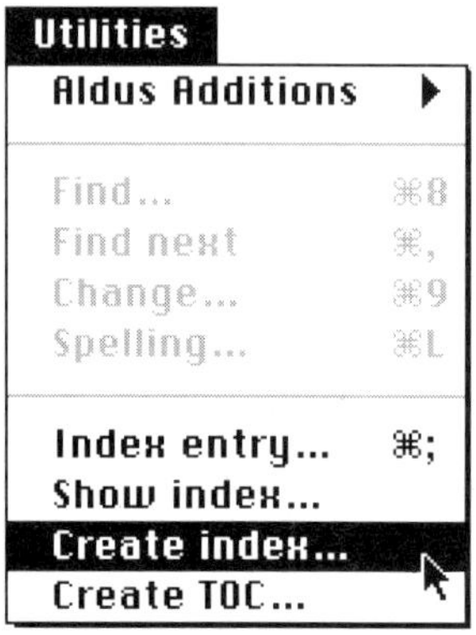

Figure 18. Use the *Create index* command to generate the index, once you have entered, cross-referenced, and edited all your index entries. This opens the *Create index* dialog box.

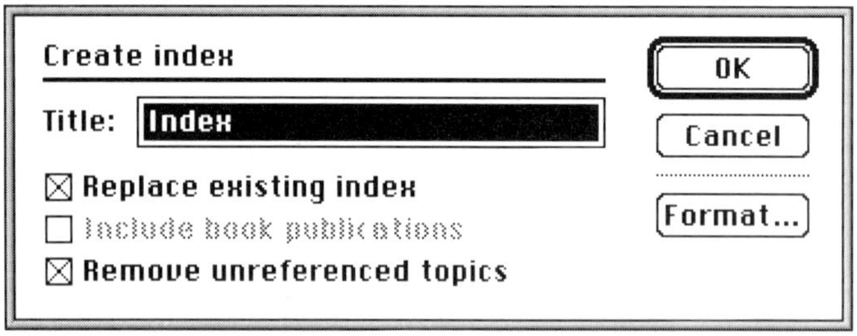

Figure 19. The default title shown here is *Index*. You can delete this and include your own—up to 30 characters. *Replace existing index* is unchecked only if this is the first index you have created. You can uncheck this if you want to keep the existing index.

You can select the *Include book publications* option if the open publication has a book list and you want the full book list indexed. Uncheck it if you want only the single publication index.

The *Remove unreferenced topics* option excludes any index entries that do not have a page number or cross-reference.

Clicking on *OK* generates the index. Clicking the *Format* button gives you the *Index format* dialog box.

Figure 20. Use the *Index format* dialog box to determine

- what sections and headings are included in the index.
- whether the index format is a nested (indented entries) or run-in (entries in a single paragraph). Examples of the *Nested* or *Run-in* format are shown at the bottom of the dialog box as you choose each option.
- what characters separate index entries. More details of these are in Appendix A of the *PageMaker User Manual.*

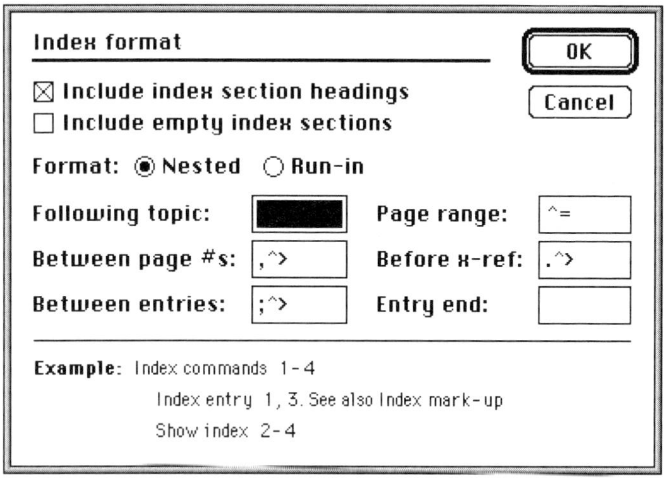

Figure 21. Once you have generated the index, place the index text file on the page as you would any other text file.

You can modify the styles (which are generated by PageMaker) and the text as you would normally.

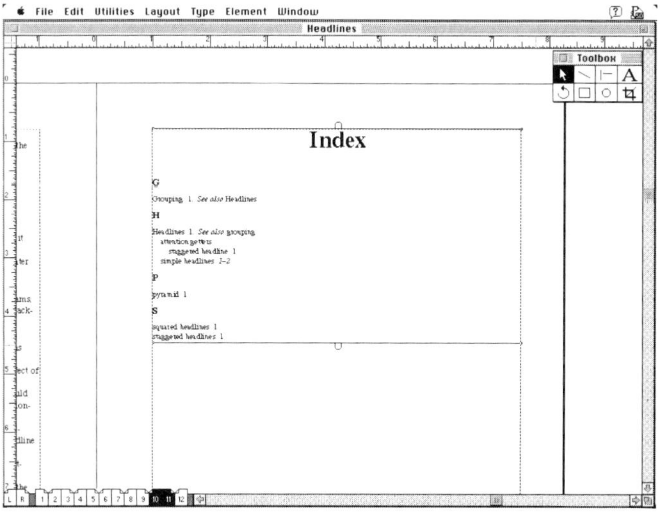

UTILITIES 17

DICTIONARY EDITOR

The Dictionary Editor is a separate utility that you can use to add, edit, find and hyphenate words in PageMaker's user dictionary. PageMaker uses the dictionary for spell checking and hyphenating (see Chapter 4 for more information on spell checking and hyphenation). You can also create your own dictionary.

STARTING DICTIONARY EDITOR

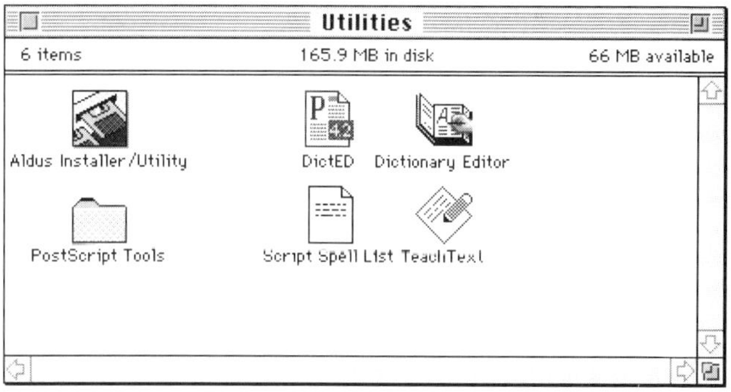

Figure 1. To start Dictionary Editor, find the Dictionary Editor in the *Utilities* folder in the *Aldus* folder in the *System folder.*

OPENING AND CREATING DICTIONARIES

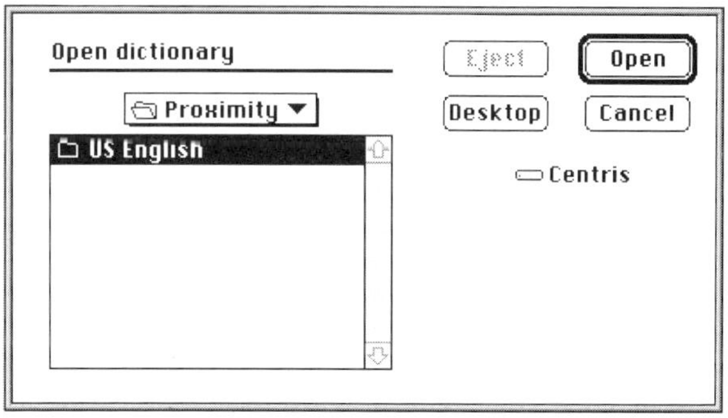

Figure 2. To open an existing dictionary, select *Open* from the **File** menu and choose the dictionary you want to edit. To create a new dictionary, select *New* from the **File** menu.

Importing Text Files

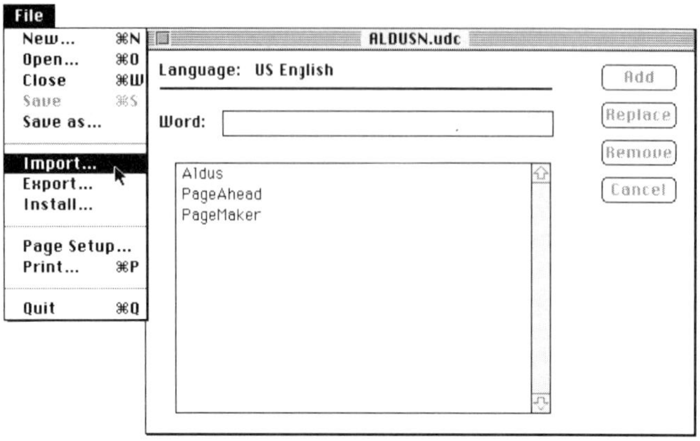

Figure 3. After you have selected a dictionary, this dialog box appears. If you have not added any words to the user dictionary through the *Hyphenation* or the *Spelling* commands, this dialog box will be empty. You can, however, add words, or import text-only files that contain a list of words separated by carriage returns, tabs, or spaces. To do this, select *Import* from the **File** menu.

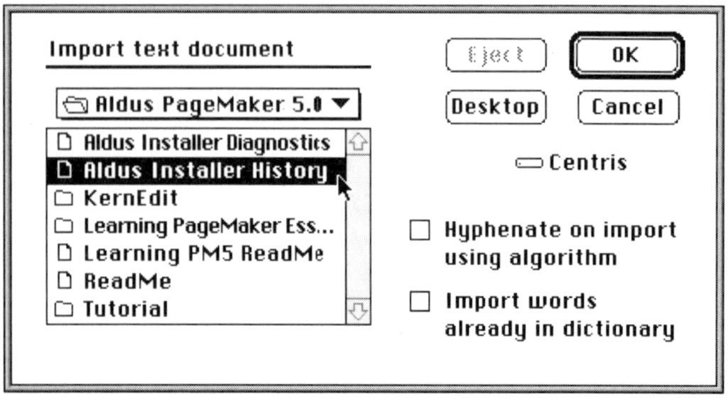

Figure 4. When the *Import text document* dialog box appears, find and double-click on the text file you want to import.

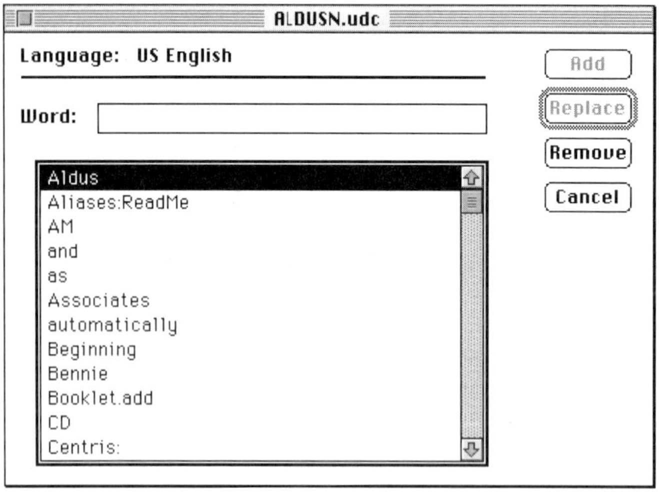

Figure 5. When you return to the *Dictionary Editor* dialog box, you see a list of words in the word list.

Selecting and Editing Words

Figure 6. To select a word from the list, double-click on it. It appears in the *Word* text box. You can then make any spelling or hyphenation changes in this text box (see Chapter 4 for more information on hyphenating words). To save your changes, click on the *Replace* button. Clicking on the *Clear* button removes the word and the changes from the *Word* text box.

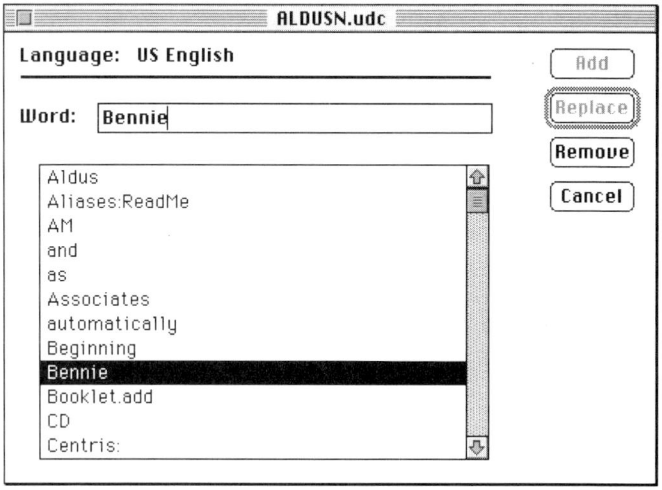

Removing Words

To remove a word, double-click on it and click on the *Remove* button.

Finding Words

Figure 7. To find a word without having to scroll, select *Find* from the **Edit** menu. Type the word into the *Find what* text box and click on the *Find* button.

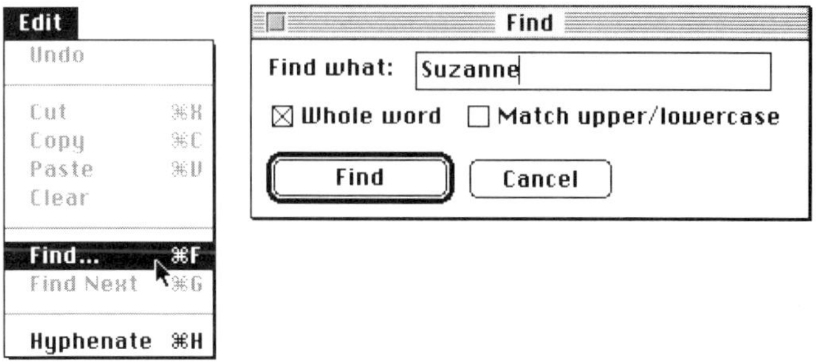

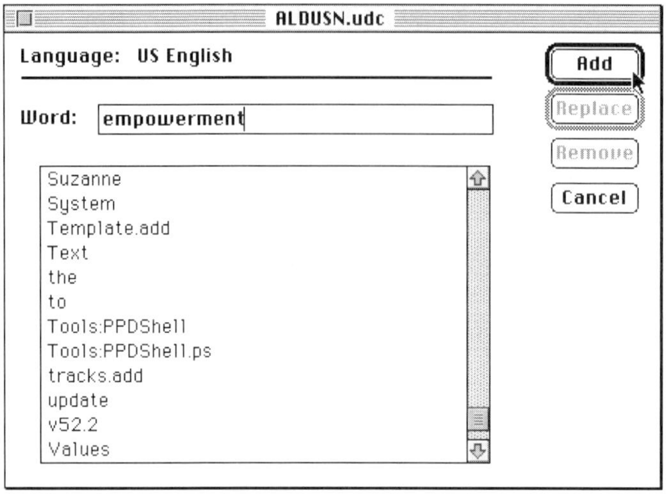

ADDING SINGLE WORDS

Figure 8. Type the word you want to add in the *Word* text box with the exact spelling and capitalization and click on the *Add* button. PageMaker adds this word to the list.

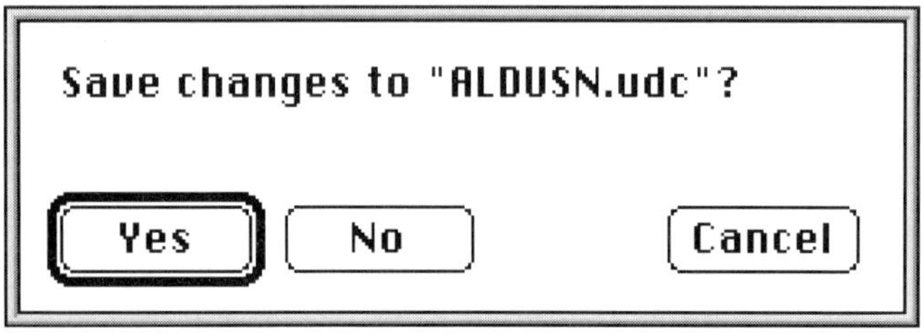

QUITTING DICTIONARY EDITOR

Figure 9. You can leave the Dictionary Editor using the *Quit* command in the **File** menu. If you have not saved the changes you have made, you are prompted to save changes to the current dictionary.

Index

A

B

C

D

E

K

L

M

N

O

T

U

W

More from Peachpit Press. . .

Art of Darkness

Erfert Fenton

This book is the perfect companion to AFTER DARK, the world's most popular screen saver and one of the top-selling utility programs of all time. It explains how to install, operate, and customize the program, as well as how to create modules for new screen savers. Included are nine new AFTER DARK modules created exclusively for this book. *(128 pages, includes disk)*

Everyone's Guide to Successful Publications

Elizabeth Adler

This comprehensive reference book pulls together all the information essential to developing and producing printed materials that will get your message across. Packed with ideas, practical advice, concrete examples, and hundreds of photographs and illustrations, it discusses planning the printed piece, writing strong copy, basic design, desktop publishing, preparation for printing, and distribution. *(412 pages)*

Desktop Publisher's Survival Kit

David Blatner

Here is a book that provides insights into desktop publishing on the Macintosh: trouble-shooting print jobs, working with color, scanning, and selecting fonts. A disk containing 12 top desktop publishing utilities, 400K of clip art, and two fonts is included in this package. *(176 pages, includes disk)*

Illustrator Illuminated

Clay Andres

This book is for people who want to know more about Adobe Illustrator than the manuals can tell them. It uses full-color graphics to show how professional artists use Illustrator's tools to create a variety of stylesand effects. Each chapter shows the creationof a specific illustration from concept through completion. Additionally, it covers using Illustrator in conjunction with Adobe Streamline and Photoshop. *(200 pages)*

The Little Mac Book, 3rd Edition

Robin Williams

Praised by scores of magazines and user group newsletters, this concise, beautifully written book covers the basics of Macintosh operation. It provides useful reference information, including charts of typefaces, special characters, and keyboard shortcuts. Totally updated for System 7. *(336 pages)*

The Little Mac Word Book

Helmut Kobler

Here's a fast way to learn Word 5.0 basics. This book provides concise and clear information about formatting text; using Word with Apple's new System 7 operating system; taking advantage of Word's writing tools; setting up complex tables, and much more! *(240 pages)*

The Little QuicKeys Book

Steve Roth and Don Sellers

This handy guide to CE Software's QuicKeys 2.0 explores the QuicKeys keysets and the different libraries QuicKeys creates for each application; shows how to link together functions and extensions; and provides an abundance of useful macros. *(288 pages)*

The Macintosh Bible, 4th Edition

Arthur Naiman, Nancy E. Dunn, Susan McAllister, John Kadyk, and a cast of thousands

It's more than just a book—it's a phenomenon. Even Apple's own customer support staff uses it. Now the Fourth Edition is here, and its 1,248 pages are crammed with tips, tricks, and shortcuts to get the most out of your Mac. And to make sure the book doesn't get out-of-date, three 30-page updates are included in the price (we mail them to you free of charge). Every Mac owner should have one. *(1,248 pages)*

Mac Classic & SE Upgrade and Repair Secrets

Larry Pina

When your Mac goes down—or you want to upgrade its power—then what? Scratch your head, make a few phone calls, then haul if off to the shop (hoping for the best)? Now there's a definitive guide, covering 95% of all common failures, upgrades and adjustments. Every instruction is simple and direct, taking a "when your machine does X, then Y is usually the cause and here's how to fix it" approach. Covers Mac Classic/Classic II, Mac SE, SE FDHD and SE/30 computers. *(300 pages)*

The Macintosh Bible "What Do I Do Now?" Book, 3rd Edition

Charles Rubin

Completely updated, this bestseller covers just about every sort of basic problem a Mac user can encounter. The book shows the error message exactly as it appears on screen, explains the problem (or problems) that can produce the message, and discusses what to do. This book is geared for beginners and experienced users alike. *(352 pages)*

The Mac is not a typewriter

Robin Williams

This best-selling, elegant guide to typesetting on the Mac has received rave reviews for its clearly presented information, friendly tone, and easy access. Twenty quick and easy chapters cover what you need to know to make your documents look clean and professional. *(72 pages)*

Photoshop 2.5: Visual QuickStart Guide

Elaine Weinmann and Peter Lourekas

The author of our award-winning *QuarkXPress 3.2: Visual QuickStart Guide* does it again. This is an indispensable guide for Mac users who want to get started in Adobe Photoshop but who don't have a lot of time to read books. Covers how to use masks, filters, colors, tools, and much more. *(264 pages)*

The Photoshop Wow! Book

Linnea Dayton and Jack Davis

This book is really two books in one: first, an easy-to-follow, step-by-step tutorial of Photoshop fundamentals; and second, over 150 pages of tips and techniques for getting the most out of Photoshop version 2.5. Full color throughout, *The Photoshop Wow! Book* shows exactly how professional artists employ the software, with explanations every step of the way. Includes a disk containing Photoshop filters and utilities. *(264 pages, includes disk)*

QuarkXPress 3.3: Visual QuickStart Guide (Mac Edition)

Elaine Weinmann

Winner of the 1992 Benjamin Franklin Award, this book is a terrific way to get introduced to QuarkXPress in just a couple of hours. Lots of illustrations and screen shots make each feature of the program absolutely clear. This book is helpful to both beginners and intermediate Quark users. *(248 pages)*

Real World FreeHand 4

Olav Martin Kvern

The ultimate insider's guide to FreeHand, this authoritative and entertaining book first lays out the basics and then concentrates on advanced techniques. *(528 pages)*

Real World Scanning and Halftones
David Blatner and Steve Roth

Master the digital halftone process—from scanning images to tweaking them on your Mac or PC to imagesetting them. Learn about optical character recognition, gamma control, sharpening, PostScript halftones, Photo CD and image-manipulating applications like Photoshop and PhotoStyler. *(296 pages)*

Silicon Mirage
Steve Aukstakalnis and David Blatner

Virtual reality is the amazing new technology of "pretend worlds," where individuals can completely immerse themselves in computer-generated environments. *Silicon Mirage* provides an easily understandable explanation of the "virtual senses" already possible, the strikingly broad array of fields where virtual reality is having an impact, and the breathtaking horizons yet to be discovered. *(300 pages)*

The Underground Guide to Laser Printers
The editors of Flash Magazine

Over the lifespan of your laser printer, you're likely to spend more on supplies and repairs than on the original equipment. This book shows you how to save your hard-earned coins with inside information on toner recharges, laser printer repairs, and other hot, money-saving topics. It's also packed with great tips for doing things with your laser printer you've never imagined, including printing on mugs, mouse pads and T-shirts, making plate-ready negatives, and much more. *(180 pages)*

Order Information:

How soon will I get my books?

UPS Ground orders arrive within 10 days on the West Coast and within three weeks on the East Coast. UPS Blue orders arrive within two working days anywhere in the U.S., provided we receive a fax or a phone call by 11 a.m. Pacific Time.

What about backorders?

Any book that is not available yet will be shipped separately when it is printed. *Requesting such books will not hold up your regular order.*

What if I don't like it?

Since we're asking you to buy our books sight unseen, we back them with an *unconditional money-back guarantee.* Whether you're a first time or a repeat customer, we want you to be completely satisfied in all your dealings with Peachpit Press.

What about shipping to Canada and overseas?

Shipping to Canada and overseas is via air mail. Orders must be prepaid in U.S. dollars.

Order Form

To order, call:

(800) 283-9444 or (510) 548-4393 (M-F) • (510) 548-5991 fax

#	TITLE	Price	Total
	Art of Darkness (with disk)	19.95	
	Desktop Publisher's Survival Kit (with disk)	22.95	
	Everyone's Guide to Successful Publications	28.00	
	Illustrator Illuminated	24.95	
	The Little Mac Book, 3rd Edition	16.00	
	The Little Mac Word Book	15.95	
	The Little QuicKeys Book	18.95	
	The Macintosh Bible, 4th Edition	32.00	
	Mac Classic & SE Upgrade and Repair Secrets	28.00	
	The Mac is not a typewriter	9.95	
	PageMaker 5: Visual QuickStart Guide (Macintosh)	14.95	
	Photoshop 2.5: Visual QuickStart Guide (Mac Edition)	18.00	
	The Photoshop Wow! Book (with disk)	35.00	
	The QuarkXPress Book, 4th Edition (Macintosh)	29.95	
	QuarkXPress 3.3: Visual QuickStart Guide (Mac Edition)	15.95	
	Real World FreeHand 4 (available March 1994)	29.95	
	Real World Scanning and Halftones	24.95	
	Silicon Mirage	15.00	
	The Underground Guide to Laser Printers	12.00	

SHIPPING:	First Item	Each Additional
UPS Ground	$ 4	$ 1
UPS Blue	$ 8	$ 2
Canada	$ 6	$ 4
Overseas	$14	$14

Subtotal	
8.25% Tax (CA only)	
Shipping	
TOTAL	

Name		
Company		
Address		
City	State	Zip
Phone	Fax	
☐ Check enclosed	☐ Visa	☐ MasterCard
Company purchase order #		
Credit card #	Expiration Date	

Peachpit Press, Inc. • 2414 Sixth Street • Berkeley, CA • 94710

Your satisfaction is guaranteed or your money will be cheerfully refunded!